ones of
ing fast
sents an
n for a

aims. It
getting
ring no
duction

ory and
careful
r losing
points
political
to the
ory add
signifi-
es how
Chapter
s using
t social
oratory
hapters.
he main
nd the
ries.

nic and
of East
(1992).
rsity of

GAME THEORY

A Critical Introduction

Shaun P. Hargreaves Heap and Yanis Varoufakis

London and New York

First published 1995
by Routledge
11 New Fetter Lane, London EC4P 4EE

Simultaneously published in the USA and Canada
by Routledge
29 West 35th Street, New York, NY 10001

Typeset in Garamond by
J&L Composition Ltd, Filey, North Yorkshire

Printed and bound in Great Britain by Biddles Ltd, Guildford and King's Lynn

British Library Cataloguing in Publication Data

A catalogue record for this book is available from the British Library.

Library of Congress Cataloging in Publication Data

Heap, Shaun Hargreaves, 1951–
Game theory: a critical introduction / Shaun P. Hargreaves Heap
and Yanis Varoufakis.
p.   cm.
Includes bibliographical references and index.
1. Social sciences – Mathematics.   2. Game theory.   I. Varoufakis,
Yanis.   II. Title.
H61.25.H4   1994
519.3–dc20   94–22051

ISBN 0–415–09402–X (hbk)
ISBN 0–415–09403–8 (pbk)

CONTENTS

CONTENTS

LIST OF BOXES

PREFACE

As ever there are people and cats to thank. There is also on this occasion electronic mail. The first draft of this book took shape in various cafeterias in Florence during YV's visit to Europe in 1992 and matured on beaches and in restaurants during SHH's visit to Sydney in 1993. Since then the mail wires between Sydney and Norwich, or wherever they are, have rarely been anything other than warm to hot, and of course we shall claim that this might account for any mistakes.

The genesis of the book goes back much longer. We were colleagues together at the University of East Anglia, where game theory has long been the object of interdisciplinary scrutiny. Both of us have been toying with game theory in an idiosyncratic way (see SHH's 1989 and YV's 1991 books) – it was a matter of time before we did so in an organised manner. The excuse for the book developed out of some joint work which we were undertaking during SHH's visit to Sydney in 1990. During the gestation period colleagues both at Sydney and at UEA exerted their strong influence. Martin Hollis and Bob Sugden, at UEA, were obvious sources of ideas while Don Wright, at Sydney, read the first draft and sprinkled it with liberal doses of the same question: 'Who are you writing this for?' (Ourselves of course Don!) Robin Cubbitt from UEA deserves a special mention for being a constant source of helpful advice throughout the last stages. We are also grateful to the Australian Research Council for grant 24657 which allowed us to carry out the experiments mentioned in Chapter 8.

It is natural to reflect on whether the writing of a book exemplifies its theme. Has the production of this book been a game? In a sense it has. The opportunities for conflict abounded within a two-person interaction which would have not generated this book unless strategic compromise was reached and cooperation prevailed. In another sense, however, this was definitely no game. The point about games is that objectives and rules are known in advance. The writing of a book by two authors is a different type of game, one that game theory does not consider. It not only involves moving within the rules, but also it requires the ongoing creation of the rules. And if this were not enough, it involves the ever shifting profile of objectives, beliefs and concerns of each author as the writing proceeds. Our one important thought in this book is that game theory will remain deficient until it develops an interest in games like the one we experienced over the last two years. Is it any wonder that this is *A Critical Introduction*?

Lastly, there are the people and the cats: Lucky, Margarita, Pandora, Sue, Thibeau and Tolstoy – thank you.

Shaun P. Hargreaves Heap
Yanis Varoufakis
May 1994

1

AN OVERVIEW

1.1 INTRODUCTION

1.1.1 Why study game theory?

Game theory is everywhere these days. After thrilling a whole generation of post–1970 economists, it is spreading like a bushfire through the social sciences. Two prominent game theorists, Robert Aumann and Oliver Hart, explain the attraction in the following way:

> Game Theory may be viewed as a sort of umbrella or 'unified field' theory for the rational side of social science . . . [it] does not use different, ad hoc constructs . . . it develops methodologies that apply in principle to all interactive situations.
>
> (Aumann and Hart, 1992)

Of course, you might say, two practitioners would say that, wouldn't they. But the view is widely held, even among apparently disinterested parties. Jon Elster, for instance, a well-known social theorist with very diverse interests, remarks in a similar fashion:

> if one accepts that interaction is the essence of social life, then . . . game theory provides solid microfoundations for the study of social structure and social change.
>
> (Elster, 1982)

In many respects this enthusiasm is not difficult to understand. Game theory was probably born with the publication of *The Theory of Games and Economic Behaviour* by John von Neumann and Oskar Morgenstern (first published in 1944 with second and third editions in 1947 and 1953). They defined a game as any interaction between agents that is governed by a set of rules specifying the possible moves for each participant and a set of outcomes for each possible combination of moves. One is hard put to find an example of social phenomenon that cannot be so described. Thus a theory of games promises to apply to almost any social interaction where

1

individuals have some understanding of how the outcome for one is affected not only by his or her own actions but also by the actions of others. This is quite extraordinary. From crossing the road in traffic, to decisions to disarm, raise prices, give to charity, join a union, produce a commodity, have children, and so on, it seems we will now be able to draw on a single mode of analysis: the theory of games.

At the outset, we should make clear that we doubt such a claim is warranted. This is a *critical* guide to game theory. Make no mistake though, we enjoy game theory and have spent many hours pondering its various twists and turns. Indeed it has helped us on many issues. However, we believe that this is predominantly how game theory makes a contribution. It is useful mainly because it helps clarify some fundamental issues and debates in social science, for instance those within and around the political theory of liberal individualism. In this sense, we believe the contribution of game theory to be largely pedagogical. Such contributions are not to be sneezed at.

If game theory does make a further substantial contribution, then we believe that it is a negative one. The contribution comes through demonstrating the limits of a particular form of individualism in social science: one based *exclusively* on the model of persons as preference satisfiers. This model is often regarded as the direct heir of David Hume's (the 18th century philosopher) conceptualisation of human reasoning and motivation. It is principally associated with what is known today as rational choice theory, or with the (neoclassical) economic approach to social life (see Downs, 1957, and Becker, 1976). Our main conclusion on this theme (which we will develop through the book) can be rephrased accordingly: we believe that game theory reveals the limits of 'rational choice' and of the (neoclassical) economic approach to life. In other words, game theory does not actually deliver Jon Elster's 'solid microfoundations' for all social science; and this tells us something about the inadequacy of its chosen 'microfoundations'.

The next section (1.2) sketches the philosophical moorings of game theory, discussing in turn its three key assumptions: **agents are instrumentally rational (section 1.2.1); they have common knowledge of this rationality (section 1.2.2); and they know the rules of the game (section 1.2.3)**. These assumptions set out where game theory stands on the big questions of the sort 'who am I, what am I doing here and how can I know about either?'. The first and third are ontological.[1] They establish what game theory takes as the material of social science: in particular, what it takes to be the essence of individuals and their relation in society. The second raises epistemological issues[2] (and in some games it is not essential for the analysis). It is concerned with what can be inferred about the beliefs which people will hold about how games will be played when they have common knowledge of their rationality.

2

We spend more time discussing these assumptions than is perhaps usual in texts on game theory because we believe that the assumptions are both controversial and problematic, in their own terms, when cast as general propositions concerning interactions between individuals. This is one respect in which this is a critical introduction. The discussions of instrumental rationality and common knowledge of instrumental rationality (sections 1.2.1 and 1.2.2), in particular, are indispensable for anyone interested in game theory. In comparison section 1.2.3 will appeal more to those who are concerned with where game theory fits in to the wider debates within social science. Likewise, section 1.3 develops this broader interest by focusing on the potential contribution which game theory makes to an evaluation of the political theory of liberal individualism. We hope you will read these later sections, not least because the political theory of liberal individualism is extremely influential. Nevertheless, we recognise that these sections are not central to the exposition of game theory *per se* and they presuppose some familiarity with these wider debates within social science. For this reason some readers may prefer to skip through these sections now and return to them later.

Finally, section 1.4 offers an outline of the rest of the book. It begins by introducing the reader to actual games by means of three classic examples which have fascinated game theorists and which allow us to illustrate some of the ideas from sections 1.2 and 1.3. It concludes with a chapter-by-chapter guide to the book.

1.1.2 Why read this book?

In recent years the number of texts on game theory has multiplied. For example, Rasmussen (1989) is a good 'user's manual' with many economic illustrations. Binmore (1990) comprises lengthy, technical but stimulating essays on aspects of the theory. Kreps (1990) is a delightful book and an excellent eclectic introduction to game theory's strengths and problems. More recently, Myerson (1991), Fudenberg and Tirole (1991) and Binmore (1992) have been added to the burgeoning set. Dixit and Nalebuff (1993) contribute a more informal guide while Brams (1993) is a revisionist offering. One of our favourite books, despite its age and the fact that it is not an extensive guide to game theory, is Thomas Schelling's *The Strategy of Conflict*, first published in 1960. It is highly readable and packed with insights few other books can offer. However, *none* of these books locates game theory in the wider debates within social science. This is unfortunate for two reasons.

Firstly, it is liable to encourage further the insouciance among economists with respect to what is happening elsewhere in the social sciences. This is a pity because mainstream economics is actually founded on philosophically controversial premises and game theory is potentially in rather a good position to reveal some of these foundational difficulties. In other words, what appear as 'puzzles' or 'tricky issues' to many game theorists are actually echoes of fundamental philosophical dispute; and so it would be unfortunate to overlook this invitation to more philosophical reflection.

Secondly, there is a danger that other social sciences will greet game theory as the latest manifestation of economic imperialism, to be championed only by those who prize technique most highly. Again this would be unfortunate because game theory really does speak to some of the fundamental disputes in social science and as such it should be an aid to all social scientists. Indeed, for those who are suspicious of economic imperialism within the social sciences, game theory is, somewhat ironically, a potential ally. Thus it would be a shame for those who feel embattled by the onward march of neoclassical economics if the potential services of an apostate within the very camp of economics itself were to be denied.

This book addresses these worries. It has been written for all social scientists. It does not claim to be an authoritative textbook on game theory. There are some highways and byways in game theory which are not travelled. But it does focus on the central concepts of game theory, and it aims to discuss them critically and simply while remaining faithful to their subtleties. Thus we have trimmed the technicalities to a minimum (you will only need a bit of algebra now and then) and our aim has been to lead with the ideas. We hope thereby to have written a book which will introduce game theory to students of economics and the other social sciences. In addition, we hope that, by connecting game theory to the wider debates within social science, the book will encourage both the interest of non-economists in game theory and the interest of economists to venture beyond their traditional and narrow philosophical basis.

1.2 THE ASSUMPTIONS OF GAME THEORY

Imagine you observe people playing with some cards. The activity appears to have some structure and you want to make sense of what is going on; who is doing what and why. It seems natural to break the problem into component parts. First we need to know the rules of the game because these will tell us what actions are permitted at any time. Then we need to know how people select an action from those that are permitted. This is the approach of game theory and the first two assumptions in this section address the last part of the problem: how people select an action. One focuses on what we should assume about what motivates each person (for instance, are they playing to win or are they just mucking about?) and the other is designed to help with the tricky issue of what each thinks the other will do in any set of circumstances.

1.2.1 Individual action is instrumentally rational

Individuals who are instrumentally rational have preferences over various 'things', e.g. bread over toast, toast and honey over bread and butter, rock over classical music, etc., and they are deemed rational because they select actions which will best satisfy those preferences. One of the virtues of this model is that very little needs to be assumed about a person's preferences. Rationality is cast in a means–end framework with the task of selecting the most appropriate means for achieving certain ends (i.e. preference satisfaction); and for this purpose, preferences (or 'ends') must be coherent in only a weak sense that we must be able to talk about satisfying them more or less. Technically we must have a 'preference ordering' because it is only when preferences are ordered that we will be able to begin to make judgements about how different actions satisfy our preferences in different degrees. In fact this need entail no more than a simple consistency of the sort that when rock music is preferred to classical and classical is preferred to muzak, then rock should also be preferred to muzak (the interested reader may consult Box 1.1 on this point).[3]

Thus it appears a promisingly general model of action. For instance, it could apply to any type of player of games and not just individuals. So long as the State or the working class or the police have a consistent set of objectives/preferences, then we could assume that it (or they) too act instrumentally so as to achieve those ends. Likewise it does not matter what ends a person pursues: they can be selfish, weird, altruistic or whatever; so long as they consistently motivate then people can still act so as to satisfy them best.

Readers familiar with neoclassical *Homo economicus* will need no further introduction. This is the model found in standard introductory texts, where preferences are represented by indifference curves (or utility functions) and agents are assumed rational because they select the action which attains the highest feasible indifference curve (maximises utility). For readers who have not come across these standard texts or who have forgotten them, it is worth explaining that preferences are sometimes represented mathematically by a utility function. As a result, acting instrumentally to satisfy best one's preferences becomes the equivalent of utility maximising behaviour. In short, the assumption of instrumental rationality cashes in as an assumption of utility maximising behaviour. Since game theory standardly employs the metaphor of utility maximisation in this way, and since this metaphor is open to misunderstanding, it is sensible to expand on this way of modelling instrumentally rational behaviour before we discuss some of its difficulties.

Ordinal utilities, cardinal utilities and expected utilities

Suppose a person is confronted by a choice between driving to work or catching the train (and they both cost the same). Driving means less waiting in queues and greater privacy while catching the train allows one to read while on the move and is quicker. Economists assume we have a preference ordering: each one of us, perhaps after spending some time thinking about the dilemma, will rank the two possibilities (in case of indifference an equal ranking is given). The metaphor of utility maximisation then works in the following way. Suppose you prefer driving to catching the train and so choose to drive. We could say equivalently that you derive X utils from driving and Y from travelling on the train and you choose driving because this maximises the utils generated, as $X > Y$.

Box 1.1

UTILITY MAXIMISATION AND CONSISTENT CHOICE

Suppose that a person is choosing between different possible alternatives which we label x_1, x_2, etc. We shall use the following notation to describe the preferences which inform these choices: $x_1 \quad x_2$ means that the person 'prefers x_1 to x_2 **or** is indifferent between them'; $x_1 \geq x_2$ means that he or she 'prefers x_1 to x_2'; and $x_1 = x_2$ means that he or she is 'indifferent between the two'. A person is deemed *instrumentally rational* if he or she has preferences which satisfy the following conditions:

(1) *Reflexivity:*   For any x_i, $x_i \geq x_i$
(2) *Completeness:* For any x_i, x_j, either $x_i \geq x_j$ or $x_i \leq x_j$
(3) *Transitivity:*   For any x_i, x_j, x_k, if $x_i \geq x_j$ **and** $x_j \geq x_k$, then $x_i \geq x_k$
(4) *Continuity:*   For any x_i, x_j, x_k, if $x_i > x_j > x_k$, then there must exist some 'composite' of x_i and x_k, say y, which gives the same amount of utility as x_j; that is, $y = x_j$ and our individual is indifferent between them.

In the definition of *continuity* above there are more than one way of interpreting the 'composite' alternative denoted by y. One is to think of y as a basket containing bits of x_i and bits of x_j. For example, if x_i is '5 croissant', x_j is '3 bagels' and x_k is '10 bread rolls', then some combination of croissant and bread rolls (e.g. 2 croissant and 4 bread rolls) must be equally valued as the 3 bagels. Another interpretation of y is probabilistic. Imagine that y is a lottery which gives the individual x_i with probability p ($0 < p < 1$) and x_k with probability $1 - p$. Then the continuity axiom says that there exists some probability p (e.g. 0.3) such that this lottery (that is, alternative y) is valued by the individual exactly as much as x_j.

When axioms (1), (2) and (3) hold, then the individual has a well-defined preference ordering. When (4) also holds, this preference ordering can be represented by a utility function. (A utility function takes what the individual has, e.g. x_i, and translates it into a unique level of utility. Its mathematical representation in this case is $U(x_i)$.) Thus the individual who makes choices with a view to satisfying his or her preference ordering can be conceived as one who is maximising this utility function.

Box 1.2

REFLECTIONS ON INSTRUMENTAL RATIONALITY

Instrumental rationality is identified with the capacity to choose actions which best satisfy a person's objectives. Although there is a tradition of instrumental thinking which goes back to the pre-Socratic philosophers, it is David Hume's *Treatise on Human Nature* which provides the clearest philosophical source. He argued that 'passions' motivate a person to act and 'reason' is their servant.

> We speak not strictly and philosophically when we talk of the combat of passion and reason. Reason is, and ought only to be the slave of the passions, and can never pretend to any other office than to serve and obey them.

Thus reason does not judge or attempt to modify our 'passions', as some might think. This, of course, does not mean that our 'passions' might not be 'good', 'bad', 'wishy-washy' when judged by some light or other. The point is that it is not the role of reason to form such judgements. Reason on this account merely guides action by selecting the best way to satisfy our 'passions'.

This hypothesis has been extremely influential in the social sciences. For instance, the mainstream, neoclassical school of economics has accepted this Humean view with some modification. They have substituted preferences for passions and they have required that these preferences should be consistent. This, in turn, yields a very precise interpretation for how instrumental reason goes to work. It is as if we had various desires or passions which when satisfied yield something in common; call it 'utility'. Thus the fact that different actions are liable to satisfy our different desires in varying degrees (for instance, eating some beans will assuage our desire for nourishment while listening to music will satisfy a desire for entertainment) presents no special problem for instrumental reason. Each action yields the same currency of pleasure ('utils') and so we can decide which action best satisfies our desires by seeing which generates the most 'utility' (see Box 1.1 on consistent choice).

This maximising, calculative view of instrumental reason is common in economics, but it needs careful handling because it is liable to suggest an unwarranted connection with the social philosophy of 'utilitarianism' as presented by Jeremy Bentham and later John Stewart Mill (especially since J.S. Mill is a key figure associated with both the beginnings of neoclassical economics and the social philosophy of utilitarianism). The key difference is that Bentham's social philosophy envisioned a universal currency of happiness for all people. Everything in people's lives either adds to the sum total of utility in society (i.e. it is pleasurable) or subtracts from it (i.e. is painful) and the good society is the one that maximises the sum of those utilities, or average utility (see also Box 4.5 in Chapter 4). This was a radical view at the time because it broke with the tradition of using some external authority (God, the Church, the Monarch) to judge social

7

outcomes, but it is plainly controversial now because it presumes we can compare one person's utility with another's. Neither neoclassical economics nor Humean philosophy is committed to such a view as the utility indices are purely personal assessments on these accounts and cannot be compared one with another.

The influence of instrumental reasoning stretches well beyond economics. Neoclassical economists have themselves exported this model of 'rational choice' to many other parts of the social sciences through the so-called 'economic' or 'rational choice' models of politics, marriage, divorce, suicide, etc. (see Becker, 1976). There is even the 'rational choice' version of Marxism (see Elster, 1986b). In turn, these efforts join forces with those of other social theorists. For example, Max Weber famously sees purposive rational action as one of the ideal types through which we can develop a rational understanding of individual action; and he regards the way that western institutions increasingly embody the character of calculative reason as one of the hallmarks of 'modernity'.

However, while (neoclassical) economists typically work only with instrumental reason, social theorists, like Weber and Jürgen Habermas, recognise other motivations. Thus instrumental reason is to be contrasted for Weber with 'value rational' action: that is, action which is to be understood *not* as a means to an end but as valuable in its own right. Likewise for Habermas the 'life form' of the human being cannot be simply reduced to the mastery over nature which is symptomatic of purposive (instrumentally) rational action. Our life form is distinguished by the fact that we reach understanding through language and this is the source of another kind of rationality, the rationality of communicative action. This recognition of alternative types of rationality enriches the work of these social theorists in ways which are typically lost on economists. For example, it creates the possibility of tensions developing between the different types of reason and it offers a vantage point from which to assess both instrumental reasoning and 'modernity'.

It will be obvious though that this assignment of utility numbers is arbitrary in the sense that any X and Y will do provided $X > Y$. For this reason these utility numbers are known as *ordinal utility* as they convey nothing more than information on the ordering of preferences.

Two consequences of this arbitrariness in the ordinal utility numbers are worth noting. Firstly the numbers convey nothing about strength of preference. It is as if a friend were to tell you that she prefers Verdi to Mozart. Her preference may be marginal or it could be that she adores Verdi and loathes Mozart. Based on ordinal utility information you will never know. Secondly there is no way that one person's ordinal utility from Verdi can be compared with another's from Mozart. Since the ordinal utility number is meaningful only in relation to the *same* person's satisfaction from something else, it is meaningless across persons. This is why the talk of utility maximisation does not automatically connect neoclassical economics and game theory to traditional utilitarianism (see Box 1.2 on the philosophical origins of instrumental rationality).

Ordinal utilities are sufficient in many of the simpler decision problems and games. However, there are many other cases where they are not enough. Imagine for instance that you are about to leave the house and must decide on whether to drive to your destination or to walk. You would clearly like to walk but there is a chance of rain which would make walking awfully unpleasant. Let us say that the predicted chance of rain by the weather bureau is 50–50. What does one do? The answer must depend on the strength of preference for walking in the dry over driving in the dry, driving in the wet and walking in the wet. If, for instance, you relish the idea of walking in the dry a great deal more than you fear getting drenched, then you may very well risk it and leave the car in the garage. Thus, we need information on strength of preference.

Cardinal utilities provide such information. If 'walking in the dry', 'driving in the wet', 'driving in the dry' and 'walking in the wet' correspond to 10, 6, 1 and 0 cardinal utils respectively, then not only do we have information regarding ordering, but also of how much one outcome is preferred over the next. Walking in the dry is ten times better for you than driving in the dry. Such cardinal utilities allow the calculus of desire to convert the decision problem from one of utility maximisation to one of utility maximisation *on average*; that is, to the maximisation of *expected utility*. It works as follows (see Box 1.3 on how expected utility maximisation is an extension of the idea of consistent choice to uncertain decision settings).

In the previous example, we took for granted that the probability of rain is $\frac{1}{2}$. If you walk there is, therefore, a 50% chance that you will receive 10 cardinal utils and a 50% chance that you will receive 0 utils. On average your tally will be 5 utils. If, by contrast, you drive, there is a 50% chance of getting 6 utils (if it rains) and a 50% chance of ending up with only 1 cardinal util. On average driving will give you 3.5 utils. If you act as if to maximise average utility, your decision is clear: you will walk. So far we conclude that in cases where the outcome is uncertain cardinal utilities are necessary and expected utility maximisation provides the metaphor for what drives action. As a corollary, note for future reference that whenever we encounter expected utility, cardinal (and not ordinal) utilities are implied. The reason is that it would be nonsense to multiply probabilities with ordinal utility measures whose actual magnitude is inconsequential since they do not reveal strength of preference. Finally notice that, although cardinal utility takes us closer to 19th century utilitarianism, we are still a long way off because one person's cardinal utility numbers are still incomparable with another's. Thus, when we say that your cardinal utility from walking in the dry is 10, this is meaningful only in relation to the 6 utils you receive from driving in the wet. It cannot be compared with a similar

Box 1.3

CONSISTENT CHOICE UNDER RISK AND EXPECTED UTILITY MAXIMISATION

Suppose the actions which a person must choose between have uncertain outcomes in the following sense. Each action has various possible outcomes associated with it, each with some probability. For example, the purchase of a lottery ticket for $1 where there is a probability of $\frac{1}{100}$ of winning $50 is an action with an uncertain outcome. One could either lose $1 or gain a net $49 when buying the ticket and the respective probabilities of each outcome are $\frac{99}{100}$ and $\frac{1}{100}$. Notationally we call this action a *prospect* and we represent it as a pairing of the possible outcomes with their respective probabilities: $(-\$1, \$49; \frac{99}{100}, \frac{1}{100})$. Then the question is: how do people choose between (risky) prospects?

As we saw in Box 1.1, the theory of instrumentally rational choices specifies certain conditions (or axioms) which the preferences of an individual must satisfy if they are to be consistent. The following axioms need to be added to the list in Box 1.1 in order to make preferences over prospects consistent also.

(1), (2) and (3) remain as in Box 1.1.

(4) *Continuity* also remains as in Box 1.1 but with a minor alteration to extend its relevance to preferences over prospects. Consider three prospects y_i, y_j and y_k and imagine that the individual prefers the first to the second and the second to the third. Then there exists *some* probability p such that if we were to let the individual have prospect y_i with probability p and prospect y_k with probability $1 - p$, then our individual would be equally happy with this situation as he or she would be with prospect y_j. (Notice the similarity with the second interpretation of the continuity axiom in Box 1.1.)

(5) *Preference increasing with probability*: If $y_i > y_j$ and $y_m = (y_i, y_j; p_1, 1 - p_1)$, $y_n = (y_i, y_j; p_2, 1 - p_2)$, then $y_m > y_n$ only if $p_1 > p_2$.

(6) *Independence*: For three prospects y_i, y_j, y_k, if $y_i > y_j$, then there exists a probability λ such that a $(\lambda, 1 - \lambda)$ probability mix of y_i and y_j must be at least as good as a $(\lambda, 1 - \lambda)$ probability mix of y_i and y_j. In our notation for prospects, $(y_i, y_j; \lambda, 1 - \lambda) \geq (y_i, y_k; \lambda, 1 - \lambda)$.

The theory of instrumentally rational choice shows that if an individual's preferences satisfy conditions (1) to (6) then an individual who acts on his or her preference ordering acts *as if* in order to maximise his or her *expected utility function*.

number relating somebody else's cardinal utility from driving in the wet, walking in the dry and so on.

Cardinal utilities and the assumption of expected utility maximisation to game theory are important because uncertainty is ubiquitous in games.

Consider the following variant of an earlier example. You must choose between walking to work or driving. Only this time your concern is not the weather but a friend of yours who also faces the same decision in the morning. Assume your friend is not on the phone (and that you have made no prior arrangements) and you look forward to meeting up with him or her while strolling to work (and if both of you choose to walk, your paths are bound to converge early on in the walk). In particular your first preference is that you walk together. Last in your preference ordering is that you walk only to find out that your friend has driven to work. Of equal second best ranking is that you drive when your friend walks and when your friend drives. We will capture these preferences in matrix form – see Figure 1.1.

If the numbers in the matrix were ordinal utilities, it would be impossible to know what you will do. If you expect your friend to drive then you will also drive as this would give you 1 util as opposed to 0 utils from walking alone. If on the other hand you expect your friend to walk then you will also walk (this would give you 2 utils as opposed to only 1 from driving). Thus your decision will depend on what you expect your friend to do and we need some way of incorporating these expectations (that is, the uncertainty surrounding your friend's behaviour) into your decision making process.

Suppose that, from past experience, you believe that there is $\frac{2}{3}$ chance that your friend will walk. This information is useless unless we know how much you prefer the accompanied walk *over* the solitary drive; that is, unless your utilities are of the cardinal variety. So, imagine that the utils in the matrix of Figure 1.1 are cardinal and you decide to choose an action on the basis of expected utility maximisation. You know that if you drive, you will certainly receive 1 util, regardless of your friend's choice (notice that the first row is full of ones). But if you walk, there is a $\frac{2}{3}$ chance that you will meet up with your friend (yielding 2 utils for you) and a $\frac{1}{3}$ chance of walking alone (0 utils). On average, walking will give you $\frac{4}{3}$ utils ($\frac{2}{3}$ times 2 plus $\frac{1}{3}$ times 0). More generally, if your belief about the probability of your friend walking is p (p having some value between 0 and 1, e.g. $\frac{2}{3}$) then your expected utility from walking is $2p$ and that from driving is 1. Hence an expected utility maximiser will always walk as long as p exceeds $\frac{1}{2}$.

Game theory follows precisely such a strategy. It assumes that it is 'as if'

		Friend	
		Drive	Walk
You	Drive	1	1
	Walk	0	2

Figure 1.1

11

you had a cardinal utility function and you act so as to maximise expected utility. There are a number of reasons why many theorists are unhappy with this assumption.

The critics of expected utility theory (instrumental rationality)

(a) Internal critique and the empirical evidence

The first type of worry is found within mainstream economics (and psychology) and stems from empirical challenges to some of the assumptions about choice (the axioms in Box 1.3) on which the theory rests. For instance, there is a growing literature that has tested the predictions of expected utility theory in experiments and which is providing a long list of failures. Some care is required with these results because when people play games the uncertainty attached to decision making is bound up with anticipating what others will do and as we shall see in a moment this introduces a number of complications which in turn can make it difficult to interpret the experimental results. So perhaps the most telling tests are not actually those conducted on people playing games. Uncertainty in other settings is simpler when it takes the form of a lottery which is well understood and apparently there are still major violations of expected utility theory. Box 1.4 gives a flavour of these experimental results.

Of course, any piece of empirical evidence requires careful interpretation and even if these adverse results were taken at their face value then it would still be possible to claim that expected utility theory was a prescriptive theory with respect to rational action. Thus it is not undermined by evidence which suggests that we fail in practice to live up to this ideal. Of course, in so far as this defence is adopted by game theorists when they use the expected utility model, then it would also turn game theory into a prescriptive rather than explanatory theory. This in turn would greatly undermine the attraction of game theory since the arresting claim of the theory is precisely that it can be used to explain social interactions.

In addition, there are more general empirical worries over whether all human projects can be represented instrumentally as action on a preference ordering (see Sen, 1977). For example, there are worries that something like 'being spontaneous', which some people value highly, cannot be fitted into the means–ends model of instrumentally rational action (see Elster, 1983). The point is: how can you decide to 'be spontaneous' without undermining the objective of spontaneity? Likewise, can all motives be reduced to a utility representation? Is honour no different to human thirst and hunger (see Hollis, 1987, 1991)? Such questions quickly become philosophical and so we turn explicitly in this direction.

Box 1.4

THE ALLAIS PARADOX

Kahneman and Tversky (1979) offer the following reworking of the famous study in Allais (1953) (see also Sugden (1991) for an up to date survey of the literature).

You are asked to choose between two lotteries, lottery 1 and lottery 2.

Lottery 1 $2500 with probability 33%
$2400 with probability 66%
0 with probability 1%
Lottery 2 $2400 with certainty

(Notice that lottery 2 is a lottery only in name since it offers a certain pay-off.)

Which do you choose? Once you have made a choice consider two other lotteries:

Lottery 3 $2500 with probability 33%
0 with probability 67%
Lottery 4 $2400 with probability 34%
0 with probability 66%

Which do you choose now? Many people choose lotteries 2 and 3. It seems that in choosing between lotteries 1 and 2 they are not prepared to take the small risk of receiving nothing in order to have a small chance of getting an extra $100. They prefer the safety of the second lottery instead. However, when it comes to a choice between lotteries 3 and 4, lottery 3 seems only slightly riskier than lottery 4 and people are more willing to take that extra risk in order to boost their pay-offs.

However, expected utility theory is categorical here. If you have chosen lottery 1 you must also choose lottery 3. And if you have chosen lottery 2, you must choose lottery 4. To see why expected utility theory says this, let us rewrite the above lotteries as follows:

Lottery 1 $2400 with probability 66%
0 with probability 1%
$2500 with probability 33%
Lottery 2 $2400 with probability 66%
$2400 with probability 34%
Lottery 3 0 with probability 66%
0 with probability 1%
$2500 with probability 33%
Lottery 4 0 with probability 66%
$2400 with probability 34%

Notice that lotteries 1 and 2 contain a common 'element' in the first line: $2400 with probability 66%. Expected utility theory insists that if you have a preference between lotteries 1 and 2 then this must be so because of the other 'elements' in these lotteries. And if you were to substitute that common element with some other common element, then your original preference should be preserved. For example, suppose that you amended the first line of lotteries 1 and 2 so that instead of '$2400 with probability 66%' it read '$200 with probability 66%'. If you preferred lottery 2 to lottery 1 (say) before the amendment, expected utility theory argues that you must preserve this preference after the amendment since only the common element has been changed. This is the so-called independence axiom of expected utility theory (see Box 1.3). Now consider lotteries 3 and 4. The way we have rewritten them above, they are identical to lotteries 1 and 2 excepting the common element which has been changed from '$2400 with probability 66%' to '0 with probability 66%'. Thus, according to expected utility theory, if you prefer lottery 2 to lottery 1, you must also prefer lottery 4 to lottery 3. And yet, the majority of people participating in such experiments seem to violate the independence axiom and choose lotteries 2 and 3. The fact that expected utility theory receives little empirical support is potentially worrying for game theory because it relies so heavily on it.

(b) Philosophical and psychological discontents

This is not the place for a philosophy lesson (even if we were competent to give it!). But there are some relatively simple observations concerning rationality that can be made on the basis of common experiences and reflections which in turn connect with wider philosophical debate. We make some of those points and suggest those connections here. They are not therefore designed as decisive philosophical points against the instrumental hypothesis. Rather their purpose is to remind us that there are puzzles with respect to instrumental rationality which are openings to vibrant philosophical debate. Why bother to make such reminders? Partially, as we have indicated, because economists seem almost unaware that their foundations are philosophically contentious and partially because it seems to us and others that the only way to render some aspects of game theory coherent is actually by building in a richer notion of rationality than can be provided by instrumental rationality alone. For this reason, it is helpful to be aware of some alternative notions of rational agency.

Consider first a familiar scene where a parent is trying to 'reason' with a child to behave in some different manner. The child has perhaps just hit another child and taken one of his or her toys. It is interesting to reflect on what parents usually mean here when they say 'I'm going to reason with the blighter.'

'Reason' here is usually employed to distinguish the activity from something like a clip around the ear and its intent is to persuade the 'blighter' to behave differently in future. The question worth reflecting upon is: what is it about the capacity to reason that the parent hopes to be able to invoke in the child to persuade him or her to behave differently?

The contrast with the clip around the ear is quite instructive because this action would be readily intelligible if we thought that the child was only

14

instrumentally rational. If a clip around the ear is what you get when you do such things then the instrumentally rational agent will factor that into the evaluation of the action, and this should result in it being taken less often. Of course, 'reasoning' could be operating in the same way in so far as listening to parents waffling on in the name of reason is something to be avoided like a clip around the ear. Equally it could be working with the grain of instrumental rationality if the adult's intervention was an attempt to rectify some kind of faulty 'means–ends' calculation which lay behind the child's action. However, there is a line of argument sometimes used by adults which asks the child to consider how they would like it if the same thing was to happen to them; and it is not clear how a parent could think that such an argument has a purchase on the conduct of the instrumentally rational child. Why should an instrumentally rational child's reflection on their dislike of being hit discourage them from hitting others unless hitting others makes it more likely that someone will hit them in turn? Instead, it seems that the parents when they appeal to reason and use such arguments are imagining that reason works in some other way. Most plausibly, they probably hope that reason supplies some kind of internal constraint on the actions and objectives which one deems permissible, where the constraint is akin to the biblical order that you should do unto others as you would have done to yourself.

Of course, reason may not be the right word to use here. Although Weber (1947) refers to *wertrational* to describe this sort of rationality, it has to be something which the parent believes affects individual actions in a way not obviously captured by the instrumental model. Furthermore there is a philosophical tradition which has associated reason with supplying just such additional constraints. It is the tradition initiated by Immanuel Kant which famously holds that reason is ill equipped to do the Humean thing of making us happy by serving our passions.

> Now in a being which has reason and will, if the proper object of nature were its conservation, its welfare, in a word, its happiness, then nature would have hit upon a very bad arrangement in selecting reason to carry out this purpose. . . . For reason is not competent to guide the will with certainty in regard to its objects and the satisfaction of all our wants (which to some extent it even multiplies) . . . . its true destination must be to produce a will, not merely good as a means to something else, but good in itself, for which reason was absolutely necessary.
>
> (Kant, 1788, pp. 11–12).

Thus reason is instead supposed to guide the ends we pursue. In other words, to return to the case of the child taking the toy, reason might help us to see that we should not want to take another child's toy. How might it specifically do this? By supplying a negative constraint is Kant's answer. For Kant it is never going to be clear what reason specifically instructs, but

---

Box 1.5

KANT'S CATEGORICAL IMPERATIVE

Kant summarises the categorical imperative thus: 'Act only on that maxim whereby thou canst at the time will that it should become a universal law.'

As an example of how the categorical imperative might be applied and how it differs from instrumental reasoning, consider a person wondering whether to pay his or her taxes. Non-payment could be instrumentally rational in so far as the person is concerned only with his or her welfare and the chances of being fined for non-payment are slight. However, such an action would not pass the test of the categorical imperative. If the person were (hypothetically) to consider not paying his or her taxes while at the same time accepting the premise that others are similarly rational, then he or she would be committed to the predictable result that society would break down and life would become nasty, brutish and probably short as government support for law and order, health care, road building, etc., collapsed without the necessary funding from taxes. Thus for Kant the rational person should not allow reason to be a slave to the passions (which might lead to non-payment); instead our rationality, and the fact that we share it, should lead us to the categorical imperative and the payment of taxes.

---

since we are all equipped with reason, we can see that reason could only ever tell us to do something which it would be possible for everyone to do. This is the test provided by the categorical imperative (see Box 1.5) and reason guides us by telling us to exclude those objectives which do not pass the test. Thus we should not want to do something which we could not wish would be done by everyone; and this might plausibly explain why reason could be invoked to persuade the child not to steal another child's toy.

Even when we accept the Kantian argument, it is plain that reason's guidance is liable to depend on characteristics of time and place. For example, consider the objective of 'owning another person'. This obviously does not pass the test of the categorical imperative since all persons could not all own a person. Does this mean then we should reject slave-holding? At first glance, the answer seems to be obvious: of course, it does! But notice it will only do this if slaves are considered people. Of course we consider slaves people and this is in part why we abhor slavery, but ancient Greece did not consider slaves as people and so ancient Greeks would not have been disturbed in their practice of slavery by an application of the categorical imperative.

This type of dependence of what is rational on time and place is a feature of many philosophical traditions. For instance, Hegel has reason evolving historically and Marx tied reason to the expediency of particular modes of production. It is also a feature of the later Wittgenstein who proposes a rather different assault on the conventional model of instrumental reason. As we shall say more about this in section 1.2.3, it suffices for now to note that Wittgenstein suggests that if you want to know why people act in the way that they do, then ultimately you are often forced in a somewhat circular fashion to say that such actions are part of the practices of the society in which those persons find themselves. In other words, it is the fact that people behave in a particular way in society which supplies the reason for the individual person to act: or, if you like, actions often supply their own reasons. This is shorthand description rather than explanation of Wittgenstein's argument, but it serves to make the connection to an influential body of psychological theory which makes a rather similar point.

Festinger's (1957) cognitive dissonance theory proposes a model where reason works to 'rationalise' action rather than guide it. The point is that we often seem to have no reason for acting the way that we do. For instance, we may recognise one reason for acting in a particular way, but we can equally recognise the pull of a reason for acting in a contrary fashion. Alternatively, we may simply see no reason for acting one way rather than another. In such circumstances, Festinger suggests that we experience psychological distress. It comes from the dissonance between our self-image as individuals who are authors of our own action and our manifest lack of reason for acting. It is like a crisis of self-respect and we seek to remove it by creating reasons. In short we often rationalise our actions *ex post* rather than reason *ex ante* to take them as the instrumental model suggests.

This type of dissonance has probably been experienced by all of us at one time or another and there is much evidence that we both change our preferences and change our beliefs about how actions contribute to preference satisfaction so as to rationalise the actions we have taken (see Aronson, 1988). Some of the classic examples of this are where smokers have systematically biased views of the dangers of smoking or workers in risky occupations similarly underestimate the risks of their jobs. Indeed in a modified form, we will all be familiar with a problem of consumer choice when it seems impossible to decide between different brands. You consult consumer reports, specialist magazines and the like and it does not help because all this extra information only reveals how uncertain you are about what you want. The problem is you do not know whether safety features of a car, for instance, matter to you more than looks or speed or cost. And when you choose one rather than another you are in part choosing to make, say, 'safety' one of your motives. Research has shown that people seek out and read advertisements for the brand of car they have just bought. Indeed, to return us to economics, it is precisely this insight which has been at the heart of one of the Austrian and other critiques of the central planning system when it is argued that planning can never substitute for the market

17

because it presupposes information regarding preferences which is in part created in markets when consumers choose.

(c) The source of beliefs

You will recall in the example contained in Figure 1.1 that in deciding what to do you had to form an expectation regarding the chances that your friend would walk to work. Likewise in an earlier example your decision over whether to walk or drive depended on an expectation: the probability of rain. The question we wish to explore here is where these beliefs come from; and for this purpose, the contrast between the two decision problems is instructive.

At first sight it seems plausible to think of the two problems as similar. In both instances we can use previous experience to generate expectations. Previous experience with the weather provides probabilistic beliefs in the one case, and experience with other people provides it in the other. However, we wish to sound a caution. There is an important difference because the weather is not concerned at all about what you think of it whereas other people often are. This is important because while your beliefs about the weather do not affect the weather, your beliefs about others can affect their behaviour when those beliefs lead them to expect that you will act in particular ways. For instance, if your friend is similarly motivated and thinks that you will walk then he or she will want to walk; and you will walk if you think he or she will walk. So what he or she thinks you think will in fact influence what he or she does!

To give an illustration of how this can complicate matters from a slightly different angle, consider what makes a good meteorological model. A good model will be proved to be good in practice: if it predicts the weather well it will be proclaimed a success, otherwise it will be dumped. On the other hand in the social world, even a great model of traffic congestion, for instance, may be contradicted by reality simply because it has a good reputation. If it predicts a terrible jam on a particular stretch of road and this prediction is broadcast on radio and television, drivers are likely to avoid that spot and thus render the prediction false. This suggests that proving or disproving beliefs about the social world is liable to be trickier than those about the natural world and this in turn could make it unclear how to acquire beliefs rationally.

Actually most game theorists seem to agree on one aspect of the problem of belief formation in the social world: how to update beliefs in the presence of new information. They assume agents will use *Bayes's rule*. This is explained in Box 1.6. We note there some difficulties with transplanting a technique from the natural sciences to the social world which are related to the observation we have just made. We focus here on a slightly

Box 1.6

BAYES'S RULE

Two examples:

(a) How seriously do you take a medical diagnosis?

Imagine you have just taken a test for a dreaded disease X and your doctor has just gloomily informed you that you have tested positive. Suppose that it is known beyond doubt that 0.1% of the population are affected by X and that 100,000 tests have been administered so far. Also it is known that the test is correct 99% of the time (that is, the test is positive 99% of the time for someone who has X and negative 99% of the time for someone who does not have it). How depressed should you be? What are the chances that you really have X?

At first sight, it seems that there is a 99% chance that you have X since you tested positive and the test is 99% accurate. Bayes's rule gives you (a scientific) cause to rejoice; at least to postpone despair. Let us reconsider the data. Of the 100,000 people tested, 0.1% will have X; that is, 100 people on average. Of those 100 X-affected people who have taken the test, 99 will prove positive (recall the test is 99% accurate). However, of the 99,900 healthy people 1% will also test positive owing to the 1% error margin of the test, i.e. 999 healthy people will have tested positive. Thus, of a total of 1098 positive tests (999 healthy plus the 99 affected people) only 99 have X. Thus the probability that you have X given (or conditional on the fact) that you have tested positive is 99/1098 which is only about 9%!

The above captures the logic of Bayes's rule for amending initial probabilistic beliefs in the light of new evidence. The initial beliefs were that (a) the probability that you have X is 0.1%; (b) the probability that you have X if the test proves positive $Pr(X|$ test is positive$) = 99\%$ – notice that | stands for 'given that'. The new bit of information is that you tested positive. How do you amend the probability that you have X in the light of this information?

In general, Thomas Bayes suggested the following rule which codifies our earlier calculations: the probability that event A has occurred given that event B has just been observed is written as $Pr(A|B)$ (this is known as a conditional probability) and equals

$$Pr(A|B) = [Pr(B|A)Pr(A)]/[Pr(B|A)Pr(A) + Pr(B|\text{not }A)Pr(\text{not }A)]$$

(where 'not A' means that event A did not occur).

To see how it applies in our example, think of event B as the new information, namely B: 'You tested positive for disease X.' Then the question is, what is $Pr(A|B)$? That is, what is the probability that you have X given that the test was positive? Let us put together the right hand side of Bayes's rule. $Pr(B|A)$ is the probability that you will test positive given that you have X. It equals 99% (from (b) above). $Pr(A)$ is the probability that you have X as assessed before the test (i.e. the new information): it equals 0.1% (from (a) above). Thus the numerator equals 99% times 0.1%, i.e. 9.9%. The denominator equals 9.9% plus $Pr(B|\text{not }A)$ times

19

Pr(not A). The probability of 'not A', i.e. that you do not have X, is 99.9% while the probability of testing positive if you do not have it (i.e. Pr(B|not A)) equals 1%. Therefore the whole denominator equals 109.8%. It turns out that the probability that you have X given that you tested positive equals 9.9/109.8, which is exactly what we found earlier; a touch above 9%.

(b) Should you prosecute?

Let us suppose that you are the district attorney who must decide whether to prosecute the person who the police say has committed the crime. You adopt a simple rule of thumb: if it seems that there is more than a 50% chance, based on the evidence presented by the police, that the person did commit the crime then you prosecute. Here are the details of the case. It is known almost beyond doubt that the crime was committed by one person in a group of six people. So before any police evidence is presented, you believe that there is something fractionally less than a one-in-six chance that the person identified by the police actually did commit the crime (to allow for just some doubt that the crime could have been committed by someone outside the group), say 0.15. The police offer one piece of evidence to support their claim that their candidate committed the crime: this person's confession. It is also 'well known' that what people say to the police is only 80% reliable. Should you prosecute?

Bayes's rule tells us that the probability that the person is G (guilty) conditional on the information C (the evidence of a confession) is given by

$$\text{Pr}(G|C) = \text{Pr}(G \text{ and } C)/\text{Pr}(C) =$$
$$\text{Pr}(C|G)\text{Pr}(G)/[\text{Pr}(C|G)\text{Pr}(G)+\text{Pr}(C|NG)\text{Pr}(NG)]$$

where Pr(C|G) is the probability of confessing when guilty (which is the 80% reliability rate), Pr(C|NG) is the probability of the person confessing when not guilty (that is, the unreliability rate of 20%) and the Pr(G) and Pr(NG) are the prior probability assessments of guilty and not guilty (respectively 15 and 85%).

When the substitutions are performed, Bayes's rule yields the inference that the probability of guilt is revised to 0.41, which is less than the 50% and the DA tells the police to get more evidence if they want a prosecution! The result is perhaps somewhat surprising but you can see how it is derived by imagining a population of 100 people with 15 guilty people in it. You ask each to confess and given the 80% reliability rate, 12 of the guilty will and 3 will not, and 68 of the 85 innocents will not confess (= 80% reliable) and 17 innocents will confess. Thus there are 29 confessions altogether, but only 12 (that is, a proportion equal to 0.41) come from people who are genuinely guilty.

There are a couple of points to notice about Bayes's rule. The first is that it is a rule of statistical inference and it will only apply to stationary probability distributions. So in this instance you cannot apply it if the chance of the guilty person coming from the group of six suspects, rather than some larger group, kept changing. Secondly, the rule can only be applied when the new information, the event, has a prior probability assessment of zero (this can be seen from the expression above because it is not defined when the probability of a confession is zero). In other

> words, if something happens which you had never anticipated, but which is actually relevant, then you cannot use Bayes's rule to take it into account.

different problem. Bayes provides a rule for updating, but where do the original (prior) expectations come from? Or to put the question in a different way: in the absence of evidence, how do agents form probability assessments governing events like the behaviour of others?

There are two approaches in the economics literature. One responds by suggesting that people do not just passively have expectations. They do not just wait for information to fall from trees. Instead they make a conscious decision over how much information to look for. Of course, one must have started from somewhere, but this is less important than the fact that the acquisition of information will have transformed these original 'prejudices'. The crucial question, on this account, then becomes: what determines the amount of effort agents put into looking for information? This is deceptively easy to answer in a manner consistent with instrumental rationality. The instrumentally rational agent will keep on acquiring information to the point where the last bit of search effort costs her or him in utility terms the same amount as the amount of utility he or she expects to get from the information gained by this last bit of effort. The reason is simple. As long as a little bit more effort is likely to give the agent more utility than it costs, then it will be adding to the sum of utilities which the agent is seeking to maximise.

This looks promising and entirely consistent with the definition of instrumentally rational behaviour. But it begs the question of how the agent knows how to evaluate the potential utility gains from a bit more information *prior to gaining that information*. Perhaps he or she has formulated expectations of the value of a little bit more information and can act on that. But then the problem has been elevated to a higher level rather than solved. How did he or she acquire that expectation about the value of information? 'By acquiring information about the value of information up to the point where the marginal benefits of this (second-order) information were equal to the costs', is the obvious answer. But the moment it is offered, we have the beginnings of an infinite regress as we ask the same question of how the agent knows the value of this second-order information. To prevent this infinite regress, we must be guided by something *in addition* to instrumental calculation. But this means that the paradigm of instrumentally rational choices is incomplete. The only alternative would be to assume that the individual *knows* the benefits that he or she can expect on average from a little more search (i.e. the expected marginal benefits)

21

Box 1.7

THE ELLSBERG PARADOX, UNCERTAINTY, PROBABILITY ASSESS-MENTS, AND CONFIDENCE

Suppose you are shown an urn with 90 balls in it and you are told that 30 are red and that the remaining 60 balls are either black or yellow. One ball is going to be selected at random and you are given the following choice. Option I will give you $100 if a red ball is drawn and nothing if either a black or a yellow ball is drawn; option II will give you $100 if a black ball and nothing if a red or a yellow ball is drawn. Here is a summary of the options:

	Red	Black	Yellow
Option I	$100	0	0
Option II	0	$100	0

Make a note of your choice and then consider another two options based on the same random draw from this urn:

	Red	Black	Yellow
Option III	$100	0	$100
Option IV	0	$100	$100

Which of these would you choose?

Ellsberg (1961) reports that, when presented with this pair of choices, most people select options I and IV. Adopting the approach of expected utility theory (see Box 1.3), this reveals a clear inconsistency in probability assessments. On this interpretation, when a person chooses option I over option II, he or she is revealing a higher subjective probability assessment of a 'red' than a 'black'. However, when the same person prefers option IV to III, he or she reveals that his or her subjective probability assessment of 'black' or 'yellow' is higher than a 'red' or 'yellow', and this implies that a 'black' has a higher probability assessment than a 'red'!

Perhaps the simplest explanation of this pair of choices turns on the confidence which a person attaches to probability assessments. For example, when choosing between options I and II, if the person opts for I he or she knows the *exact* probability of winning $100: it is $\frac{1}{3}$. By contrast, were he or she to choose option II, the probability of winning would have been unknown. Now look again at options III and IV. By choosing option IV one knows the exact probability of winning: $\frac{2}{3}$. On the other hand, the probability of winning $100 when choosing option III is ambiguous. In other words, the choices of I and IV can be explained by an aversion to ambiguity and a preference for prospects which come with precise, objective, information about the probability of winning or losing. This kind of preference violates expected utility theory but can by no means be dismissed as irrational.

In so far as this explanation seems plausible, then the Ellsberg paradox points to a deeper problem with respect to the conventional expected utility maximising model because it suggests that probability assessments inadequately capture the way that uncertainty enters into decision making. In fact, it is precisely this observation which lies at the famous distinction between risk (i.e. as in lotteries where you do not know what will happen but you know all the possible outcomes and the probability for each) and uncertainty (i.e. cases in which you are in the dark) in economics (see Knight, 1921, and Keynes, 1936).

because he or she knows the full information set. But then there is no problem of how much information to acquire because the person knows everything!

The second response by neoclassical economists to the question 'Where do beliefs come from?' is to treat them as purely subjective assessments (following Savage, 1954). This has the virtue of avoiding the problem of rational information acquisition by turning subjective assessments into data which is given from outside the model along with the agents' preferences. They are what they are; and they are only revealed *ex post* by the choices people make (see Box 1.7 for some experimental evidence which casts doubt on the consistency of such subjective assessments and more generally on the probabilistic representations of uncertainty). The distinct disadvantage of this is that it might license almost any kind of action and so could render the instrumental model of action close to vacuous. To see the point, if expectations are purely subjective, perhaps any action could result in the analysis of games, since any subjective assessment is as good as another. Actually game theory has increasingly followed Savage (1954), by regarding the probability assessments as purely subjective, but it has hoped to prevent this turning itself into a vacuous statement (to the effect that 'anything goes') by supplementing the assumption of *instrumental rationality* with the assumption of *common knowledge of rationality* (CKR). The purpose of the latter is to place some constraints on people's subjective expectations regarding the actions of others.

1.2.2 Common knowledge of rationality (CKR) and consistent alignment of beliefs (CAB)

We have seen how expectations regarding what others will do are likely to influence what it is (instrumentally) rational for you to do. Thus fixing the beliefs that rational agents hold about each other is likely to provide the key to the analysis of rational action in games. The contribution of CKR in this respect comes in the following way.

If you want to form an expectation about what somebody does, what could be more natural than to model what determines their behaviour and then use the model to predict what they will do in the circumstances that interest you? You could assume the person is an idiot or a robot or whatever, but most of the time you will be playing games with people who are instrumentally rational like yourself and so it will make sense to model your opponent as instrumentally rational. This is the idea that is built into the analysis of games to cover how players form expectations. We assume that there is common knowledge of rationality held by the players. It is at once both a simple and complex approach to the problem of expectation formation. The complication arises because with common knowledge of rationality I know that you are instrumentally rational and since you are rational and know that I am rational you will also know that I know that you are rational and since I know that you are rational and that you know that I am rational I will also know that you know that I know that you are rational and so on . . . . This is what common knowledge of rationality means. Formally it is an infinite chain given by

(a) that each person is instrumentally rational
(b) that each person knows (a)
(c) that each person knows (b)
(d) that each person knows (c) And so on *ad infinitum*.

This is what makes the term *common knowledge* one of the most demanding in game theory. It is difficult to pin down because common knowledge of X (whatever X may be) cannot be converted into a finite phrase beginning with 'I know . . .'. The best one can do is to say that if Jack and Jill have common knowledge of X then 'Jack knows that Jill knows that Jack knows . . . that Jill knows that Jack knows . . . X' – an infinite sentence. The idea reminds one of what happens when a camera is pointing to a television screen that conveys the image recorded by the very same camera: an infinite self-reflection. Put in this way, what looked a promising assumption suddenly actually seems capable of leading you anywhere.

To see how an assumption that we are similarly motivated might not be so helpful in more detail, take an extreme case where you have a desire to be fashionable (or even unfashionable). So long as you treat other people as things, parameters like the weather, you can plausibly collect information on how they behave and update your beliefs using the rules of statistical inference, like Bayes's rule (or plain observation). But the moment you have to take account of other people as like-minded agents concerned with being fashionable, which seems to be the strategy of CKR, the difficulties multiply. You need to take account of what others will wear and, with a group of like-minded fashion hounds, what each of them wears will depend on what they expect others (including you) to wear, and what each expects others to wear depends on what each expects each other will expect others to wear, and so on . . . . The problem of expectation formation spins hopelessly out of control.

Nevertheless game theorists typically assume CKR and many of them, and certainly most people who apply game theory in economics and other disciplines, take it further: in order to come up with precise predictions on rational behaviour they assume not only CKR, but also they make (what we call) the assumption of consistently aligned beliefs (CAB). In other words they assume that everybody's beliefs are consistent with everybody else's. CAB gives great analytical power to the theorist, as we will see in later chapters. Nevertheless, the jump from CKR to CAB is controversial, even among game theorists (see Kreps, 1990, Bernheim, 1984, and Pearce, 1984).

Put informally, the notion of *consistent alignment of beliefs* (CAB) means that no instrumentally rational person can expect another similarly rational person who has the same information to develop different thought processes. Or, alternatively, that no rational person expects to be surprised by another rational person. The point is that if the other person's thought is genuinely moving along rational lines, then since you know the person is rational and you are also rational then your thoughts about what your rational opponent might be doing will take you on the same lines as his or her own thoughts. The same thing applies to others provided they respect *your* thoughts. So your beliefs about what your opponents will do are consistently aligned in the sense that if you actually knew their plans, you would not want to change your beliefs; and if they knew your plans they would not want to change the beliefs they hold about you and which support their own planned actions.

Note that this does not mean that everything can be deterministically predicted. For example, both you and others may be expecting good weather with probability $\frac{3}{4}$. In that sense your beliefs are consistently aligned. Yet it rains. You may be disappointed but you are not surprised, since there was always a $\frac{1}{4}$ chance of rain. What partially underpins the jump from CKR to CAB is the so-called Harsanyi doctrine. This follows from John Harsanyi's famous declaration that when two rational individuals have the same information, they **must** draw the same inferences and come, independently, to the same conclusion. So, to return to the fashion game, this means that when two rational fashion hounds confront the same information regarding the fashion game played among fashion hounds, they should come to the same conclusion about what rational players will wear.

As stated this would still seem to leave it open for different agents to entertain different expectations (and so genuinely surprise one another) since it only requires that rational agents draw the same inferences from the same information but they need not enjoy the same information. To make the transition from CKR to CAB complete, Robert Aumann takes the argument a stage further by suggesting that rational players will come to hold the same information so that in the example involving the expectations on whether it will rain or not, rational agents could not 'agree to disagree' about the probability of rain. (See Box 1.8 for the complete argument.) One can almost discern a dialectical argument here; where

---

Box 1.8

ROBERT AUMANN'S DEFENCE OF THE ASSUMPTION OF A CONSISTENT ALIGNMENT OF BELIEFS

Suppose you believe that the probability of rain tomorrow is $\frac{3}{4}$. And suppose that I believe it to be $\frac{1}{4}$. On this basis, you could agree to pay me $1 if it does not rain and I could agree to pay you $1 if it does. Sounds reasonable? Not to game theorists in this tradition. Notice that although the final payoff tomorrow will sum to zero (that is, what I will win/lose and what you will lose/win sum to zero), this is not so with the pay-offs we expect today. Each one of us expects payoffs: $1 with probability $\frac{3}{4}$ and $-$1 with probability $\frac{1}{4}$. On average, each expects to make 50 cents [$1 $\times$ $(\frac{3}{4})$ $-$ $1 $\times$ $(\frac{1}{4})$ = $(\frac{1}{2})$]. Thus our expectations are inconsistent with each other. If we are both rational we can only disagree because we have different evidence or information sets. In offering to make the bet, each one of us reveals to the other some of what was previously 'privately' held information. You reveal that you have evidence which ought to temper my confidence that it will be dry tomorrow and similarly I reveal to you some of my evidence which ought to temper your confidence in rain. Consequently each will want to revise their expectation of rain tomorrow. This exchange of information will continue so long as we disagree and with each exchange the disagreement narrows until finally it disappears. Thus according to Aumann, rational agents cannot agree to disagree.

---

following Socrates, who thought unique truths can be arrived at through dialogue, we assume that an opposition of incompatible positions will give way to a uniform position acceptable to both sides once time and communication have worked their elixir. Thus, CKR spawns CAB.

Such a defence of CAB is not implausible, but it does turn on the idea of an explicit dialogue in real (i.e. historical) time. Aumann does not specify how and where this dialogue will take place, and without such a process there need be no agreement (Socrates' own ending confirms this). This would seem to create a problem for Aumann's argument at least as far as one-shot games are concerned (that is, interactions which occur between the same players only once and in the absence of communication). You play the game once and then you might discover *ex post* that you must have been holding some divergent expectations. But this will only be helpful if you play the same game again because you cannot go back and play the original game afresh.

Furthermore, there is something distinctly optimistic about the first (Harsanyi) part of the argument. Why should we expect rational agents faced with the same information to draw the same conclusions? After all, we do not seem to expect the same fixtures will be draws when we complete the football pools; nor do we enjoy the same subjective expectations about the prospects of different horses when some bet on the favourite and others on the outsider. Of course, some of these differences might stem from differences in information, but it is difficult to believe that this accounts for all of them. What is more, on reflection, would you really expect our fashion hounds to select the same clothing when each only knows that the other is a fashion hound playing the fashion game?

These observations are only designed to signal possible trouble ahead and we shall examine this issue in greater detail in Chapters 2 and 3. We conclude the discussion now with a pointer to wider philosophical currents. Many decades before the appearance of game theory, the German philosophers G.F.W. Hegel and Immanuel Kant had already considered the notion of the self-conscious reflection of human reasoning on itself. Their main question was: can our reasoning faculty turn on itself and, if it can, what can it infer? Reason can certainly help persons develop ways of cultivating the land and, therefore, escape the tyranny of hunger. But can it understand how it, itself, works? In game theory we are not exactly concerned with this issue but the question of what follows from common knowledge of rationality has a similar sort of reflexive structure. When reason knowingly encounters itself in a game, does this tell us anything about what reason should expect of itself?

What is revealing about the comparison between game theory and thinkers like Kant and Hegel is that, unlike them, game theory offers something settled in the form of CAB. What is a source of delight, puzzlement and uncertainty for the German philosophers is treated as a problem solved by game theory. For instance, Hegel sees reason reflecting on reason as it reflects on itself as part of the restlessness which drives human history. This means that for him there are no answers to the question of what reason demands of reason in other people outside of human history. Instead history offers a changing set of answers. Likewise Kant supplies a weak answer to the question. Rather than giving substantial advice, reason supplies a negative constraint which any principle of knowledge must satisfy if it is to be shared by a community of rational people: any rational principle of thought must be capable of being followed by all. O'Neill (1989) puts the point in the following way:

[Kant] denies not only that we have access to transcendent metaphysical truths, such as the claims of rational theology, but also that reason has intrinsic or transcendent vindication, or is given in consciousness. He does not deify reason. The only route by which we can vindicate certain ways of thinking and acting, and claim that those ways have authority, is by considering how we must discipline our thinking if we are to think or act at all. This disciplining leads us not to algorithms of reason, but to certain constraints on all thinking, communication and interaction among any plurality. In particular we are led to the principle of rejecting thought, act or communication that is guided by principles that others cannot adopt.

(O'Neill p. 27)

To summarise, game theory is avowedly Humean in orientation. Nevertheless a disciple of Hume will protest two aspects of game theory rather strongly. The first we have already mentioned in Box 1.2: by substituting desire and preference for the passions, game theory takes a narrower view of human nature than Hume. The second is that game theorists seem to assume *too much* on behalf of reason. Hume saw reason acting like a pair of scales to weigh the pros and cons of a certain action so as to enable the selection of the one that serves a person's passions best. Game theory demands rather more from reason when starting from CKR it moves to CAB and the inference that rational players will always draw the same conclusions from the same information. Thus when the information comprises a particular game, rational players will draw the same inference regarding how rational players will play the game. Would Hume have sanctioned such a conclusion? It seems doubtful (see Sugden, 1991). After all, even Kant and Hegel, who attach much greater significance than Hume to the part played by reason, were not convinced that reason would ever give either a settled or a unique answer to the question of what reflection of reason on itself would come up with.

1.2.3 Action within the rules of games

There are two further aspects of the way that game theorists model social interaction which strike many social scientists as peculiar. The first is the assumption that individuals know the rules of the game – that is, they know all the possible actions and how the actions combine to yield particular pay-offs for each player. The second, and slightly less visible one, is that a person's motive for choosing a particular action is strictly independent of the rules of the game which structure the opportunities for action.

Consider the first peculiarity: how realistic is the assumption that each player knows all the possible moves which might be made in some game? Surely, in loosely structured interactions (games) players often invent moves. And even when they do not, perhaps it is asking too much to assume that a person knows both how the moves combine to affect their own utility pay-offs and the pay-offs of other players. After all, our motives are not always transparent to ourselves, so how can they be transparent to others?

There are several issues here. Game theory must concede that it is concerned with analysing interactions where the menu of possible actions for each player is known by everyone. It would be unfair of us to expect game theory to do more. Indeed this may not be so hard to swallow since each person must know that 'such and such' is a possible action before they can *decide* to take it. Of course people often blunder into things and they often discover completely new ways of action, but neither of these types of acts could have been decided upon. Blundering is blundering and game theory is concerned with conscious decision making. Likewise, you can only decide to do something when that something is known to be an option, and genuinely creative acts create something which was not known about before the action. The more worrying complaint appears to be the one regarding knowledge of other people's utility pay-offs (in other words, their preferences).

Fortunately though, game theory is not committed to assuming that agents know the rules of the game in this sense with certainty. It is true that the assumption is frequently made (it distinguishes games where information is complete from those in which it is incomplete) but, according to game theorists, it is not essential. The assumption is only made because it is 'relatively easy' to transform any game of incomplete information into one of complete information. Harsanyi (1967/1968) is again responsible for the argument. Chapter 2 gives a full account of the argument, but in outline it works like this. Suppose there are a number of different 'types' of player in the world where each type of player has different preferences and so will value the outcomes of a game in different ways. In this way we can view your uncertainty about your opponent's utility pay-offs as deriving from your uncertainty about your opponent's 'type'. Now all that is needed is that you hold common prior expectations with your opponent (the Harsanyi/Aumann doctrine) about the likelihood of your opponent turning out to be one type of player or another and the game has become one of complete information.

The information is complete because you know exactly how likely it is that your opponent will be a player of one type or another and your opponent also knows what you believe this likelihood to be. Again it is easy to see how once this assumption has been made, the analysis of play in this game will be essentially the same as the case where there is no uncertainty about your opponent's identity. We have argued before that you will choose the action which yields the highest expected utility. This requires that you work out the probability of your opponent taking various actions because their action affects the pay-offs to you from each of your actions. When you know the identity of your opponent, this means you have to work out the probability of that kind of an opponent taking any particular action. The only difference now is that the probability of your opponent taking any particular action depends not only on the probability that a rational opponent of some type, say A, takes this action but also on the probability of your opponent being type A in the first place.

The difficult thing in all likelihood, as we have argued above, is to know always what a rational opponent of known preferences will do. But so long as we have sorted this out for each type of player and we know the chances of encountering each type, then the fact that we do not know the identity of the opponent is a complication, but not a serious one. To see the point, suppose we know left-footed people are slower moving to the right than the left and vice versa. Then we know the best thing to do in soccer is to try and dribble past a left-footed opponent on their right and vice versa. If you do not know whether your opponent is left or right footed, then this is, of course, a complication. But you can still decide what to do for the best in the sense of being most likely to get past your opponent. All you have to know are the relative chances of your opponent being left or right footed and you can decide which way to swerve for the best.

Moving on, game theory is not unusual in distinguishing between actions and rules of the game. The distinction reflects the thought that we are often constrained in the actions that we take. For instance, nobody would doubt the everyday experience that common law and the laws of Parliament, the rules of clubs or institutions that we belong to and countless informal rules of conduct provide a structure to what we can and cannot do. Likewise social theory commonly recognises that these so-called 'structures' constrain our actions. However, the way that action is separated from the rules of the game (or 'structures') positions game theory in a very particular way in discussions in social theory regarding the relation between 'action' and 'structure'.

To be specific, game theory accepts the strict separation of action from structure. The structure is provided by the rules of the game and action is analysed under the constraints provided by the structure. This may be a common way of conceiving the relation between the two, but it is not the only one. It is as if structures provide architectural constraints on action. They are like brick walls which you bump into every now and then as you walk about the social landscape. The alternative metaphor comes from language. For example Giddens (1979) suggests that action involves some shared rules just as speaking requires shared language rules. These rules constrain what can be done (or said), but it makes no sense to think of them as separate from action since they are also enabling. Action cannot be taken without background rules, just as sentences cannot be uttered without the rules of language. Equally rules cannot be understood independently of the actions which exemplify them. In other words, there is an organic or holistic view of the relation between action and structure.

The idea behind Giddens' argument can be traced to an important theme in the philosophy of Wittgenstein: the idea that action and structure are mutually constituted in the practices of a society. This returns us to a point which was made earlier with respect to how actions can supply their own reasons. To bring this out, consider a person hitting a home run in baseball with the bases loaded or scoring a four with a reverse sweep in cricket. Part of the satisfaction of both actions comes, of course, from their potential contribution to winning the game. In this sense, part of the reason for both actions is strictly external to the game. You want to win and the game simply constrains how you go about it.

However, a part of the satisfaction actually comes from what it means in baseball to 'hit a home run with the bases loaded' or what it means in cricket to 'score a four with a reverse sweep'. Neither actions are simply ways of increasing the team's score by four. The one is an achievement which marks a unique conjunction between team effort (in getting the bases loaded) and individual prowess (in hitting the home run); while the other is a particularly audacious and cheeky way of scoring runs. What makes both actions special in this respect are the rules and traditions of the respective games; and here is the rub because the rules begin to help supply the reasons for the action. In other words, the rules of these games both help to constitute and regulate actions. Game theory deals in only one aspect of this, the regulative aspect, and this is well captured by the metaphor of brick walls. Wittgenstein's language games, by contrast, deal with the constitutive aspect of rules and who is to say which best captures the rules of social interaction.

The question is ontological and it connects directly with the earlier discussion of instrumental rationality. Just as instrumental rationality is not the only ontological view of what is the essence of human rationality, there is more than one ontological view regarding the essence of social interaction. Game theory works with one view of social interaction, which meshes well with the instrumental account of human rationality; but equally there are other views (inspired by Kant, Hegel, Marx, Wittgenstein) which in turn require different models of (rational) action.

1.3 LIBERAL INDIVIDUALISM, THE STATE AND GAME THEORY

1.3.1 Methodological individualism

Some social scientists, particularly those who are committed to individualism, like the strict separation of choice and structure found in game theory because it gives an active edge to choice. Individuals *qua* individuals are plainly doing something on this account, although how much will depend on what can be said about what is likely to happen in such interactions. Game theory promises to tell a great deal on this. By comparison other traditions of political philosophy (ranging from Marx's dialectical feedback between structure and action to Wittgenstein's shared rules) work with models of human agents who seem more passive and whose contribution merges seamlessly with that of other social factors. Nevertheless the strict separation raises a difficulty regarding the origin of structures (which, at least, on other accounts are no more mysterious than action and choice).

Where do structures come from when they are separate from actions? An ambitious response which distinguishes methodological individualists of all types is that the structures are merely the deposits of previous interactions (potentially understood, of course, as games). This answer may seem to threaten an infinite regress in the sense that the structures of the previous interaction must also be explained and so on. But, the individualist will want to claim that ultimately all social structures spring from interactions between some set of *a*social individuals; this is why it is 'individualist'. These claims are usually grounded in a 'state of nature' argument, where the point is to show how particular structures (institutional constraints on action) could have arisen from the interaction between *a*social individuals. Some of these 'institutions' are generated *spontaneously* through conventions which emerge and govern behaviour in repeated social interactions. For example, one thinks of the customs and habits which inform the tradition of common law. Others may arise through individuals consciously entering into contracts with each other to create the institutions of collective decision making (which enact, for example statute law). Perhaps the most famous example of this type of institutional creation comes from the early English philosopher Thomas Hobbes who suggested in *Leviathan* that, out of fear of each other, individuals would contract with each other to form a State. In short, they would accept the absolute power of a sovereign because the sovereign's ability to enforce contracts enables each individual to transcend the dog-eat-dog world of the state of nature, where no one could trust anyone and life was 'short, nasty and brutish'.

Thus, the key individualist move is to draw attention to the way that structures not only constrain; they also enable (at least those who are in a position to create them). It is the fact that they enable which persuades individuals consciously (as in State formation) or unconsciously (in the case of those which are generated spontaneously) to build them. To bring out this point and see how it connects with the earlier discussion of the relation between action and structure it may be helpful to contrast Hobbes with Rousseau. Hobbes has the State emerging from a contract between individuals because it serves the interests of those individuals. Rousseau also talked of a social contract between individuals, but he did not speak this individualist language. For him, the political (democratic) process was not a mere means of serving persons' interests by satisfying their preferences. It was also a process which *changed* people's preferences. People were socialised, if you like, and democracy helped to create a new human being, more tolerant, less selfish, better educated and capable of cherishing the new values of the era of Enlightenment. By contrast, Hobbes' men and women were the same people before and after the contract which created the State.[4]

Returning to game theory's potential contribution, we can see that, in so far as individuals are modelled as Humean agents, game theory is well placed to help assess the claims of methodological individualists. After all, game theory purports to analyse social interaction between individuals who, as Hume argued, have passions and a reason to serve them. Thus game theory should enable us to examine the claim that, beginning from a situation with no institutions (or structures), the self-interested behaviour of these instrumentally rational agents will either bring about institutions or fuel their evolution. An examination of the explanatory power of game theory in such settings is one way of testing the individualist claims.

In fact, as we shall see in subsequent chapters, the recurring difficulty with the analysis of many games is that there are too many potential plausible outcomes. There are a variety of disparate outcomes which are consistent with (Humean) individuals *qua* individuals interacting. Which one of a set of potential outcomes should we expect to materialise? We simply do not know. Such pluralism might seem a strength. On the other hand, however, it may be taken to signify that the selection of one historical outcome is not simply a matter of instrumentally rational individuals interacting. There must be something more to it outside the individuals' preferences, their constraints and their capacity to maximise utility. The question is: what? It seems to us that either the conception of the 'individual' will have to be amended to take account of this extra source of influence (whatever it is) or it will have to be admitted that there are non-individualistic (that is, holistic) elements which are part of the explanation of what happens when people interact. In short, game theory offers the lesson that methodological individualism can only survive by expanding the notion of rational agency. The challenge is whether there are changes of this sort which will preserve the individualist premise.

1.3.2 Game theory's contribution to liberal individualism

Suppose we take the methodological individualist route and see institutions as the deposits of previous interactions between individuals. Individualists are not bound to find that the institutions which emerge in this way are fair or just. Indeed, in practice, many institutions reflect the fact that they were created by one group of people and then imposed on other groups. All that any methodological individualist is committed to is being able to find the origin of institutions in the acts of individuals *qua* individuals. The political theory of liberal individualism goes a stage further and tries to pass judgement on the legitimacy of particular institutions. Institutions in this view are to be regarded as legitimate in so far as all individuals who are governed by them would have broadly 'agreed' to their creation.

Naturally, much will turn on how 'agreement' is to be judged because people in desperate situations will often 'agree' to the most desperate of outcomes. Thus there are disputes over what constitutes the appropriate reference point (the equivalent to Hobbes's state of nature) for judging whether people would have agreed to such and such an arrangement. We set aside a host of further problems which emerge the moment one steps outside liberal individualist premises and casts doubt over whether people's preferences have been autonomously chosen. Game theory has little to contribute to this aspect of the dispute. However, it does make two significant contributions to the discussions in liberal individualism with respect to how we might judge 'agreement'.

Firstly, there is the general problem that game theory reveals with respect to all (Humean) individualist explanations: the failure to predict unique outcomes in some games (a failure which was the source of doubt, expressed at the end of section 1.3.1, about methodological individualism). This is an insight which has a special relevance for the discussion in the political theory of liberal individualism concerning the conscious creation of institutions through 'agreement'. If the test of legitimacy is 'would individuals agree to such and such?' then we need a model which tells us what individuals will agree to when they interact. In principle there are probably many models which might be used for this purpose. But, if one accepts a basic Humean model of individual action, then it seems natural to model the 'negotiation' as a game and interpret the outcome of the game as the terms of the 'agreement'. Hence we need to know the likely outcome of such games in order to have a standard for judging whether the institutions in question might have been agreed to. Thus when game theory fails to yield a prediction of what will happen in such games, it will make it very difficult for a liberal political theory premised on Humean underpinnings to come to any judgement with respect to the legitimacy of particular institutions.

Secondly game theory casts light on a contemporary debate central to liberal theory: the appropriate role for the State, or more generally any collective action agency, such as public health care systems, educational institutions, industrial relations regulations, etc. From our earlier remarks you will recall that individualists can explain institutions either as acts of conscious construction (e.g. the establishment of a tax system) or as a form of 'spontaneous order' which has been generated through repeated interaction (as in the tradition which interprets common law as the reflection of conventions which have emerged in society). The difference is important. In the past two decades the New Right has argued against the conscious construction of institutions through the actions of the State, preferring instead to rely on spontaneous order.

One of the arguments of the New Right draws on Robert Nozick's (1974) view that the condition of 'agreement', in effect, is satisfied when outcomes result from a voluntary exchange between individuals. There is no need for grand negotiations involving all of society on this view: anything goes so long as it emerges from a process of voluntary exchange. We shall say nothing on this here. But this line of argument draws further support from the Austrian school of economics, especially Friedrich von Hayek, when they argue that the benefits of institution creation (for instance the avoidance of Hobbes's dog-eat-dog world) can be achieved 'spontaneously' through the conventions which emerge when individuals repeatedly interact with one another. In other words, to escape from Hobbes's nightmare, we do not need to create a collective action agency like the State according to the New Right wing of liberalism; and again game theory is well placed through the study of repeated games to examine this claim.

1.4 A GUIDE TO THE REST OF THE BOOK

1.4.1 Three classic games: chicken, coordination and the prisoners' dilemma games

There are three particular games that have been extensively discussed in game theory and which have fascinated social scientists. The reason is simple: they appear to capture some of the elemental features of all social interactions. They can be found both within existing familiar 'structures' and plausibly in 'states of nature'. Thus the analysis of these games promises to test the claims of individualists. In other words, how much can be said about the outcome of these games will tell us much about how much of the social world can be explained in instrumentally rational, individualist terms.

The first contains a mixture of conflict and cooperation: it is called *chicken* or *hawk–dove*. For instance, two people, Bill and Jill, come across a $100 note on the pavement and each has a basic choice between demanding the lion's share (playing hawk) or acquiescing in the other person taking the lion's share (playing dove). Suppose in this instance a lion's share is $90 and when both play dove, they share the $100 equally, while when they both act hawkishly a fight ensues and the $100 gets destroyed. The options can be represented as we did before along with the consequences for each. This is done in Figure 1.2; the pay-off to the row player, Jill, is the first sum and the pay-off to the column player, Bill, is the second sum.

Plainly both parties will benefit if they can avoid simultaneous hawk-like behaviour, so there are gains from some sort of cooperation. On the other hand, there is also conflict because depending on how the fight is avoided the benefits of cooperation will be differently distributed between the two

		Bill	
		Hawk	Dove
Jill	Hawk	0, 0	90, 10
	Dove	10, 90	50, 50

Figure 1.2

players. The interesting questions are: do the players avoid the fight, and if they do how is the $100 divided?

To illustrate a *coordination game*, suppose in our earlier example of your attempt to walk to work along with a friend (Figure 1.1) that your friend has similar preferences and is trying to make a similar decision. Thus Figure 1.3 represents the joint decision problem.

		Friend	
		Drive	Walk
You	Drive	1, 1	0, 0
	Walk	0, 0	2, 2

Figure 1.3

Will you coordinate your decision and, if you do, will you walk together or drive separately?

Finally there is the *prisoners' dilemma* game (to which we have dedicated the whole of Chapter 5 and much of Chapter 6). Recall the time when there were still two superpowers each of which would like to dominate the other, if possible. They each faced a choice between arming and disarming. When both arm or both disarm, neither is able to dominate the other. Since arming is costly, when both decide to arm this is plainly worse than when both decide to disarm. However, since we have assumed each would like to dominate the other, it is possible that the best outcome for each party is when that party arms and the other disarms since although this is costly it allows the arming side to dominate the other. These preferences are reflected in the 'arbitrary' utility pay-offs depicted in Figure 1.4.

Game theory makes a rather stark prediction in this game: both players will arm (the reasons will be given later). It is a paradoxical result because each does what is in their own interest and yet their actions are collectively self-defeating in the sense that mutual armament is plainly worse than the alternative of mutual disarmament which was available to them (pay-off 1 theory of games.' The inspector may not have thought it worth his while, o the sergeant's, to explain this 'theory of games', but it is surely significan that game theory now features as part of the vocabulary of a popula television drama.

In an assessment of game theory, Tullock (1992) has remarked somewhat similarly that,

game theory has been important in that it has affected our vocabulary and our methods of thinking about certain problems.

Of course, he was thinking of the vocabulary of the social scientist. However, the observation is even more telling when the same theory also enters into a popular vocabulary, as it seems to have done. As a result, the need to understand what that theory tells us 'about certain problems' becomes all the more pressing. In short, we need to understand what game theory says, if for no other reason than that many people are thinking about the world in that way and using it to shape their actions.

		Column player	
		Disarm	Arm
Row Player	Disarm	2, 2	0, 3
	Arm	3, 0	1, 1

Figure 1.4

for each rather than 2). The existence of this type of interaction together with the inference that both will arm has provided one of the strongest arguments for the creation of a State. This is, in effect, Thomas Hobbes's argument in *Leviathan*. And since our players here are themselves States, both countries should agree to submit to the authority of a higher State which will enforce an agreement to disarm (an argument for a strong, independent, United Nations?).

1.4.2 Chapter-by-chapter guide

The next two chapters set out the key elements of game theory. For the most part the discussion here relates to games in the abstract. There are few concrete examples of the sort that 'Jack and Jill must decide how to fill a pail of water'. Our aim is to introduce the central organising ideas as simply and as clearly as possible so that we can draw out the sometimes controversial way in which game theory applies abstract reasoning.

Chapter 2 introduces the basics: the logical weeding out of strategies which are not compatible with instrumental rationality (i.e. dominance reasoning), the most famous concept that game theory has produced for dissecting games (the equilibrium concept developed by John Nash in the 1950s) and the idea of players choosing strategies *as if* at random when they are in situations where they cannot be certain about what they ought to do (these are the so-called mixed strategies). John Nash's equilibrium idea proved to be central in game theory and, thus, we discuss its meaning and uses extensively. Much attention is also paid to the critical aspects of its use. In particular, we take up some of the issues foreshadowed in sections 1.2.1 and 1.2.2 above (as well as the special problems associated with combining this equilibrium concept with the idea of mixed strategies).

The chapter also introduces two ideas which have been central to the project of refining Nash's equilibrium notion. The purpose of refining it was to make it more efficient in distinguishing between 'good' and 'not-so-good' strategies. The first refinement concerns the way that game theorists have identified the admissible sets of beliefs and strategies. Effectively, they only admit beliefs which are compatible with the assumption of CAB (see section 1.2.2), and strategies compatible with such beliefs. This first refinement is illustrated with a type of solution (the Bayesian equilibrium concept) which applies to games of incomplete information (that is, when you do not know the pay-offs of your opponent) in which some learning is possible. The second refinement relates to the possibility of the occasional mistake (or 'tremble' as it is known in the trade) affecting the execution of a strategy choice. It is introduced in order to help the game theorist reduce the number of possible solutions to games which do not feature clear-cut outcomes.

Chapter 3 extends the analysis of games to those interactions in which players take turns to act (dynamic games). It is in the context of these dynamic games that most of the refinements to the standard way of analysing games (the Nash equilibrium, that is) have been developed. For example, this chapter explains terms which have become fashionable recently, and which have the capacity to dishearten the casual observer; terms such as subgame perfection, sequential equilibria, proper equilibria and the ideas of backward and forward induction. The chapter concludes with an assessment of the place and role of the Nash equilibrium concept in game theory.

Chapter 4 is devoted to the analysis of bargaining games. These are games which have a structure which is similar to the chicken (or the hawk–dove) game above. Somewhat confusingly, John Nash proposed a particular solution for this type of game which has nothing to do with his earlier equilibrium concept (although this solution does emerge as a Nash equilibrium in the bargaining game). So be warned: the Nash solution to a bargaining game in Chapter 4 is not the same thing as the Nash equilibrium concept in Chapters 2 and 3. Much of the most recent work on this type of game has taken place in the context of an explicit dynamic version of the interaction and so Chapter 4 also provides some immediate concrete illustrations of this.

Chapter 4 also introduces the distinction between **cooperative** and **non-cooperative game theory**. The distinction relates to whether agreements made between players are binding. **Cooperative game theory** assumes that such agreements are binding, whereas **non-cooperative game theory** does not. For the most part the distinction is waning because most sophisticated **cooperative game theory** is now based on a series of **non-cooperative** games for the simple reason that if we want to assume binding agreements we shall want to know what makes such agreements binding and this will require a **non-cooperative** approach. In line with this trend, and apart from the discussion contained in Chapter 4, this book is concerned only with **non-cooperative game theory**.

The next three chapters continue in the vein of Chapter 4. They look at how the basic ideas of game theory have been applied and refined in the analysis of one or other of the three classic games.

Chapter 5 focuses on the prisoners' dilemma game. It discusses a variety

of instances of the game and a number of proposals for overc sub-optimal outcome. These range from the introduction through Immanuel Kant's rationality to David Gauthier's idea o a disposition towards constrained maximisation.

Chapter 6 deals with dynamic games of a very particular concerned with games which are repeated. The difference wh tion makes is that it enables people to develop much more c strategies. For example, there is the scope for punishing playe they have done in the past and there are opportunities for reputations for playing the game in a particular way. These richer types of behaviour than are possible in one-shot game tempting to think that these repeated games provide a model fo explanation. In fact, the richness of play comes with a pr anything can happen in these repeated games! In other word games pose even more sharply the earlier problem of Nash selection; that is, knowing what is (rationally) possible.

Chapter 7 is concerned with the evolutionary approach t games. This approach potentially both provides an answer to tl of how actual historical outcomes come into being (when a outcomes could have occurred) and it circumvents some of doubts expressed in Chapters 2, 3 and 4. It does this by a assumption of common knowledge (instrumental) rationality — analysis of evolutionary games is particularly useful in assessing in liberal theory regarding 'spontaneous order'. We have also Chapter 7 a discussion of the nature of history, the differenc history and evolution, as well as on morality and the social e norms and institutions.

Chapter 8 concludes the book with a brief survey of t empirical evidence on how people actually play games undei experimental conditions.

In the following chapters we have tried to provide the re helpful mix of pure, simple game theory and of a commentary v appeal to the social scientist. In some chapters the mix is n biased towards the technical exposition (e.g. Chapters 2 and 3 we have emphasised those matters which will appeal mostly to are keen to investigate the implications of game theory for s (e.g. Chapters 4–7).

1.5 CONCLUSION

There was a scene in a recent BBC prime time drama series police inspector smiling as he told a sergeant, 'That puts prisoner's dilemma.' The sergeant asked what 'this dilemma' inspector replied as he walked off, 'Oh it's something from t

2

THE ELEMENTS OF GAME
THEORY

2.1 INTRODUCTION

This chapter introduces the central ideas in game theory. It begins by showing how rational players can logically weed out strategies which are strategically inferior (sections 2.3 and 2.4). Such elimination of strategies relies on what game theory refers to as *dominance reasoning* and it sometimes requires the assumption of common knowledge of rationality (CKR). It is important because it yields clear predictions of what instrumentally rational players will do in some games by means of a step-by-step logic. However, in many games dominance reasoning offers no clear (or useful) predictions of what might happen. In these circumstances, game theorists commonly turn to the Nash equilibrium solution concept, named after its creator John Nash (section 2.5). The basic idea behind this concept is that rational players should not want to change their strategies if they knew what each of them had chosen to do.

This solution concept helps to refine the predictions of game theory. However, there is a cost in terms of generality. The step to Nash seems to require rather more than the assumptions of rationality and CKR. In section 1.2.2 of the previous chapter we described the essence of the extra requirement: the assumption that players' beliefs will be consistently aligned (CAB). In some games even this move does not generate predictions adequately because there are some games in which no specific set of strategies is recommended by the Nash equilibrium. In the jargon, there are games in which there is either no Nash equilibrium in pure strategies, or there are many.[1] Thus predictions made using the Nash equilibrium concept can be either non-existent or indeterminate.

As a result game theorists have attempted to refine the Nash equilibrium concept. We present two such refinements: the Bayesian Nash equilibrium concept for games of incomplete information (section 2.6) and the idea of trembling hand perfect equilibria (section 2.7). They embody two of the central ideas which have been at play in the project of refining the Nash equilibrium to overcome the problems it encounters in many games.

2.2 THE REPRESENTATION OF GAMES AND SOME NOTATION

Game theorists represent games in two ways. The first is called the **normal (or matrix) form** of a game. What it does is to associate combinations of choices (also referred to as moves or, more commonly, strategies) with outcomes by means of a matrix showing each player's pay-offs (or preferences) for each combination of choices/strategies – see Figure 2.1.

	C1	C2
R1	$^+$10, 4	$^+$1, 5$^-$
R2	9, 9$^-$	0, 3

The ($^+$, $^-$) marks next to pay-offs indicate 'best response' strategies – see the first definition in the text below

Figure 2.1

In this book the player choosing between the rows (or columns) will be labelled the row (or column) player, henceforth abbreviated as R (or C). R will be thought of as female and C as male. R's first strategy option is the first row denoted by R1. And so on. Now suppose R chooses R2 and C chooses C1. The corresponding outcome is (R2, C1). In this example, R receives 9 utils and so does C. The first entry in any element of the pay-off matrix is R's utility pay-off while the second belongs to C. For instance, outcome (R2, C2) gives 3 utils to C and nothing to R.

The second type of representation of a game is called the **extensive (or dynamic, or tree-diagram) form**. Nothing is said about the process, or sequence, of the game in the normal form and the implication is that players move simultaneously. Suppose we wish to indicate that R chooses her strategy a few moments before C gets a chance to do the same. The normal form cannot represent such a sequence; and this is where the extensive form comes in handy. In Figure 2.2 we represent two versions of the above game, one in which R moves first and one in which C takes the first step. Depending on the chosen path from one node to the other (nodes are represented with circles, with the initial node being the only one which is not full), we gravitate towards the final outcome at the bottom of the tree diagram. To preserve the analogy with the normal form representation, the first pay-off refers to R and the second to C.

There is one marking on these diagrams to note well: the broken line that appears when R is called upon to choose, Figure 2.2(b). This line joins the nodes in which R could be at. It defines what is called R's **information set** when this stretches across more than one decision node. In this instance its presence means that R does *not* know when called upon to play whether C

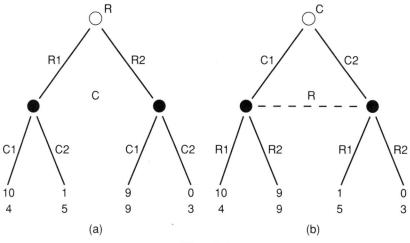

Figure 2.2

played C1 or C2; thus R could be at either of the linked decision nodes. The contrast in figure 2.2(a) where there is no broken line means that C knows which node he is at when called upon to play. So he knows whether R played R1 or R2 before he decides what to play.

It is worth noting (for more complicated games) that there is convention when drawing a game in extensive form which precludes branches looping back into one another. In other words, the sequence of decisions is always drawn in an 'arboresque' or tree-like manner with branches growing out (and not into one another). So even when an individual faces the same choice (between, say, R1 and R2) after several possible sequences of previous choices by the players, the choice must be seperately identified for each of the possible sequences leading up to it. The point is that even when people face the same choice, we wish to distinguish them when they have different histories and this is what the prohibition on looping back ensures.

2.3 DOMINANCE AND EQUILIBRIUM

How should (or would) a person play a game like the one depicted in Figure 2.1? A first glance may not be very revealing but on closer inspection, it appears that R's choice of action is obvious: play strategy R1. Why? To see this, let us first define a best response (or reply) strategy.

Definition: A strategy for player R is **best response (or reply)** to one of C's, say strategy C_i, if it gives R the largest pay-off given that C has played C_i. Similarly for player C.

Looking back at Figure 2.1, were C to play strategy C1, R1 would give R 10 utils, while R2 would only produce 9. Thus R1 is R's best response to C1.

Likewise if C were to choose C2, R1 still generates a higher pay-off for R than R2 (1 as opposed to 0). We have marked with a ($^+$) sign R's highest pay-off corresponding to each of C's strategies. This explains the ($^+$) sign next to the 10 and 1 pay-offs of player R: they indicate that R1 is the best response to C1 and C2 (notice how these signs coincide on the first row, i.e. strategy R1). Similarly we used a ($^-$) sign for C's highest pay-offs corresponding to each of R's strategies.

From the ($^-$) markings corresponding to C's best response strategies, we find that (unlike R) player C has two different best responses: C1 is best response to R1 and C2 is best response to R2 (notice how the ($^-$) markings lie in different columns, i.e. different C-strategies are best responses to different R-strategies). So, what C will do depends on what he thinks R will do. If he expects R1, he will play C1.

> **Definition:** A strategy is **dominated** if it is *not* a best response strategy whatever the strategy choice of the opposition. Conversely, a strategy is **dominant** if it is a best strategy (i.e. it maximises a player's utility pay-off) regardless of the opposition's choice of strategy.

In the language of the above definition, R2 is a dominated strategy and therefore R1 is dominant. Thus an instrumentally rational player R will be choosing R1 regardless of her thoughts about C's choice. We see that this prediction requires no degree of common knowledge rationality (CKR) whatsoever. Even if playing against a monkey, a rational player selects his or her dominant strategy (provided one exists).

> **Definition: Zero-order CKR** describes a situation in which players are instrumentally rational but they know nothing about each other's rationality. By contrast, **first-order CKR** means that not only are they instrumentally rational but also each believes that the other is rational in this manner. It follows that, if *n* is an even number, **nth-order CKR** conveys the following sentence: 'R believes that C believes that R that . . . C believes that R is instrumentally rational'; a sentence containing the verb 'believes' *n* times. When *n* is odd, then *n*th-order CKR means: 'R believes that C believes that R that . . . that C is instrumentally rational'; a sentence containing the verb 'believes' *n* times.

Returning to the game in Figure 2.1, we see that zero-order CKR is sufficient to predict what R will do: she will choose her dominant strategy R1. Indeed in games featuring one dominant strategy per player, zero-order CKR suffices. However, we need more in order to predict what a rational C will play. The reason of course is that he has no dominant strategy, meaning that what he does depends on what he expects R to do.[2] And before he can form such expectations he needs to know something about R's thoughts. It is easy to see that first-order CKR provides the necessary information. For if C knew that R is instrumentally rational, he would expect her to choose R1 as he can see (just as well as we can) that R1 is dominant. His best response then emerges: strategy C2.

The above can be summarised as follows: if we allow the set of signs (:, b) to denote the verbs 'chooses' and 'believes' respectively, then

zero-order CKR means that R : R1, while first-order CKR implies that C b R : R1, and therefore C : C2.

The fact that one of the two players has a dominant strategy allows the theorist, as well as the players, to pinpoint a single outcome as the only solution for the game. We call this an *equilibrium* solution because it is the only outcome not threatened by increasingly intelligent analysis of the situation. The more the players think of their situation, the more likely they are to converge on outcome (R1, C2).

Definition: An outcome is an **equilibrium** if it is brought about by strategies that agents have good reason to follow.

Of course the above is a minimal definition of an equilibrium outcome. It is minimalist because it offers no clue as to what constitutes a 'good reason'. In the game of Figure 2.1, we found that each player had a reason to choose a particular strategy. It was based on the presence of a dominant strategy and first-order CKR.

Definition: A **dominant strategy equilibrium** is one which emerges when the existence of a dominant strategy for at least one of the two players provides a reason for each player to choose a particular strategy.

2.4 RATIONALISABLE BELIEFS AND ACTIONS

Let us augment the game in Figure 2.1 by adding a third strategy for each player, as in Figure 2.3.

What will happen here? Does (instrumentally) rational play recommend

	C1	C2	C3
R1	+10, 4	+1, 5−	98, 4
R2	9, 9−	0, 3	99, 8
R3	1, 98	0, 100−	+100, 98

Figure 2.3

different strategies to those of Figure 2.1? The remarkable answer is: no! The newly available outcomes, (R3, C3), offer rich rewards to both parties, yet neither strategy will be undertaken by players with some degree of confidence in each other's instrumental rationality.

To see why, consider whether C would ever choose C3. The answer is never, because C3 is not a best response to any of R's strategies. That is, player C can *always* do better by playing either C1 or C2: C3 is a **dominated** strategy (notice that no ($^-$) mark corresponds to any pay-off for C in the third column). Similarly notice that R2 is dominated for player R. Thus far we see that zero-order CKR has eliminated two strategies: R2 and C3. What about the rest? Would, for example, R ever play R3? Yes, provided that she expects C to play C3 (you can see this because of the ($^+$) marking that can be found next to 100 on the bottom right of the matrix). However, she would not expect that if she knew that C is instrumentally rational (since C3, we just concluded, is a dominated strategy for C). Therefore first-order CKR eliminates the possibility that R will choose R3 and leaves R1 as the only strategic option open to R.

What will C do under first-order CKR? We know that he will not play C3 under any circumstances. And we know that whether he will choose C1 or C2 depends on whether he expects R to choose R1, R2 or R3. First-order CKR means that he will not expect R to choose R2 (since a rational R never chooses R2 and first-order CKR means that C knows R is rational). It seems that C is left with only one option: C2. We conclude that the equilibrium of this game is the outcome corresponding to strategies (R1, C2), and that it is arrived at by assuming only first-order CKR. Notice, however, that for the players to *expect* this equilibrium to materialise with certainty, we need more than first-order CKR. The reason is that C chooses C2 only because he does not expect R to go for R2. Still, he does not know, so far, whether R will opt for R1 or R3, even though C2 is a best reply to either. If, however, we assume second-order CKR, suddenly it becomes clear to him that R will choose R1. For if C believes that R believes C to be instrumentally rational, then C does not expect R to expect him to play C3, in which case he does not expect R to play R3. It is clear that second-order CKR fixes C's beliefs on the unshakeable expectation that R will choose R1. Notice that R's beliefs are still not that precise. She knows (through first-order CKR) that C3 is not on the cards, but is not sure as to whether C1 or C2 will be played. This uncertainty makes no difference to her strategy since, in either case, her best reply is R1. But before R can form a certain view about whether C will go for C1 or C2, we need third-order CKR. That is, R must know that C's thoughts are subject to second-order CKR, or to put it differently R must expect C to expect R to play R1 before she can be certain that C will choose C2. This is the same as assuming third-order CKR.

In conclusion, there is an equilibrium in this game (Figure 2.3) which will materialise if players are subject to first-order CKR. In our shorthand notation, R and C are rational (zero-order CKR); C b R to be rational and R b C to be rational (first-order CKR) which means that C b R : R1 and R b C : C2. Hence outcome (R1, C2). Moreover, for C to be sure that it will materialise, we need second-order CKR. And to be sure that R will know this also we need third-order CKR.

Definition: The **process of successive elimination of dominated strategies** works as follows. At the beginning, each player identifies his or her dominated strategies and those of his or her opponent. These are eliminated (zero-order CKR). Then each eliminates those other strategies which are best responses to strategies eliminated in the previous round (first-order CKR). In the next round, more strategies are eliminated if they appear to be best responses to recently eliminated strategies (second-order CKR). And so on until no strategies can be further eliminated.

Another example where this type of (iterated) dominance reasoning can be applied is given by the game in Figure 2.4.

	C1	C2	C3	C4
R1	5, 10	0, 11	1, 2 0	10, 10
R2	4, 0	1, 1	2, 0	20, 0
R3	3, 2	0, 4	4, 3	50, 1
R4	2, 93	0, 92	0, 91	100, 90

Figure 2.4

The successive deletion of dominant strategies now works through the following steps:

(zero-order CKR)　　　Step 1: C eliminates C4 (notice that C4 is *always* worse as a strategy for C than C1, C2 or C3; i.e. C4 is dominated).

(first-order CKR)　　　Step 2: R eliminates R4 (since the only reason for playing R4 is that it is a good reply to C4, which was eliminated in step 1).

(second-order CKR)　Step 3: C eliminates C1 (because C1 makes sense only as a good reply to R4, which was eliminated in step 2).

(third-order CKR)　　Step 4: R eliminates R1 (R1 being rationally playable only if there is a threat that C1 will be played by C. But C1 was eliminated in step 3).

(fourth-order CKR)   Step 5:   C eliminates C3 (which was leaning on R1 that was eliminated in step 4).

(fifth-order CKR)   Step 6:   Now that C is only left with strategy C2, R opts for R2 (i.e. her best response to C2)

We conclude that (R2, C2) form the (iterated) dominant equilibrium in this game. Such strategies are sometimes also referred to as **rationalisable strategies** (after Bernheim, 1984, and Pearce, 1984).

> **Definition: Rationalisable strategies** are those strategies that are left in a two-person game after the process of successive elimination of dominated strategies is completed.

The term *rationalisable* has been used to describe such strategies because a player can defend his or her choice (i.e. rationalise it) on the basis of beliefs about the beliefs of the opponent which are *not* inconsistent with the game's data. However, to pull this off, we need 'more' commonly known rationality than in the simpler games in Figures 2.1 and 2.3. Looking at Figure 2.4 we see that outcome (100, 90) is much more inviting than the rationalisable outcome (1, 1). It is the deepening confidence in each other's instrumental rationality (fifth-order CKR, to be precise) which leads our players to (1, 1). In summary notation, the rationalisable strategies R2, C2 are supported by the following train of thinking (which reflects the six steps described earlier):

(a) R b C is rational; C b R is rational
(b) R b C b R b C : C2 and C b R b C b R : R2

One might think that rather too much believing about believing is required here, but is this not the hallmark of strategic thinking?

Of course, this process of (iterated) dominance reasoning will not always yield a unique equilibrium. Put differently, more than one strategy per player may turn out to be rationalisable. Figure 2.5 contains two examples:

	C1	C2	C3	C4
R1	+5, 10	0, 11	1, 10	10, 20⁻
R2	4, 0	+1, 0	2, 0	20, 1⁻
R3	3, 2	0, 4⁻	+4, 3	50, 1
R4	2, 93⁻	0, 92	0, 91	+100, 90

Figure 2.5

In Figure 2.5 the process of elimination begins with the dominated C3 and throws out strategies R2, R3 and C2. This leaves R with R1 and R4, and C with C1 and C4. Each player can rationally play one of two strategies and the game is indeterminate. Or to put this slightly differently there are four **rationalisable strategies** R1, R4, C1 and C4 and so we might reasonably expect any of the four possible RC combinations from this group might be played. Perhaps we should be grateful; at the least four strategies were eliminated. But even this is not always possible. In the game of Figure 2.6, *all* strategies are rationalisable because no strategy is dominated – therefore CKR of however large order can offer no guidance to players.

	C1	C2	C3
R1	⁺100, 100	0, 0	50, 101⁻
R2	50, 0	⁺1, 1⁻	60, 0
R3	0, 300⁻	0, 0	⁺200, 200

Figure 2.6

Box 2.1

A BRIEF HISTORY OF GAME THEORY

It is rare for someone to be universally acclaimed a genius by their peers, but John von Neumann (1903–57), who wrote with Oskar Morgenstern the key early book on game theory, was such a rarity. He was a brilliant Hungarian mathematician who emigrated to the USA in 1930. It is equally rare for the fame of a mathematician to stretch far beyond the groves of academe, but again von Neumann was the exception. He was well known as a result of his crucial mathematical contributions to the Manhattan Project for the development of atomic weapons during the Second World War and for his pioneering work on the modern computer. He was also a member, at the end of his life, of the influential Atomic Energy Commission and his attendance at meetings in a wheelchair (as he struggled with cancer) has provoked speculation that he was the model for Dr Strangelove in Stanley Kubrick's 1963 film of that name.

Reputedly, von Neumann became interested in the general problem of what to do where what seems best depends on what other persons think you might do, as a result of playing poker. A similar interest in poker (and the role of bluffing) was the inspiration for what is often taken to be the earliest contribution to modern game theory by the French mathematician Borel in the early 1920s. By comparison, von Neumann's first paper, entitled 'The theory of parlour games', appeared later, in 1928; and he

49

combined with the economist Morgenstern at Princeton even later to produce the landmark book on game theory in 1944.

After the Second World War, game theory became closely associated with the Rand Corporation. The Rand (standing for R and D) Corporation was a private company spun off from the US Air Force at the end of the war and it was specifically concerned with the prospects of intercontinental nuclear warfare. Game theory was obviously relevant to this task and as a result the organisation championed its development by hiring as consultants von Neumann and other central figures in the development of game theory, like John Nash, Duncan Luce and Howard Raiffa.

Von Neumann and Morgenstern's book had dealt with zero-sum non-cooperative games (as well as a variety of cooperative games, which only concern us briefly here in Chapter 4). These are games where one player's gain/loss is always the other player's loss/gain as the returns sum to zero. They showed that playing the maximin strategy is the rational thing to do in these games (i.e. you look at the worst outcome each of your strategies may bring and then choose the strategy with the best such 'worst' outcome). Zero-sum games are, however, more curious than ubiquitous in social life and consequently non-cooperative game theorists rapidly switched attention to what should be done in non-zero-sum games. The immediate result was the famous Nash equilibrium concept, after John Nash, which is discussed extensively in this book. The basic idea is that rational players should select strategies which are best replies to each other because the selection of such strategy pairs will not cause either player to regret their choice. Interestingly this equilibrium concept was first tested in some experiments at Rand by the game theorists Flood and Dresher and they used a game which has the form that later became famously known as the prisoners' dilemma (see Poundstone, 1993).

Game theory has been likened to Kriegspiel, the notorious game popularised by Prussian military schools as a 'training for war', because of the association with Rand and its Dr Strangelove image (see Poundstone, 1993). Indeed, Rand was charged with 'thinking the unthinkable' and not unsurprisingly during these early days, game theory often seemed tainted by its connection with the Rand plans for nuclear war and pre-emptive nuclear strikes. Perhaps this explains in part why game theory suffered an eclipse in its fortunes in the late 1950s. What is not in doubt is the decline of game theory over this decade. By 1957, Luce and Raiffa, in what remains a classic text on game theory, express the point clearly.

> We have the historical fact that many social scientists have become disillusioned with game theory. Initially there was a naive bandwagon feeling that game theory solved innumerable problems in sociology and economics, or that, at least it made their solution a practical matter of a few years' work. This has not turned out to be the case.
>
> (1957, p. 10)

Game theory languished for the next 20 years. There were important contributions along the way, of course (from Harsanyi and Selten, in particular), but it was not until the 1980s that game theory took off again; and this time it soared!

2.5 NASH STRATEGIES AND NASH EQUILIBRIUM SOLUTIONS

2.5.1 The role of common knowledge rationality (CKR) and the Harsanyi doctrine

This section introduces the most powerful, popular and controversial tool of game theory. It comes from John Nash who gave game theory, through a number of seminal papers in the 1950s, an impetus and character that it retains (see Box 2.1 for a potted history of game theory). In these papers he addresses precisely the problem of multiple rationalisable strategies by seeking to place further restrictions on the beliefs which a rational person will entertain. To illustrate his argument, consider strategy R1 in the game of Figure 2.6. The following monologue by R is the only set of beliefs that can *rationalise* the choice of R1.

I will play R1 because I expect C to play C1. Why do I expect this? Because C has got me wrong and he expects that I will be playing R3 (rather than the R1 which I intend to play). You can ask me why *I* think that *he* will think that. Well, perhaps because he expects that I will mistakenly think that he is about to play C3, when in reality I expect him to play C1. Of course, if he knew that I was planning to play R1, he ought to play C3. But he does not know this and, for this reason, and given my expectations, R1 is the right choice for me. Of course, had he known I will play R1, I should not do so. It is my conjecture, however, that he expects me to play R3 thinking I expect him to play C3. The reality is that I expect him to play C1 and I plan to play R1.

It can be summarised using the shorthand described earlier as follows:

R : R1 because   R b C :   C1 because (see next line)
                   R b C b R : R3 because (see next line)
                   R b C b R b C : C3 because (see next line)
                   R b C b R b C b R : R1 (and this loops back to the beginning)

We see that fourth-order CKR is sufficient for a belief to be developed which is consistent with this particular strategy. Increasing the order of CKR does not change things as the above loop will be repeated every four iterations. Thus strategy R1 can be based on expectations which are sustainable even under infinite-order CKR. Different, but equally internally consistent, trains of thought exist to support R2 and R3. For example, R3 is supported by a story very similar to the above. We offer only its shorthand exposition:

R : R3 because   R b C : C3 because (see next line)
                   R b C b R : R1 because (see next line)

R b C b R b C : C1 because (see next line)
R b C b R b C b R : R3 (and so loops back to the beginning)

Now consider the equivalent rationalisation of R2:

I will play R2 because I believe that C will play C2. And why do I believe that C will play C2? Because he thinks that I will play R2, thinking that I expect him to play C2. And so on.

This is much simpler than the one required to justify R1 or R3: witness its simplicity in shorthand form, which reveals that the loop of beliefs only takes two orders of CKR to produce.

R : R2 because   R b C : C2 because
R b C b R : R2 (and so loops back to the beginning)

John Nash (1951) picks out R2 as the more salient strategy not only because it is simpler but because it *is the only strategy supported by beliefs which do not presume that one's opponent will make a mistake by expecting something which R does not intend to do.* Compare the stories told in support of R1 and R3 on the one hand, and R2 on the other, and it is obvious that R1 and R3 can only be played rationally when R assumes that C has got R's thought processes wrong (for example, R1 is played when R believes that C believes that R will play R3). By contrast, R2 requires no such assumption. Indeed, R2 demands that R expects C to guess her thoughts correctly. You will recall our discussion from section 1.2.2 in Chapter 1 in which the so-called Harsanyi doctrine was presented. That doctrine (together with the Aumann argument over the impossibility of agreeing to disagree) means beliefs are consistently aligned as in the Nash equilibrium strategies (R2, C2) above. Thus if we accept the argument that players' beliefs must be consistently aligned (CAB), then we will follow Nash and expect (R2, C2) in this game.

> **Definition:** Beliefs are **inconsistently aligned** when action emanating from these beliefs can potentially 'upset' them. A belief of one player (say X) is 'upset' when another player (say Y) takes an action with a probability which player X has miscalculated. By constrast, beliefs are **consistently aligned (CAB)** when the actions taken by each player (based on the beliefs they hold about the other) are constrained so that they do not upset those beliefs.

The same analysis applies for player C. Strategies C1 and C3, in this example, are rationalisable only if C expects R to get some things wrong, whereas C2 is played when C respects R's capacity to forecast accurately his thoughts. It turns out that in Figure 2.6 the only outcome which corresponds to mutual respect of the capacity of one's opponent to prophesy correctly (but also to know that the other knows . . . that each can prophesy accurately) is (R2, C2), the **Nash equilibrium** (produced by the **Nash strategies**).

> **Definition:** A set of rationalisable strategies (one for each player) are in a **Nash equilibrium** if their implementation confirms the expectations of each player about the other's choice. Put differently, **Nash strategies** are the only rationalisable ones which, if implemented, confirm the expectations on which they were based. This is why they are often referred to as self-confirming strategies or why it can be said that this equilibrium concept requires that players' beliefs are consistently aligned (CAB).

It may help to notice that a corollary of this definition is that Nash equilibria are formed by strategy pairs which are best replies to each other because this reveals the connection between the Nash equilibrium concept and CAB from another angle. If we accept the Harsanyi doctrine and both players face the same information set given by the knowledge of the rules of the game, then we will accept that both players will draw the same inference about how rational players will play this game. Thus there is a unique way for rational players to play the game. We assume CKR so both players will expect that the uniquely rational way of playing the game will be followed. The question is what is it? Well if there is one way for rational agents to play and they are both instrumentally rational, then it follows that the uniquely rational way must satisfy the condition of specifying strategies which are best replies to each other. Otherwise one player, by not selecting a best reply, will not be acting instrumentally rationally. Thus we may not be able to say immediately what the uniquely rational way of playing the game is, but we can narrow the answer down because we know that when there is a uniquely rational way then it will have to be formed by strategies which are best replies to each other; that is, they must be in Nash equilibrium.

The thinking behind the Nash equilibrium is in some respects quite brilliant. It cuts through the knot of webs of beliefs and arrives at a simple conclusion that happens to correspond to the highest degree of mutual respect of everyone's mental capacities. In more practical terms, it can furnish unique solutions where there were many (e.g. Figure 2.6). It is thus no wonder that game theorists, as well as many social theorists, have embraced the Nash concept. There are, however, reasons for being cautious.

Box 2.2

COURNOT'S OLIGOPOLY THEORY IN THE LIGHT OF GAME THEORY

The first example of interdependent decision making that students of economics are introduced to explicitly is the case of oligopoly; that is, a market in which there are few sellers who (by virtue of their size relative to the market) have the capacity to affect price through their output decisions. Long before game theory, a famous model of this situation was suggested by a 19th century French economist: the Cournot equilibrium.

Suppose that there are two firms only: firm 1 and firm 2. Each tries to maximise profits by selecting the appropriate level of output. However, the market price of the commodity they are producing (and subsequently selling) depends on the total level of output. If p denotes price, then p is a function of Q, where $Q = q_1 + q_2$ is total output and q_i is the level of output chosen by firm i (i is 1 or 2). The problem here is that each firm influences price and therefore a firm's revenue pq_i depends not only on its choice of output (q_i) but also on the output choice of its competitor. As a result, the profits of each firm are a function of the combination of output strategies (q_1, q_2). To keep things simple, consider the one-shot non-cooperative version of this game: firms make a single decision about output levels and do not communicate with each other prior to making it. Of course in reality firms make many such decisions after observing the behaviour of the competition. But this would require a repeated game analysis which we reserve for Chapter 6. To motivate the current example, we may think of the output choice as equivalent to having to decide the size of the plant. Once one makes such a decision, it cannot be changed (at least in the short run) and thus the game is of the one-shot variety.

Assuming that these firms are trying to maximise profits, it is easy to show that, given (a) a demand function (linking total output Q to market price p) and (b) a cost function for each firm (which computes the total cost of production for a firm for each level of output by that firm) there exist simple relations $q_1 = f(q_2)$ and $q_2 = g(q_1)$ translating into a best reply the expectations of each concerning the level of output of the other. In other words, function $f(.)$ tells firm 1 how much to produce (i.e. sets q_1) if it expects (for some reason) firm 2 to produce q_2. Function $g(.)$ similarly tells firm 2 which level of q_2 maximises its profits if it expects (for some reason) firm 1 to produce q_1. The next analytical task is to find reasons for expecting one level of output by your competitor rather than another. Pinpointing the beliefs which are likely to generate some kind of solution is best understood in the context of this chapter's sections 2.3, 2.4 and 2.5.

In the figure opposite the two axes depict the potential quantity strategies of the two firms. The flatter line labelled g represents the best replies of firm 2 to all possible q_2 choices by firm 1. For example, if firm 2 expects firm 1 to choose q_1^2, its best strategy is q_2^1. Similarly, line f captures the best responses of firm 1 to each potential strategy (q_2) of firm 2. (Below we show how these lines are derived mathematically.) It becomes immediately noticeable that, in view of the definition of the two

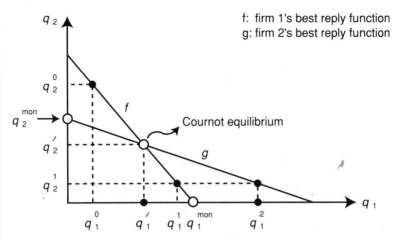

lines $f(.)$ and $g(.)$, the strategy combination (q'_1, q'_2) is a Nash equilibrium. The reason is that q'_1 is firm 1's best reply to q'_2 while the latter is firm 2's best reply to q'_1 – notice how in the above diagram point (q'_1, q'_2) belongs to f and g simultaneously. _consistent alignment of belief_

Under what conditions will the Nash equilibrium (q'_1, q'_2) materialise? Do we need to assume CAB or will CKR suffice? The answer is in the diagram above: CKR will suffice as there is no need for CAB. Let us explain. Is there a strategy for firm 1 other than q'_1 which is rationalisable? If there is, then only the assumption of CAB will support the Nash equilibrium over other rationalisable strategies. Consider some other strategy, say q^0_1. Could firm 1 choose it rationally? The answer is negative since the only belief that would motivate such a choice is that firm 2 would choose q^0_2. However, firm 2 would never choose to produce so much since line g (the second firm's best reply line) cuts the vertical axis at a point below q^0_2 at level q^{mon}_2. After all q^{mon}_2 is the output firm 2 would produce if firm 1 was not around (i.e. if $q_1 = 0$); that is, firm 2's monopoly output. Firm 2 will never produce more than that!

Thus firm 1 cannot rationally choose q^0_1. How about output q^1_1? To choose this rationally, firm 1 must expect firm 2 to produce q^1_2. Is this possible? At first sight, yes (since it is less than q^{mon}_2). However, the question then becomes 'Does firm 1 have a good reason to expect firm 2 to produce q^1_2?' Firm 2 will select this level of output only if it expects firm 1 to produce q^2_1. But it would be silly for firm 2 to expect firm 1 to do so as this would mean that firm 1 would be producing above its monopoly output q^{mon}_1. In conclusion, the choice of q^1_1 cannot be justified by a train of plausible beliefs; at some order of common knowledge of rationality (CKR) one of the two firms must anticipate a level of production by another firm exceeding what that firm would have produced if it had the market to itself (which is implausible). It transpires that, through repeated application of this logic, the only set of quantity strategies which can be defended by trains of plausible beliefs is the equilibrium outcome (q'_1, q'_2). _common knowledge of rationality_

Two remarks: firstly, the Cournot equilibrium above is a Nash equilibrium but it did not require the CAB assumption. In this sense, it is similar to the equilibrium outcomes in the games of Figures 2.3 and 2.4

55

which were brought about by the successive elimination of dominated strategies. In this example, the dominated strategies which were eliminated initially are $q_2 > q_2^{mon}$ and $q_1 > q_1^{mon}$, since neither firm will produce in a situation of duopolistic competition more than it would have had it monopolised the market. No order of CKR was necessary for this elimination. CKR is used at the next level when all the strategies of firm 1 (or 2) which depend on expectations of q_2 (or q_1) exceeding q_2^{mon} (or q_1^{mon}) are eliminated. If we go far enough, the only strategies left untouched are the equilibrium strategies q_1' and q_2'. As in the examples of Figures 2.3 and 2.4, an equilibrium was found based on the assumption of CKR (of some order) with no need to make the draconian CAB assumption. Only in this case (unlike the games of Figures 2.3 and 2.4), the number of potential strategies is infinite (since the strategy set is continuous) making necessary an infinite order of CKR in order to arrive at the equilibrium.

Secondly, we arrived at the Cournot equilibrium in what is known as *logical time* (as opposed to historical time). That is, the convergence to (q_1', q_2') was not a result of a sequence of decisions but of a sequence of beliefs. This is a one-shot game involving a single decision by each firm. If we want an analysis of what happens when firms make a sequence of interdependent decisions, we need a totally upgraded model. As we show in Chapter 6, repetition creates many equilibria which the above diagram is ill-equipped to illustrate.

Some algebra follows.

Let the inverse demand function be $p = a - bQ$ where $Q = q_1 + q_2$. Then firm 1 tries to maximise the profit function $V_1 = [a - b(q_1 + q_2)]q_1 - c_1q_1$ subject to q_1, while firm 2 maximises profit function $V_2 = [a - b(q_1 + q_2)]q_2 - c_2q_2$ subject to q_2. Parameters c_1 and c_2 are the (assumed constant) costs of producing one unit of output by each of the two firms. The condition for the maximisation of profits is that the derivatives of V_1 and V_2 are set equal to zero. Hence $a - 2bq_1 - bq_2 - c_1 = 0$ and $a - 2bq_2 - bq_1 - c_2 = 0$ are the conditions which must be satisfied so that each firm maximises its profits. Rewriting, we get two functions of q^1:

$$f: q_2 = (a - c_1)/b - 2q_1$$
$$g: q_2 = (a - c_2)/2b - (1/2)q_1$$

These linear equations are the best reply functions (as depicted in the diagram) of firms 1 and 2 respectively. The fact that they are linear (owing to the linearity of the demand and cost functions) ensures that the intersection point between them can be supported by trains of thought which do not cross over into the implausible area $q_2 > q_2^{mon}$ and $q_1 > q_1^{mon}$. Lastly, it is interesting to ask how Cournot thought of this solution without any game theory: he simply observed that if each firm treated the other parametrically (that is, if it ignored the fact that its decision would affect the other) relations f and g emerge. If seen as a system of two equations in two unknowns, there is only one solution. Intriguingly, we get the same solution if we assume that each side has no idea that its decisions affect those of the other (which is what Cournot did) as we do when we assume that they are fully aware of their interdependence and totally respectful of each other's rationality (i.e. CKR)!

2.5.2 Some logical objections to the Nash equilibrium concept

Why assume that rational players always hold mutually consistent beliefs when every strategy of each player can be supported with a set of internally consistent beliefs? The answer that Nash would give (and it is appealing) is that, because they are rational and respect each other's rationality, they are naturally drawn to the Nash equilibrium since the latter is the only one that respects equally every one's rationality. Internal consistency is not enough when the game is to be played under CKR; mutual respect of the highest order requires that the beliefs should also be mutually consistent (CAB).

In the same spirit, it is sometimes argued (borrowing a line from John von Neumann and Oskar Morgenstern) that the objective of any analysis of games is the equivalent of writing a book on how to play games; and the minimum condition which any piece of advice on how to play a game must satisfy is simple: the advice must remain good advice once the book has been published. In other words, it could not really be good advice if people would not want to follow it once the advice was widely known. On this test, only (R2, C2) pass, since when the R player follows the book's advice, the C player would want to follow it as well, and vice versa. The same cannot be said of the other rationalisable strategies. For instance, suppose (R1, C1) was recommended: then R would not want to follow the advice when C is expected to follow it by selecting C1 and likewise, if R was expected to follow the advice, C would not want to.

Both versions of the argument with respect to what mutual rationality entails seem plausible. Yet, there is something odd here. Does respect for each other's rationality lead each person to believe that neither will make a mistake in a game? Anyone who has talked to good chess players (perhaps *the* masters of strategic thinking) will testify that rational persons pitted against equally rational opponents (whose rationality they respect) do not immediately assume that their opposition will never make errors. On the contrary, the point in chess is to *engender* such errors! Are chess players irrational then?

One is inclined to answer no, but why? And what is the difference as compared with the earlier Nash intuition?

The difference resides in whether it is rational for players to think that they might outwit their opponent, in the sense that they act on a belief that their opponent thinks they will do something other than what they are going to do. Nash says this is not rational, while chess players seem to think it is; and both answers can make sense. It all depends on whether you believe there is a uniquely rational way to play the game. If there is then Nash is right since a combination of rational players and a uniquely rational course of action leaves no reason for one to expect that the other will play in some different way without contravening the assumption of CKR. However, when there is no uniquely rational way to play the game (which is certainly what chess players seem to think), then it is unclear what either player should expect of the other and so it is perfectly possible for a player to act on a belief that their opponent will think they are going to play something completely different. In these circumstances, the only restraint on what you expect your opponent to believe about you, is that your opponent cannot expect you to play a dominated strategy as this would contravene the assumption of CKR.

In other words, any rationalisable strategy is consistent with CKR and the move from CKR to Nash requires the further assumption that beliefs must be consistently aligned (CAB). In turn this only makes sense when there is a uniquely rational way to play the game.

David Kreps (1990) sums the problem up nicely:

> We may believe that each player has his own conception of how his opponents will act, and we may believe that each plays optimally with respect to his conception, but it is much more dubious to expect that in all cases those various conceptions and responses will be 'aligned' or nearly aligned in the sense of an equilibrium, each player anticipating that others will do what those others indeed plan to do.

It might be possible to leave it at that. Perhaps some games have uniquely rational ways to be played and others do not; and so be it. However, defenders of the generality of the Nash equilibrium concept make a stronger argument by appealing to the **Harsanyi doctrine**. It will be recalled that this doctrine suggests (see also section 1.2.2) that, given the same information set regarding some event, rational agents must always draw the same conclusion (that is, expectations of what will happen). Of course, it is possible that agents have different information sets and so draw different conclusions. But it will be recalled from section 1.2.2 that Robert Aumann, in defence of Harsanyi, discounts this possibility because two agents could not agree to disagree in such a manner, since the moment rational agents discover that they are holding inconsistent expectations each has a reason to revise their beliefs until they converge and become consistent. Thus the Harsanyi–Aumann combination implies that rational agents, when faced by the same information with respect to the game (the event in this case), should hold the same beliefs about how the game will be played by rational agents. In short there must be a unique set of beliefs which rational players will hold about how a game is played rationally.

There are problems with both parts of the argument and we have referred to them in Chapter 1. We risk repetition because the Nash equilibrium concept gives us an opportunity to recast and develop these objections. The Harsanyi doctrine seems to depend on a powerfully algorithmic and controversial view of reason. Reason on this account (at least in an important part) is akin to a set of rules of inference which can be used in moving from evidence to expectations. That is why people using reason (because they are using the same algorithms) should come to the same conclusion. However, there is genuine puzzlement over whether such an algorithmic view of reason can apply to all circumstances. Can any finite set of rules contain rules for their own application to all possible circumstances? The answer seems to be no, since under some sufficiently detailed level of description there will be a question of whether the rule applies to this event and so we shall need rules for applying the rules for applying the rules. And as there is no limit to the detail of the description of events, we shall need rules for applying the rules for applying the rules, and so on to infinity. In other words, every set of rules will require creative interpretation in some circumstances and so in these cases it is perfectly possible for two individuals who share the same rules to hold divergent expectations.

This puts a familiar observation from John Maynard Keynes and Frank Knight regarding genuine uncertainty in a slightly different way, but nevertheless it yields the same conclusion. There will be circumstances under which individuals are unable to decide rationally what probability assessment to attach to events because the events are uncertain and so it should not be surprising to find that they disagree. Likewise, the admiration for entrepreneurship found among economists of the Austrian school depends on the existence of uncertainty. Entrepreneurship is highly valued precisely because, as a result of uncertainty, people can hold different expectations regarding the future. In this context, the entrepreneurs are those who back their judgement against that of others and succeed. In other words, there would be no job for entrepreneurs if we all held common expectations in a world ruled by CAB!

A similar conclusion regarding ineliminable uncertainty is shared by social theorists who have been influenced by the philosophy of Kant. They deny that reason should be understood algorithmically or that it always supplies answers as to what to do. For Kantians reason supplies a critique of itself which is the source of negative restraints on what we can believe rather than positive instructions as to what we should believe. Thus the categorical imperative (see section 1.2.1), which according to Kant ought to determine many of our significant choices, is a sieve for beliefs and it rarely singles out one belief. Instead, there are often many which pass the test and so there is plenty of room for disagreement over what beliefs to hold.

Perhaps somewhat surprisingly though, a part of Kant's argument might lend support to the Nash equilibrium concept. In particular Kant thought that rational agents should only hold beliefs which are capable of being universalised. This idea, taken by itself, might prove a powerful ally of Nash. The beliefs which support R1 and R3 in Figure 2.6 for the R player do not pass this test since if C were to hold those beliefs as well, C would knowingly hold contradictory beliefs regarding what R would do. In comparison, the beliefs which support R2 and C2 are mutually consistent and so can be held by both players without contradiction. Of course, a full Kantian perspective is likely to demand rather more than this and it is not typically adopted by game theorists. Indeed such a defence of Nash would undo much of the foundations of game theory: for the categorical imperative would even recommend choosing dominated strategies if this is the type of behaviour that each wished everyone adopted. Such thoughts sit uncomfortably with the Humean foundations of game theory and we will not dwell on them for now. Instead, since the spirit of the Humean approach to reason is algorithmic, we shall continue discussing the difficulties with the Harsanyi–Aumann defence of Nash.

Robert Aumann's defence of the Harsanyi doctrine (and thus of CAB) has both logical and practical problems. The practical doubts are quite straightforward. They surface simply because the behaviour in many (especially financial) markets also suggests that people frequently hold divergent beliefs (see Box 2.3). One logical difficulty concerns the idea that disagreements yield new information for both parties which causes revisions in expectations until a convergence is achieved. It sounds plausible, but when beliefs pertain as to how to play the game and divergent beliefs are only revealed in the playing of the game, it is more than a little difficult to see how the argument is to be applied to the beliefs which agents hold prior to playing the game. Naturally when the game is repeated, the idea makes perfect sense, but for one-shot games it is difficult to see how the Aumann argument can bite. As we stated in Chapter 1, it is difficult to accept that some mental process will engender uniformity of beliefs in the absence of an actual process of interaction.

A logical difficulty also arises when information is costly to acquire. Suppose Aumann is correct and you can extract information so fully that expectations converge. Convergence means that it is 'as if' you had the same information (following Harsanyi). But if this is the case and it is costly to acquire information, why would anyone ever acquire information? Why not free-ride on other people's efforts? However, if everyone does this, then neither agent will have a reason to revise their beliefs when a disagreement is revealed because the disagreement will not reflect differences in information (since no one has acquired any). The only way to defeat this logic is by assuming that information is not transparently revealed through actions, so there is still possibly some gain to an individual through the acquisition of information rather than its extraction from other agents. But if this is the case, then expectations will not converge because agents will always hold information sets which diverge in some degree.

Thus we conclude that, unless game theorists shake off their Humean algorithmic conception of rationality (and perhaps adopt something like a Kantian consistency requirement), it will be difficult to defend the universal applicability of the Nash equilibrium concept. We draw this conclusion because it is difficult from a Humean perspective to justify a presumption

Box 2.3

AGREEING TO DISAGREE EVEN WHEN IT IS COSTLY

During the late summer of 1992, there was exceptional activity in European currency markets. First the lira was forced to devalue within the European Exchange Rate Mechanism (ERM) and then speculators turned their attentions to the pound and the Spanish peseta, selling both in the expectation that they would follow the lira.

This selling took place against a background of a deepening recession in the UK. Indeed throughout the spring and early summer as the recession in the UK economy worsened there had been renewed calls for a reduction of interest rates. But, the British government was committed to membership of the ERM and was determined to hold the exchange rate. So it kept interest rates high and it sold foreign currency from its reserves to boost the demand for pounds. There would, of course, have been no point in these circumstances in taking such actions had the government thought that the pound would eventually have to leave the ERM; since if this had been the case, then the government would have known that it was only delaying a depreciation and such a delay was obviously costly in terms of delaying interest rate cuts, and the recovery, and through the expenditure of reserves. Thus it seems we should assume that the government thought that the pound could be maintained at the old ERM rate through these actions. Equally, there would be no point in speculators selling pounds and forsaking the relatively high interest rates to be enjoyed by holding sterling rather than DMs, unless they expected that the pound would eventually depreciate.

Hence, the speculators and the British government appeared to be in fundamental disagreement through the summer of 1992 over the likely direction of sterling. This disagreement came to a spectacular head in the week beginning on 14 September. Sterling bumped along the bottom of the ERM band on Monday and Tuesday and then on Wednesday, reportedly triggered by a newspaper interview with the President of the Bundesbank, the selling of sterling reached new peaks. Indeed, as one Bank of England Official said 'I can't stress enough the sheer scale of the selling. We have never seen anything like it . . . . It was as if an avalanche was coming at us.' The Chancellor of the Exchequer raised interest rates by 2 points to 12% at 11 am; at 2.15 pm he raised them again, this time to 15%. By 4 pm, a third (about £15 billion) of the official reserves had been used in support of sterling that day alone and the defence of sterling was over. The Chancellor of the Exchequer took sterling out of the ERM, and by 5 pm on the New York market the pound had fallen by about 10% against the DM.

It is difficult to gauge the precise costs to the Bank of England, and ultimately to the British tax payer, of this disagreement over the summer of 1992. The net loss to the reserves was the (roughly) 10% depreciation on whatever reserves had been sold (or committed) in support of sterling. The precise figures here are never clear because the Bank of England takes up positions in futures markets for sterling where margins are low, but it is plain from the use of reserves on 'Black Wednesday' alone that the cost to the reserves ran into several billion pounds. In addition, there were the costs from delaying the economic recovery by pursuing high interest rates.

Of course, the other side to these costs from 'agreeing to disagree' over the summer were some spectacular speculative gains. It has been suggested, for instance, that George Soros, one of the gurus of financial markets, made a billion dollars that summer from speculating against the lira and the pound. This has not been confirmed, but as a currency dealer from the Bank of America told the *News at Ten* reporter on Wednesday evening, 'We've had an excellent day. We've made a lot of money . . . about £10 million' – not bad for 1 day's work for a few people operating in front of a computer screen!

that every game has a uniquely rational way of being played, and such a presumption appears necessary if we are to move from instrumental rationality and CKR to Nash (and CAB).

2.6 GAMES OF INCOMPLETE INFORMATION

Agents often do not know the rules of the game because they are not privy to the pay-offs of the other player. In Chapter 1 we introduced John Harsanyi's idea on how to reduce such cases of incomplete information to complete information games. To illustrate how it is done in more detail, consider the interaction between a monopoly supplier of an energy source (say coal) and a monopoly producer of electricity currently using oil-fired power stations (this is a variant of an example from Fudenberg and Tirole, 1989). The oil producer has a choice between raising price (R) or holding it steady (S) and the electricity company has a choice between building a new power station using, say, coal, so as to diversify fuel sources and remaining completely dependent on oil through not building. It is conceivable that if the costs of building a new power station are high (H) then the pay-offs

		Oil producer	
		R	S
Electricity company	B	0, −1	2, 0
	NB	2, 1	3, 0

Pay-offs when the costs of building a new power plant are high (H)

Figure 2.7

		Oil producer	
		R	S
Electricity company	B	3, −1	5, 0
	NB	2, 1	3, 0

Pay-offs when the costs of building a new power plant are low (L)

Figure 2.8

could look like those in Figure 2.7. Alternatively if costs of building are low (L) then the pay-offs could plausibly look like those in Figure 2.8.

Naturally the electricity producer knows the costs of building a new power station. If the oil company also knows this then we have a game of complete information (players know the rules of the game); and depending on whether the costs are high or low it will be given by either Figure 2.7 or 2.8. However, when the oil company does not know the costs of building a new power station, then it becomes a game of incomplete information (players are not sure about what are the rules of the game). In these circumstances, Harsanyi (1967/1968) assumed that the oil company will hold some probability assessment regarding the likelihood of building costs being high (and in general that this assessment is common knowledge) and he developed the concept of a Bayesian (Nash) equilibrium.

Such an equilibrium has the following properties: it specifies (i) an action for the electricity company (B or NB or some probability of one or the other) conditional on the knowledge of its type (H or L) which is optimal given its expectations regarding the action of the oil producer, and (ii) an action for the oil producer which is optimal given its belief p regarding type and what it expects each type will do. Finally it requires that the expectations regarding each other's behaviour are consistent with the actions planned by each agent (i.e. the CAB requirement).

In this particular game, the Bayesian equilibrium does not involve the Nash equilibrium concept because both possible versions of the game can be solved uniquely with the dominant equilibrium concept. This means that the consistency requirement is unproblematic because it follows from CKR. (In general, this will not always be the case because the potential versions of the game may not have a unique dominant equilibrium. As a result, the Bayesian equilibria often depend on the Nash equilibrium concept, in which case, and unlike the case of Figures 2.7 and 2.8, the consistency requirement depends not only on CKR but also on CAB.)

In version 2.7 (NB, R) is the dominant equilibrium because NB is a dominant strategy, while in version 2.8 the dominant equilibrium is (B, S) because B is a dominant strategy. As a result the Bayesian equilibrium can be easily computed.

> Type H electricity producers will always play NB (since it does not matter what action the oil producer takes as NB is dominant).
> Type L electricity producers will always play B (since it does not matter what action the oil producer takes as B is dominant).

Suppose that the oil producer's expectations about the electricity company are captured by probability p, where p is the probability that the costs of building a new power plant are high (H).

> The oil producer will choose R or S depending on whether $p > \frac{1}{2}$ or $p < \frac{1}{2}$ (since this is optimal given the expectation that type H electricity producers will play NB and type L will play B).

> **Definition:** The computation of a **Bayesian equilibrium** involves three steps: (a) propose a strategy combination; (b) calculate beliefs generated by these strategies; (c) check that each strategy choice is optimal.

In this particular game, the beliefs generated by the strategies (that H types play NB and L types play B, and that the oil producer will play R or S depending on p) are easily derived using CKR and they are mutually consistent with optimising behaviour. As already stated, the first two beliefs can be derived directly from CKR courtesy of the dominance argument and it is easy to check that the oil producer's actions are optimal given these beliefs. The third belief is actually irrelevant since the action of the electricity company does not depend on what it expects the oil producer to do.

For future reference, it is just worth noting that the tie-in between beliefs and strategies contained in steps (b) and (c) in the definition above is a characteristic move in the so-called Nash refinement project. We will come across it frequently in the next chapter. It will also be plain that, by construction, these steps impose CAB and so the tie-in sits quite comfortably with an equilibrium concept (that is, the Nash equilibrium) which is already premised on the move to CAB.

2.7 TREMBLING HANDS AND QUIVERING SOULS

This section continues the discussion of the Nash equilibrium concept. We suspend the doubts of section 2.5 and suppose that, for whatever reason, we are inclined to accept the Nash concept as the appropriate one for game theory. There remain two obvious problems. What happens when a game has multiple Nash equilibria? And what should be said about games which seem to have no Nash equilibria?

The potential problem when there are multiple Nash equilibria is unmistakable. In such circumstances, players who *want* to follow their Nash strategy cannot do so since there is more than one such candidate. Thus an analysis which focuses on Nash equilibria alone simply will not be telling us very much about how rational players will behave. Indeed, unless something further can be said about equilibrium selection, the appeal of game theory will be correspondingly weakened. Or to put this slightly differently: methodological individualists will not be getting much support from game theory. Against the backdrop of this reflection, it is not surprising to find that there have been various attempts to refine the Nash equilibrium concept in such a way as to reduce the number of admissible Nash equilibria. We discuss one such refinement next (others are considered in the next chapter).

The absence of a Nash equilibrium is as embarrassing as multiple Nash equilibria in the sense that players, again, get no guidance from Nash as to which strategy they ought to play. This in turn threatens to undermine the explanatory power of game theory (albeit in different ways). In fact, although there are games which do not have Nash equilibria (in pure strategies, recall note 1), there is a famous early result in game theory which shows that every game has at least one Nash equilibrium provided we are prepared to fathom a so-called mixed strategy. This type of strategy requires players to choose randomly between pure strategies and it consists of the probability with which you mix the pure strategies in this random way. For example, adopting a mixed strategy as to whether you should carry an umbrella when you leave home in the morning, boils down to the probability p with which you decide in favour of the 'pure strategy': carry the umbrella. Thus although you do not choose a specific strategy intentionally, you do choose the probability with which you will choose a specific strategy. We consider the status of mixed strategies in section 2.7.2 below.

2.7.1 Perturbed games and the trembling hand perfect equilibrium

The basic idea behind the trembling hand perfect equilibrium concept (which comes from Selten, 1975) is that a 'good' equilibrium is one which is not undermined by small mistakes. To illustrate informally how this can help narrow down the number of Nash equilibria, consider first the game given by Figure 2.9.

There are two Nash equilibria in this game: (R1, C1) and (R2, C2); observe the coincidence of the ($^+$) and ($^-$) marks on these outcomes. So far there is no obvious way to choose between them. Now suppose that Figure 2.9 is amended to the game in Figure 2.10. The players have the same two strategies as before (with the same utility pay-offs) plus a third strategy each.

The new strategies R3 and C3 seem attractive new options because when

	C1	C2
R1	⁺5, 0⁻	−1, −1
R2	−1, −1	⁺0, 5⁻

Figure 2.9

	C1	C2	C3
R1	⁺5, 0⁻	−1, −1	⁺10, −1
R2	−1, −1	⁺0, 5⁻	−1, −2
R3	−1, 10⁻	−2, −1	6, 6

Figure 2.10

played by both, they yield 6 utils to each of the two players and this is better for both than anything that was attainable in the earlier version of the game. However, when the analysis of section 2.2 is used, the game is actually indistinguishable from that of Figure 2.7. In other words, players should choose between the first two strategies as if strategies R3 and C3 were not there. The reason is simple: strategies R3 and C3 are dominated. Thus with CKR, no player *expects* another to choose the third strategy. Hence the conclusion that the games in Figures 2.9 and 2.10 are analytically identical, and we have the same problem that there are two Nash equilibria (R1, C1) and (R2, C2).

The analysis of the second version of the game is rather different, however, when a small allowance is made for the possibility of execution errors of one kind or another, or lapses in motivation which lead players to deviate from their chosen strategy. Game theorists refer to these deviations as 'trembles'. The term derives from the metaphor which has players' hands trembling at the moment of choice. Imagine that players know which strategy they want to choose, or to avoid, but at the very last moment the hand which makes the choice trembles and, accidentally, makes an unintended choice.

To see how these trembles might help to isolate one of the Nash equilibria informally, notice how player R could have more reason to favour R1 in Figure 2.10 than in Figure 2.9 when there are trembles. The reason is that R has a reason to attach some probability to player C choosing strategy C3 when there are trembles. If that were to happen, and R chooses R1, then she would receive 10 utils whereas R2 yields −1 in these circumstances. Similarly, when C expects trembles from R's hand resulting possibly in R3, then C's best response is to choose C1 (aiming also

66

for the 10 pay-off in the bottom left cell of the matrix). Therefore both R and C will be drawn to outcome (R1, C1) even if the trembles never materialise (that is, even if R3 and C3 are not chosen). Thus the very expectation that they *may* materialise is sufficient to help select one out of the two Nash equilibrium outcomes (that is, R1, C1). We shall look at this a bit more formally now.

Deriving the critical 'frequency' of trembles

Let us consider the game in Figure 2.10 from the point of view of player R. Under CKR player R does not expect C to choose C3 since the latter is dominated. She does, however, expect C1 or C2 to be chosen with positive probabilities. Let q denote R's subjective probability expectation that C will choose strategy C1. Since R does not expect C to choose C3, her complete expectations are: C1 will be chosen with probability q and C2 with probability $1 - q$. What should R do?

Using expected utility theory, if she chooses strategy R1, she will either receive pay-off 5 (with probability q, which is the probability with which C will play C1) or pay-off -1 (with probability $1 - q$). Thus her expected returns from choosing strategy R1 are given by

$$ER^{R1} = 5q - (1 - q) \qquad (2.1)$$

In a similar fashion, if she were to choose strategy R2, her expected returns from strategy R2 are

$$ER^{R2} = -1q \qquad (2.2)$$

Thus R will choose strategy R1 when $ER^{R1} > ER^{R2}$, i.e. if $q > \frac{1}{7}$. Put differently, player R will opt for the strategy which offers the prospect of getting to the (R1, C1) outcome (worth 5 utils to player R), provided she expects that player C will not try to get to outcome (R2, C2) (which is worth 5 utils to him) with a probability more than $\frac{6}{7}$.

Let us now introduce some trembles. Suppose that both players may make a mistake at the moment of choice and, without intent, choose their third strategy. Let the probability of such error equal ε. From player R's perspective, it seems that there is a probability ε of C choosing C3 and a probability $(1 - \varepsilon)$ that he will not succumb to such an error, in which case he will play (as before) C1 with probability q and C2 with probability $1 - q$. In total, the probability of C1 being chosen by C equals $(1 - \varepsilon)q$, the probability of C2 is $(1 - \varepsilon)(1 - q)$ and the probability of C3 is ε. The expected returns to player R in (2.1) and (2.2) above are amended to

$$ER^{R1} = 5(1 - \varepsilon)q - (1 - \varepsilon)(1 - q) + 10\varepsilon \qquad (2.3)$$

$$ER^{R2} = -1(1 - \varepsilon)q - \varepsilon \qquad (2.4)$$

To demonstrate the effect of the positive probability ε of such errors (or trembles), consider the following example. Suppose for instance that player R anticipates that C will want to select strategy C with probability $q = \frac{1}{7}$. We have already established that, in the absence of trembles, $q = \frac{1}{7}$ sets ER^{R1} in (2.1) equal to ER^{R2} in (2.2). This would mean that player R is totally indifferent between strategies R1 and R2 (as they entail identical expected utilities). However, it is easy to see that the moment trembles become possible, the balance of expected returns is tipped in favour of strategy R1. With $q = \frac{1}{7}$, no matter how small probability ε, if it exceeds zero, (2.3) exceeds (2.4) and player R will choose R1 over R2.

To demonstrate the role of trembles further, suppose R expects a steady (non-trembling) player C to select C1 with probability $q = \frac{1}{14}$. In the absence of trembles, R ought to choose R2 (recall that with $\varepsilon = 0$, $q < \frac{1}{7}$ sets (2.1) less than (2.2) and invites R to play R2). However, if R anticipates that C will mistakenly choose C3 with probability a touch over $\frac{7}{161}$ (i.e. $\varepsilon \geq \frac{7}{161}$), then (2.3) > (2.4) and R chooses R1 yet again.[3] In general when there are trembles towards C3 with probability ε, R will play R1 if and only if (2.3) > (2.4) or when

$$q > (\tfrac{1}{7})[(1 - 12\varepsilon)/(1 - \varepsilon)] \tag{2.5}$$

Definition: A **perturbed** version of a game is a version of the game played with 'trembles'. The introduction of the trembles means that there is always some minimum probability ε that every strategy will be played by each player. In perturbed games, players choose the probability of playing each strategy in the normal way (i.e. in a manner consistent with CKR and the Nash–Harsanyi–Aumann assumption of CAB) but subject to the condition that there are trembles. So no strategy can be chosen with probabilty 1 (or 0) due to these 'trembles'.

In conclusion we see that in the game of Figure 2.10 the possibility of mistakes (or trembles) can help steer players towards one particular Nash equilibrium when there are many. However, it does depend on the particular size of the trembles and game theorists are often loathe to make such assumptions. Suppose then we do not want to make a specific assumption about trembles, what can we say? In this game there exists some $\varepsilon > 0$ such that R2 is still optimal. That is, we cannot presume that the mere mention of the possibility that ε is positive will rid us of one of the two Nash equilibria. Hence in the game of Figure 2.10 the allusion to trembles alone does not do the trick of reducing the number of equilibria from two to one. However, there are other games in which trembles work their trick without any need to specify their magnitude. In these games we are in the happy situation where even the faintest possibility of trembles leads to a unique equilibrium outcome. We call this the *trembling hand equilibrium* which was presented by Reinhard Selten in his important 1975 paper.

Definition: A **trembling hand perfect equilibrium** is the limit of the sequence of Nash equilibria in **perturbed** versions of the game as the trembles go to zero.

So, in what type of game do trembles reduce the number of Nash equilibria simply by being mentioned (that is, as ε tends to zero)? The answer is, in games where some of the Nash equilibria rely on what we call weakly dominated strategies. Recall the strategies were dominated if they invariably produced a *worse* outcome than other strategies. Weakly dominated strategies are the ones which produce outcomes *no better* than other strategies do (albeit not necessarily worse).

Definition: A **weakly dominated strategy** is one that does as well as (but no better than) any other strategy against some of the other player's strategies, but it is inferior against at least one of the other player's strategies (see the example in Figure 2.11).

	C1	C2	C3
R1	$^+$50, 0	$^+$5, 5$^-$	$^+$1, −10,000
R2	$^+$50, 50$^-$	$^+$5, 0	0, −10,000

Figure 2.11

There are two Nash equilibria in this game: (R2, C1) and (R1, C2) (again see how the ($^+$) and the ($^-$) marks coincide in these cells). In the light of the definition above, strategy R2 is weakly dominated by R1 since it is as good as R1 when C chooses C1 or C2, but inferior to R1 when C chooses C3.

Under CKR, there is no fear that C3 will ever be played. Therefore R1 and R2 are equally likely since they yield identical pay-offs for R regardless of whether C opts for C1 or C2. However, in the presence of quite minuscule trembles which make C3 possible (even though it remain highly improbable, as ε tends to zero), all of a sudden R will lean towards R1 since she has no reason to risk R2 when C3 is a possibility (however small). This in turn eliminates any reason C may have had for playing C1. We conclude that the introduction of the possibility of trembles eliminated one of the two Nash equilibria (R2, C1) leaving only (R1, C2) standing. This happened in this game (whereas it did not happen in the game of Figure 2.10) because one of the Nash equilibria was supported by the weakly dominated strategy

R2. Given that it seems sensible (under any view regarding trembles) to allow for at least the slightest smidgen of an execution error, the trembling hand perfect equilibrium concept provides secure grounds for eliminating any Nash equilibrium which is formed by a weakly dominated strategy.

Thus the trembling hand perfect equilibrium concept is the least restrictive concept involving trembles which we could use to reduce the number of Nash equilibria because it does not require us to assume anything specific about the nature of the trembles. One might think the cost of not being restrictive in this sense is simply that we will not always be able to reduce the number of potential equilibria (for example, both (R1, C1) and (R2, C2) are trembling hand perfect equilibria in Figure 2.10 and we can only narrow matters further by making specific assumptions about the trembles). Be warned though that, even here, there are some reasons for being slightly worried about the predictions of this refinement. Consider again the game in Figure 2.11.

Granted that R2 is weakly dominated by R1, and that therefore it could never form part of a trembling hand perfect equilibrium, does this mean we should expect (R1, C2) – i.e. the unique trembling hand perfect equilibrium – to be played in this game? On reflection, is it really plausible to think that C would tremble to C3 given the dire consequences of such a tremble? Moreover, would he tremble towards C3 with the same probability as he would towards C1 or C2? Yet without such a prospect R2 ceases to be inferior to R1 . . . and surely, trembling hands notwithstanding, the attraction of the clearly superior (for both players) Nash equilibrium of (R2, C1) might privilege this Nash equilibrium in any actual play of this game.

We shall return to the question of what trembles can be 'reasonably' assumed in the next chapter. For now the example serves to flag a potential weakness with all refinements based on trembles: they need a plausible theory of trembles to go with them, one that players share.

2.7.2 Nash equilibrium mixed strategies – NEMS

A mixed strategy is a probabilistic combination of (pure) actual strategies like R1 or R2. Thus a mixed strategy for R, say, of playing R1 with probability $\frac{1}{2}$ and R2 with probability $\frac{1}{2}$ is akin to suggesting that the person decides whether to play R1 or R2 on the basis of the toss of a fair coin: heads R1, tails R2. Game theorists often distinguish between *mixed strategies* and actual strategies by referring to the latter (e.g. to R1, R2, etc.) as *pure strategies*. Mixed strategy behaviour may sound bizarre (see Box 2.4 for some examples which may help, and we shall discuss the idea in more depth later), but it is potentially an extremely useful additional type of behaviour because it both provides an alternative way of resolving situations where there is more than one plausible solution (e.g. multiple Nash equilibria) and it suggests a solution for games in which no actual (that is, pure) strategies correspond to a Nash equilibrium.

Box 2.4

MIXED STRATEGIES

The idea of mixed strategies often strikes people as a little strange. Do people really ever behave in this way by mixing probabilistically some pure strategies, by deciding what to do on a metaphorical toss of a coin? We shall discuss the possible foundation for this type of behaviour in more detail later. For now, some examples may help to bring the general idea to life. They turn on the strategic advantage of being unpredictable.

Consider a bowler in cricket or a pitcher in baseball: both types of player can have a fast and a slow ball in their repertoire and each type of ball is most effective when it is not expected. For instance, the slow ball in cricket, when slipped in among a string of fast balls, is often the one which gets the batsman out. How, then, is a bowler to achieve this unexpected effect? If the bowler always selects a pure strategy (a type of ball) in some predictable way then this will not cause surprise because the batsman will learn how the bowler decides on the type of ball; whereas if the bowler mixes the strategies by selecting the type randomly (by, say, a mental toss of a coin) then the batsman can never be quite sure which ball is coming down the pitch (just as no one can be sure how the toss of a coin will turn out).

Should you bluff in poker? If you always bluff, then the bluff will not work because others will learn that you bluff at the slightest opportunity and they will call you all the time. On the other hand, if you never bluff, then you will often become the victim of other people's bluffs. So what should you do? To enjoy the benefits of bluffing, it seems you must engage in the activity unpredictably and that means mixing bluffing with not bluffing randomly.

In a similar fashion, have you ever wondered why airlines are reluctant to tell you how many stand-by seats are available? Presumably they want to encourage marginal travellers but they do not want at the same time to encourage any of their regular passengers to switch to stand-by tickets as they might if they could predict their chances of picking up a stand-by ticket.

To see how this type of behaviour might be helpful, return to Figure 2.9 with its two Nash equilibria in pure strategies ((R1, C1) and (R2, C2)) and consider the following train of thought. It seems that neither player has a good reason to prefer one of their strategies from the other since both are potential Nash equilibrium strategies. *So players cannot possibly prefer one strategy to the other since there is no objective reason for having such a preference* (**Step 1**). What does one do when one does not have a preference between two options? *One randomises* (**Step 2**). You do not have to imagine players taking a coin out of their pocket and tossing it. Randomisation can be implicit.

Player R may choose R1 if the first person that walks through the door is a smoker, or if the first car she sees out of the window is red, white or blue. The randomisation can even be subconscious as when we somehow choose to locate ourselves in one position on a railway platform despite the fact that we do not know which is the optimal spot. We do not need to be specific about the exact mechanism by which agents randomise.

Since agents will randomise between their strategies, the problem of pinpointing the appropriate strategy becomes one of finding the best randomisation rule, i.e. the optimal probability with which to choose each strategy. Game theorists then show that *there exists only one randomisation rule per player in this game that is consistent with* **Step 1** *and* **Step 2** and so conclude that this is the solution to such games!

How is this rule determined? Returning to the game of Figure 2.9, if **Steps 1** and **2** are to be made compatible with expected utility maximisation, then R's (C's) expected returns from R1 (C1) must equal the expected returns from R2 (C2). (For if that were not the case, then **Step 1** would be false, as players would have one strategy that is better than the other on average; and, therefore, **Step 2** would be redundant.) To be specific, the expected returns to R of R1 and R2 will depend on the probabilities, say q and $1 - q$ with which C will choose C1 and C2 respectively. Through inspection these returns are given by $ER^{R1} = 5q - (1 - q)$ and $ER^{R2} = -q + 0(1 - q)$, and these will only be equal when $q = \frac{1}{7}$. (We have already come to this conclusion earlier while discussing perturbed games – see expressions (2.1) and (2.2).) Thus R will only **not** prefer one strategy from the other and resort to randomisation if C plays C1 with probability $\frac{1}{7}$ and C2 with probability $\frac{6}{7}$.

Likewise, the expected return to C of C1 and C2 will depend on the probabilities, say p and $1 - p$, of R selecting R1 and R2 respectively. These expected returns are given by $ER^{C1} = 0p - (1 - p)$ and $ER^{C2} = -p + 5(1 - p)$. Thus C will only **not** have a clear preference for one of the two strategies if R plays R1 with probability $\frac{6}{7}$ and R2 with probability $\frac{1}{7}$.

Following these two analytical steps, game theorists derive a solution concept known as a Nash equilibrium in mixed strategies (NEMS). It works as follows: **Steps 1** and **2** have players randomising in such a way that neither has a preference over their two strategies. Thus p and q are selected such that $ER^{R1} = ER^{R2}$ and $ER^{C1} = ER^{C2}$. In our example this means R chooses R1 and R2 respectively with probabilities $\frac{6}{7}$ and $\frac{1}{7}$ and C selects C1 and C2 respectively with probabilities $\frac{1}{6}$ and $\frac{6}{7}$ (the apparent symmetry reflects the fact that the pay-off matrix is symmetrical). And vice versa.

To check that these strategies are indeed in a Nash equilibrium, recall that a set of strategies is in a Nash equilibrium if the strategy which corresponds to player R is a best response to that of player C (and vice versa). Put differently, if you know that your opponent will play his or her Nash strategy, you should have no incentive to play a non-Nash strategy; and indeed when C is expected to choose $q = \frac{1}{7}$, no strategy of player R is better than the mixed strategy $p = \frac{6}{7}$.

There is a small (albeit important) difference between NEMS above and the way we defined the Nash equilibrium in section 2.5.1 which is worth highlighting. In 2.5.1 we used an example in which the Nash equilibrium ((R2, C2) in Figure 2.6) implied that, if you knew that your opponent was about to opt for his or her Nash strategy, you would *definitely* want to opt for your Nash strategy too. In the case of NEMS (described in the previous paragraph) such definite preference gives way to indifference: instead of having a direct interest in choosing your Nash strategy in response to your opponent's Nash strategy, in NEMS you simply *do not mind* choosing your Nash mixed strategy in response to your opponent's Nash mixed strategy. For instance, when C chooses $q = \frac{1}{7}$, it makes no difference to R what probabilistic combination of R1 and R2 she chooses since, once $q = \frac{1}{7}$, $ER^{R1} = ER^{R2}$; i.e. R cannot have a preference over R1 and R2 if she cares only about expected utility. This is a significant observation because it implies that the moment one expects one's opponent to play according to NEMS, there is no imperative to follow NEMS also. The best that can be said is that one does not have an incentive *not* to play NEMS.

In summary, we have built up the NEMS concept by suggesting that players might randomise when they do not know what to do and then we have noticed that there is only one pair of randomisations which is consistent with each not knowing what to do (and so they decide to randomise). Therefore there is only one pair which satisfies CAB. Another way of motivating the concept is to return directly to the Harsanyi doctrine (and thus CAB). For this purpose, notice that the game in Figure 2.9 is symmetrical. Since the players are identically placed in juxtaposition to each other, are equally rational and have access to the same pool of information, Harsanyi's doctrine (which requires that they come to the same conclusion about how equally informed and equally rational players will play the game) leads to the conclusion that they must arrive at a symmetrical Nash equilibrium (since there is no reason in the pay-offs of the game to distinguish between the two players). This removes the pure strategy equilibria (R1, C1) and (R2, C2), because neither is symmetrical in terms of pay-offs, leaving only one potentially symmetrical Nash equilibrium: NEMS, which awards equal expected returns to each player (equalling $-\frac{1}{7}$ utils).

The symmetry referred to here is, of course, only *ex ante*. What happens in reality (that is, *ex post*) depends on the actual randomisation. Even if players play according to NEMS there is always a large probability that each will receive pay-off -1 (which will happen with probability $(\frac{6}{7})^2 + (\frac{1}{7})^2 = \frac{37}{49}$). If they manage to land on one of the diagonal elements of the matrix, only one of them will receive pay-off 5. Nevertheless, many games are not even symmetrical *ex ante* and so this defence of NEMS will not always be available.

How plausible is this idea of NEMS? To appreciate why the question might need to be seriously addressed, consider a slight amendment to the game in Figure 2.9 given in Figure 2.12.

	C1	C2
R1	$^{+}5, 0^{-}$	$-5, -1$
R2	$-5, -1$	$^{+}0, 5^{-}$

Figure 2.12

Let us recompute the probabilities, p and q. We recompute p in such a way that the expected returns to player C from C1 and C2 are equal. That is, so that $ER^{C1} = ER^{C2}$, which gives $-(1 - p) = -p + 5(1 - p)$. The value that solves this equation is $p = \frac{6}{7}$, as before. Similarly, we recompute q in a way that the expected returns to player R from R1 and R2 are equal: $ER^{R1} = ER^{R2}$, which gives $5q - 5(1 - q) = -5q$. The value of q which solves this is $q = \frac{1}{3}$. This means that, according to the NEMS concept, player R will play this game in exactly the same way she played the game in Figure 2.9. As for player C, he should concede (that is, play the C1 strategy which can give him a maximum of only 0) with probability $\frac{1}{3}$. This is a puzzling result because the player who is ostensibly at a disadvantage as a result of the amendment is player R (she will lose 5 utils if the outcome is on the off diagonal of the pay-off matrix, whereas player C will lose only 1). And yet, the Nash equilibrium in mixed strategies (NEMS) suggests that C should go for the best prize in this game (pay-off 5) with probability only $\frac{2}{3}$ (which is less than in the original game) while R should be as adventurous as ever (with $p = \frac{6}{7}$)!

This result certainly seems counter intuitive and arouses suspicion which can quickly multiply. For instance, let us return to the construction of a NEMS for Figure 2.9 and suppose one player does select the NEMS probability combination. The worrying issue is why should the other do what is required by the NEMS? By definition when the one player selects the NEMS, this leaves the other indifferent between any probabilistic combination of the two pure strategies. So any probability combination is as good as another as far as that player is concerned. Of course, it is true that there is only one probability combination for the other player which will leave the original player indifferent between strategies. But why should this consideration affect the other player's selection? After all he or she is only concerned with their returns and if the original player plays NEMS this seems to provide no reason for the other to remain faithful to the probabilities specified by NEMS.

2.7.3 Nash equilibrium mixed strategies (NEMS): the Aumann defence

One response to this last worry (which is usually credited to an idea in Aumann, 1987) is that the probabilities of a NEMS are not to be interpreted as the individual's probability of selecting one pure strategy rather than another. Rather, probability p which attaches to R's behaviour should be thought of as the subjective belief which C holds about what R will do. Likewise probability q which attaches to C's behaviour reflects the subjective belief of R regarding what C will do. So players will do what players will do. And probabilities p and q (provided by NEMS) simply reflect a consistency requirement with respect to the subjective beliefs each holds about what the other will do. The requirement is the following:

(1) Given R's beliefs about C (q), then C, when forming an assessement about R (p), should not believe that R will play any strategy which is not optimal relative to those beliefs (q).
(2) Given C's beliefs about R (p), then R, when forming an assessment about C (q), should not believe that C will play any strategy which is not optimal relative to those beliefs (p).

In the game of Figure 2.9 there is only one value for q ($=\frac{1}{7}$) which could make both R1 and R2 optimal for player R (and so make the assessment of p by C something different from either 0 or 1) and there is only one value for p ($=\frac{6}{7}$) which could make both C1 and C2 rational for C (and so make the assessment of q by R something other than either 0 or 1).

The crucial question, however, which this defence of NEMS overlooks, as it stands, is how each player comes to know the beliefs that the other holds about how he or she is going to play. For instance, in (1) how does C come to know what are R's beliefs (q) about how she will play? Of course, he can work it out from (2) provided C's beliefs about R (p) are known to R. But this merely rephrases the problem: how are C's beliefs about R known to R?

The answer Aumann offers to this conundrum turns again on the Harsanyi doctrine and the CAB assumption. In our game player C will choose either C1 or C2 and one can think of some kind of event pushing C in one direction or the other (the event can be anything, it is simply whatever psychologically moves one to action in these circumstances). So there is an event of some sort which will push C in one direction or another; and following the Harsanyi doctrine, it is argued that both players must form a common prior probability assessment regarding the likelihood of the event yielding C1 or C2. So both R and C must entertain the *same* belief regarding how C will act. Of course, both players also know that there is no event which could occur which would make C take an action which was not optimal relative to his beliefs and so the value of q in (1) must also satisfy the condition set on q in (2). In other words the q in (2), which comes from recognising that C's behaviour is optimal, must be the same as the q in (1), because otherwise the two players would not be drawing the same inference from the same information set. Likewise the beliefs that C holds about R (p) must be the same as the beliefs that R holds about herself and they both know that any admissible belief must be consistent with each maximising their expected utilities.

In many respects this is an extraordinary argument. As Bob Sugden (1991) remarks

> by pure deductive analysis, using no psychological premises whatever, we have come up with a conclusion about what rational players must believe about the properties of a psychological mechanism.
> (p.798)

Yet all this depends on the Harsanyi doctrine which (following the discussion in section 2.5 of this chapter and section 1.2.2 of Chapter 1) we take to be a weakness. In mitigation perhaps, it is worth recalling that the Nash equilibrium concept in pure strategies also depends on the Harsanyi doctrine. So in this sense NEMS is no shakier or no more controversial than the Nash equilibrium concept; and if you accept the Harsanyi doctrine for one then it seems you should accept it for the other and embrace all types of Nash equilibrium equally. Alternatively, you might reject both!

Of course, another (admittedly idiosyncratic) way of founding NEMS was foreshadowed in the earlier discussion of section 2.5.2. If we take that part of Kant which demands that agents only hold beliefs that they know can be held by all without generating internal inconsistency, then this might license all Nash equilibria including NEMS.[4] In effect under this interpretation, the NEMS is the only set of beliefs which is both mutually consistent and consistent with both players being uncertain about what action will be undertaken – since with these beliefs each could take either of the possible strategies. By contrast, a *Nash equilibrium* (in pure strategies) is both mutually consistent and *consistent with each player knowing for certain which action will be undertaken.*

2.7.4 Nash equilibrium mixed strategies (NEMS): Harsanyi's Bayesian defence

Another defence of NEMS comes from Harsanyi (1973). In technical terms, the gist of his argument is that NEMS emerges in the limit as a Bayesian Nash equilibrium in a game of incomplete information. In other words, Harsanyi defends NEMS through an argument that we rarely know for certain what type of player we are playing with (see section 1.2.3 and section 2.6). Thus the Bayesian equilibrium concept often turns out to be the most appropriate equilibrium concept to use and it so happens that when the doubt in these games shrinks towards zero NEMS emerges as a Bayesian equilibrium.

The initial intuition behind this result is not strong and it will help if we develop the argument through an illustration. Figure 2.13 describes a game from Myerson (1991). It has been chosen here because there is no Nash equilibrium in pure strategies (witness the lack of coincidence of any ($^+$) with a ($^-$)). Thus the development of the Harsanyi NEMS argument will also show how NEMS is a useful addition to the Nash project because it enables the Nash equilibrium concept to be applied to games where there is no Nash equilibrium in pure strategies. The NEMS of this game is given by $p = 0.75$ (= probability of R1) and $q = 0.5$ (= probability of C1). This can be easily checked by comparing the expected return of each strategy when this is what each player believes is the likelihood governing the strategy choice of the other.

	C1	C2
R1	$0, 0^-$	$^+0, -1$
R2	$^+1, 0$	$-1, 3^-$

Figure 2.13

Suppose now that each player is drawn from a population of types, as in our metaphor above. R-players can be any type α drawn from a population which is uniformly distributed across the interval $(0, 1)$. Likewise the column players can be any type β drawn from a population which is uniformly distributed across the same interval. So each R player knows her value of α, but the C player does not know it; and likewise each C player knows his β, but the R player does not. The values of α and β affect the players' pay-offs in a small way, as shown in Figure 2.14, where ε is a suitably small number close to zero. (In other words ε reflects the 'trembles' and is an index of how the return to a player is affected by

	C1	C2
R1	$\varepsilon\alpha, \varepsilon\beta$	$\varepsilon\alpha, -1$
R2	$1, \varepsilon\beta$	$-1, 3$

Figure 2.14

the differences in type. So when ε goes to zero there is no important difference between types and the uncertainty in the game shrinks to zero.)

The Bayesian Nash equilibrium of this game is given by the following:

$$R = R1 \text{ when } \alpha > (2 + \varepsilon)/(8 + \varepsilon^2)$$
$$= R2 \text{ when } \alpha < (2 + \varepsilon)/(8 + \varepsilon^2)$$

and

$$C = C1 \text{ when } \beta > (4 - \varepsilon)/(8 + \varepsilon^2)$$
$$= C2 \text{ when } \beta < (4 - \varepsilon)/(8 + \varepsilon^2)$$

To see why this is a Bayesian equilibrium we can apply the second two steps for constructing a Bayesian equilibrium as described in the relevant definition in section 2.6.

Step (b) The probability of C playing C1 under these conjectured strategies is $[1 - (4 - \varepsilon)/(8 + \varepsilon^2)]$ (since the probability of getting a number greater than x from a uniformly distributed population across the $(0, 1)$ interval is $1 - x$), and the probability of C playing C2 is $(4-\varepsilon)/(8 + \varepsilon^2)$.

Step (c) The expected return to playing R1 given these expectations is equal to $\varepsilon\alpha$ and the expected return to playing R2 is $(1)[1 - (4 - \varepsilon)/(8 + \varepsilon^2)] + (-1)(4 - \varepsilon)/(8 + \varepsilon^2)$. Thus R1 is preferred to R2 when $\alpha > (2 + \varepsilon)/(8 + \varepsilon^2)$.

A similar demonstration of the optimality of the conjectured strategies for C is possible. Thus the conjectured strategies of C and R generate expectations which render those strategies optimal and they constitute a Bayesian equilibrium. (In effect this demonstration also reveals how the conjecture with respect to strategies was made in the first place. Since R1 becomes better for R as α increases and C1 becomes better for C as β increases, it is likely that there are some values of α and β which make each player switch between strategies. Call these values x and y. By construction, these numbers also give the respective probabilities of R playing R1 and C playing C1 and we know that for a switch to occur at these values the expected returns for each strategy available to a player must be equalised. Thus we have two equations and two unknowns, x and y, to solve for.)

Notice that as ε goes to zero, the Bayesian equilibrium converges to the NEMS of the game in Figure 2.13. (For instance, R plays R1 when $\alpha > \frac{1}{4}$, and that occurs with probability 0.75.) The construction of the Bayesian equilibrium here makes plain our earlier point that CKR is not enough: CAB is also required because each player's expectations of the other need to be made consistent with what each plans to do. In this sense the defence is very similar to Aumann's earlier one. Indeed, the only real difference is that Aumann's selection of a pure strategy turns on a psychological twitch whereas Harsanyi's selection depends on selection of the type of player. In both cases, the selection is rendered uncertain and then precise probabilities are actually attached to what people should believe as a result of applying CAB. There is only one set of beliefs regarding the likelihood of each action which can be consistently held by all.

2.8 CONCLUSION

The central solution concept in game theory is the Nash equilibrium. We hope to have shown that it cannot be justified by appealing to the assumptions of rationality and CKR. Something more is required: in effect, people must form the same (probabilistic) assessment of what is likely to happen when they go to work with the same information. When this is made clear, it will be obvious that some of the debates at the foundations of game theory touch on matters regarding the treatment of uncertainty which have always been central to debate in economics. For now we set the doubts aside. Nash is undeniably at the heart of game theory and the existence of multiple Nash equilibria in many games has set an agenda of refining Nash. The point of the refinement project is to reduce the number of Nash equilibria where possible so that the prediction of Nash is not rendered vacuous by the presence of multiple Nash equilibria in games. We have already introduced two of the essential ideas used by that refinement project in this chapter (the 'trembles' of trembling hand perfection and the tie-in between beliefs and strategies found in Bayesian equilibria) and we shall be developing these ideas further in the next chapter. We return to an assessment of Nash only at the end of that chapter.

3

DYNAMIC GAMES

Backward induction and some extensive form refinements of the Nash equilibrium

3.1 INTRODUCTION

This chapter looks at games which have a dynamic structure; that is, games in which one player makes a move *after* the other (rather than choosing strategies simultaneously). In these situations, game theory needs to specify the precise protocol of moves. Diagrammatically dynamic games resemble tree diagrams (recall section 2.2) which are known formally as the extensive form. So the extensive form representation is appropriate for a dynamic game, whereas the matrix representation (or, more formally, the normal form) which we have been using so far is suitable for interactions in which players choose simultaneously.

The next section begins with an illustration of the advantages of the extensive form as compared with the normal form for such games. It continues by showing that in some games the extensive form can help pinpoint a solution which proved elusive while the game was viewed in its matrix, or normal, form. In terms of the discussion of the previous chapter, the study of a game's dynamic structure potentially helps by reducing the number of Nash equilibria.

The hallmark of the analysis of extensive form games is the use of a type of reasoning called *backward induction*. Section 3.3 focuses on a particular refinement of the Nash equilibrium which results from a marriage of the original idea behind the Nash equilibrium and backward induction: the famous (within game theoretical circles) *subgame perfect Nash equilibrium*. Section 3.4 is devoted to some (important) controversies which result from the application of the common knowledge of rationality (CKR) axiom in dynamic (i.e. extensive form) games.

Sections 3.5 and 3.6 sketch three other major refinements of the Nash equilibrium: *sequential equilibria, proper equilibria* and those which depend on the use of *forward induction*. The chapter concludes with a critical assessment of the Nash equilibrium concept as well the attempts to refine it.

3.2 DYNAMIC GAMES, THE EXTENSIVE FORM AND BACKWARD INDUCTION

To illustrate the difference which can emerge once there is an explicit recognition of the dynamic structure of a game, consider the first game of the last chapter, given in normal form by Figure 3.1.

	C1	C2
R1	$^{+}$10, 4	$^{+}$1, 5^{-}
R2	9, 9^{-}	0, 3

Figure 3.1

It will be recalled that the analysis of this normal form game with simultaneous moves yielded the prediction that (R1, C2) would be the dominant equilibrium since strategy R2 is dominated by R1 thus forcing player C to opt for C2 (given that he could not expect a rational player R to choose R1). (Of course (R1, C2) is also a Nash equilibrium since all dominant strategy equilibria are Nash equilibria, although the opposite is not necessarily so.)

Now suppose that R chooses first and C knows her choice before he decides what to do. Figure 3.2 represents this version of the game in extensive form.

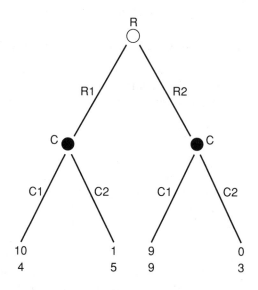

Figure 3.2

What should R choose? If she goes for R1, she may get pay-off 10. On the other hand, the best she can do if she takes R2 is 9 (recall that in the brackets at the end of the tree diagram, the first pay-off is R's and the second is C's). Does this mean she ought to play R1? The answer is, no. An instrumentally rational R will ask the following two questions:

(a) What will C do if I choose R1?
(b) What will C do if I choose R2?

The necessary answers are forthcoming following the assumption of first-order CKR. Then R answers (a) by: 'he would choose C2 because he prefers the 5 to the 4 pay-off'. The answer to (b) is, 'he would choose C1 because he prefers the 9 to the 3 pay-off'. Thus R realises that she is better off choosing R2 because (given C's rational responses to each of her choices) this yields pay-off 9 in contrast to the 1 she could expect from R1. We, therefore, see that when R's choice is known to C before he gets a chance to choose, then the equilibrium outcome is (R2, C1). For this to be proved, we only require that agents are instrumentally rational and that R knows that C is instrumentally rational (i.e. first-order CKR).

Notice that this is different to the equilibrium when the players chose simultaneously (then the equilibrium was (R1, C2)). Also, when we invite player C to choose first the equilibrium changes (you can check this for yourself). Thus the exact sequence of the game makes an enormous difference.

3.3 SUBGAME PERFECTION

3.3.1 Subgame perfection, Nash and CKR

In the last section we reasoned backwards assisted by first-order CKR. This type of reasoning is the hallmark of a particular refinement of the Nash equilibrium concept which applies to extensive form games: **subgame (Nash) perfection** (see Selten, 1975). To explain what this entails formally, we must first define a subgame.

> **Definition: A subgame** is a segment of an extensive (or dynamic game), i.e. a subset of it.[1] Consider the extensive game's tree diagram: a subset of the diagram qualifies as a subgame provided the following holds:
> (a) the subgame must start from some node, (b) it must then branch out to the successors of the initial node, (c) it must end up at the pay-offs associated with the end nodes, and finally (d) the initial node (where the subgame commenced) must be a singleton in every player's information partition.

Parts (a), (b) and (c) of the definition are straightforward. But what is the meaning of a singleton, or a player's information partition, mentioned in part (d)? Recall from Chapter 2 (section 2.2, Figure 2.2) how a player may not know exactly where he or she is in the tree diagram. In Figure 2.2(a), player C knew which branch of the tree diagram he is in when his turn comes to choose between C1 and C2. This is so because, we presume, R's choice between R1 and R2 is announced before C gets to play. However, in Figure 2.2(b) the broken line linking the two nodes of player R indicates that, when it is her turn to play, R does not know which node she is at: the one on the left or the one on the right? The reason for this uncertainty is that C's choice between C1 and C2 was not communicated to R before R was called to make a choice between R1 and R2.

At some given stage of the game, the information partition of a player represents the different positions that the player is able to distinguish from each other. So, in Figure 2.2(b) player R knows that she may be in one of two nodes (the left or the right), and hence these two nodes taken together constitute an information partition for player R. In this sense, the difference between Figures 2.2(a) and 2.2(b) is that in the former C has two distinct information partitions whereas in the latter R has only one (containing two nodes). A singleton is an information partition which contains only one node – that is, when in this information partition, the player has no doubt at all as to where in the tree diagram he or she is (which means that the player knows what action his or her opponent has taken so far).

We can now decipher part (d) of the definition of a subgame. Its purpose is to say that a subgame must start at a stage of the game where the player whose turn it is to act knows what has happened previously. From that moment onwards a new chapter in the game (that is, a subgame) begins which we can analyse separately. For example, in the game of Figure 2.2(b) the only subgame is the whole game since R's information partition (that is, at the stage where R comes into the game) contains more than one node (R does not know for certain which node she is at, the left or the right). In other words, the game has only one singleton (that is, the initial node at which C makes a choice) and thus the only subgame is the whole game. By contrast, the game in Figure 2.2(a) has three subgames: there is the game as a whole which starts from the initial decision node; there is the game which starts at C's node when R has chosen R1; and there is the game which starts at C's right hand side node when R has chosen R2. As an example consider Figure 3.5 below which contains six subgames.

The intuition behind the subgame perfect (Nash) equilibrium (SPNE) concept is that we do not want a strategy which specifies actions in some part of the game (i.e. in some subgame) which are not best replies to each other *in that subgame*. Otherwise it seems we will be entertaining behaviour which is not consistent with instrumental rationality and CKR at some stages of the game. Thus in the game of Figure 3.2 the Nash equilibrium (R1, C2) in the normal form suddenly looks untenable when the game is analysed in extensive form because it specifies an action at the subgame where C decides that is not the best reply to what has gone before. As it turns out, the only equilibrium outcome which passes this test of an analysis of the subgames is (R2, C1). Thus game theorists call it a *subgame perfect (Nash) equilibrium (SPNE)*.

> **Definition:** Strategies are in a **subgame perfect (Nash) equilibrium (SPNE)** in an extensive form game when the strategies constitute a Nash equilibrium in *each* subgame.

Some clarification of the reference to Nash in this definition may be helpful. With the original argument (R2, C1) seemed to emerge as the equilibrium because we reasoned backwards and applied CKR, whereas the definition of subgame perfection refers to Nash. Yet did the last chapter not emphasise that CKR invariably yields Nash when CAB is assumed? So why does subgame perfection refer to Nash? The answer is that *the combination of CKR together with the sequential reasoning of backward induction forces players to hold consistently aligned beliefs*, in the sense that R plays R2 believing that C will play C1 and C plays C1 because he believes R will play R2 because R recognises that C will play C1 after R1. Effectively it is backward induction, in combination with CKR, which introduces CAB through the back door.

It would be wrong, however, to assume that equilibria which emerge from backward induction *always* require CKR (or alternatively always depend on CAB). For instance, consider a very simple game in which backward induction furnishes a unique solution by itself. There are 20 cards numbered 1 to 20 and players R and C are told that the one who gets his or her hands on the 20th card, wins. The rules are simple: R starts first. She has to pick up *either* card 1 *or* card 2. If she chooses 1, then it is C's turn to choose to pick up either card 2 or 3. If on the other hand R has chosen 2, then C's options are cards 3 or 4. In general, a player can choose card number $k + 1$ *or* $k + 2$ if the other player's highest card so far is k. The first to reach 20, wins. We call this **the race to 20**.

Suppose you are R and have to choose first. What should you choose, card 1 or card 2? The answer is that you should choose card 2. To come to this conclusion, it is easiest to think backwards. Since the objective is to get to 20 first, you are home and dry if you manage to get to 17 first. For if you do, then given the rules, C can only get to 18 or 19, in which case you are bound to get to 20. Similarly, if you reach 14 before your opponent, then you can get to 17, and therefore to 20, first. Allowing this logic to unfold as far back as it goes, it soon becomes clear that the player who chooses first is certain to win since she can choose 2 and thus jump on the bandwagon that allows her to pick up cards numbered 5, 8, 11, 14, 17 and, triumphantly, 20.

The above application of backward induction is analytically equivalent to the dominance logic of section 2.3 in Chapter 2. There, we examined games in which the instrumentally rational player R knew what she ought to do without worrying about the choices of the opposition: a case in which there is a strategy that dominates all others. In our simple race-to-20 game above, the outlined strategy is a dominant strategy because it ensures victory *whatever the opposition's strategic choices*. There is no need for CKR, and backward induction without CKR carries no implication for the mutual consistency of each player's beliefs (since what one thinks that the other thinks is irrelevant).

Definition: The difference between **backward induction** and **Nash backward induction** turns on the use of CKR assumptions. The former does not require CKR whereas the latter does. By way of examples, the solution of the race-to-20 game does not depend on Nash backward induction, while that of the game in Figure 3.2 does.

3.3.2 Subgame perfection and equilibrium selection

The lesson from the last section is simple. When games have a dynamic structure, it is important to recognise this by using the extensive form. Otherwise the normal form (that is, the matrix representation) may suggest equilibria which are implausible once the game is analysed dynamically. In addition the extensive form analysis has the advantage that it sometimes reduces the number of Nash equilibria which exist in the normal form. To be specific, there are some dynamic games with multiple Nash equilibria in the normal form which have fewer subgame perfect equilibria. Thus the subgame perfection refinement and the study of a game's extensive form may help with the problem of Nash equilibrium selection which was discussed in section 2.7.

To illustrate this possibility in more detail, consider what is referred to as the chain store game. The original explanation of the game from which it derives its name has a firm (R) deciding whether to enter (R1) or stay out of (R2) the market of a monopolist (C), and the monopolist must choose between fighting an entry (C1) and acquiescing (C2). The normal form of the game is given in Figure 3.3 while the extensive form is in Figure 3.4.

	C1	C2
R1	0, 0	$^+3, 1^-$
R2	$^+2, 2^-$	2, 2^-

Figure 3.3

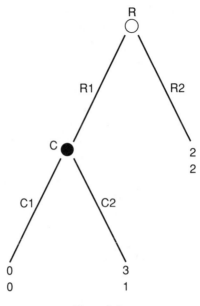

Figure 3.4

Since we shall be discussing variants of this game in some detail, it is perhaps worth noting that this type of interaction is not confined to the world of chain stores. For instance, another interaction with the same structure is found in Puccini's opera *Gianni Schicchi* (see Harper, 1991, who offers this interpretation). A wealthy man dies having willed his fortune to some monks and his relatives (C) employ someone (R) to impersonate him so as to write a new will in their favour. The impersonator must decide between willing the fortune to the relatives (R2), as he has agreed, and breaking the agreement by willing most of it to himself (R1). The relatives in turn must choose between asking the authorities to investigate the fraud of the impersonator (C1), in which case their own attempted fraud is revealed, and letting the impersonator get away with the fortune (C2). Likewise, for much of the Cold War, NATO countries were worried by the prospect of the Warsaw Pact countries invading (entering) Western Europe (R1) and they developed a potential 'fighting' strategy response (C1) of maximum nuclear retaliation leading to mutually assured destruction (MAD). R2 is the Warsaw Pact strategy of 'staying out' and C2 is the NATO response of acquiescing to an invasion.

There is no dominant equilibrium in this normal form game, but there are two Nash equilibria (R2, C1) and (R1, C2) (witness the coincidence of the ($^+$) and ($^-$) marks). However, when the game is represented in its extensive form, as in Figure 3.4, there is only one SPNE: (R1, C2). The point will be obvious since C1 is not a best reply at the subgame formed by

C's decision node and so this strategy cannot be part of an SPNE. To put the point perhaps more simply: the monopolist's threat of a fight, or the relative's threat to report Gianni's fraud, or NATO's threat to incinerate the world, is not credible; and subgame perfection excludes strategies which involve non-credible threats.

It was precisely this appreciation which led NATO eventually to change its 'fighting' response from MAD to a so-called flexible response, which had NATO 'fighting' any invasion with a response proportional to the attack. In such circumstances, it became conceivable that the returns from 'fighting' an invasion (since it now stopped short of immediate MAD) could actually yield a pay-off to NATO countries which was higher than acquiescing.

3.4 BACKWARD INDUCTION, 'OUT-OF-EQUILIBRIUM' BELIEFS AND COMMON KNOWLEDGE INSTRUMENTAL RATIONALITY (CKR)

The rationale for using backward induction seems strong. Players look forward because they recognise that what they do now will have consequences for them at the later stages of the game (subgames). To judge what those consequences might be, they assume that each will be rational in the future and on this basis they decide what to do now for the best. However, it can pose some difficulties when allied with the assumption of CKR which we now discuss.

3.4.1 'Out-of-equilibrium' beliefs and trembles

In the last section, backward induction was used to rule out Nash equilibrium (R2, C1) in the game of Figure 3.3. Strategy C1 (i.e. going to the authorities, or fighting the entry, or fighting an invasion with MAD) was not a credible threat for player C (i.e. the relatives or the monopolist or NATO) to make, and so R2 (i.e. willing the fortune to the relatives or staying out of the market or Western Europe) cannot be part of the equilibrium of this game since it is only ever a best response against C1. Thus it is the analysis of the inappropriateness of the action R2 which singles out the unique SPNE of (R1, C2).

In the jargon, strategy R2 becomes *out-of-equilibrium behaviour*. So one can say that it is the *analysis* of out-of-equilibrium behaviour which singles out (R1, C2); and yet this seems to create a puzzle. On the one hand we assume common knowledge of instrumentally rational behaviour (CKR), but, on the other, before we can establish the rational strategy we must consider what *would* happen if what turns out to be an irrational move were to be made at some point. That is, equilibrium behaviour needs to be built on an analysis of out-of-equilibrium behaviour. Put differently, we have to introduce the possibility of some lapse from rationality to explain what rationality demands. This raises two difficult interconnected questions. Is this procedure of considering lapses from rationality consistent with the assumption of CKR? Why assume that players will behave rationally when they are off the equilibrium path?

To make these questions bite, suppose we consider the plausibility of R2 as an equilibrium strategy. If R2 is rational then it must be a best reply to what C is expected to do. So to test for the rationality of R2, we need to assume something about how C will behave. But what should R assume about C's actions when R plays R2? The difficulty is that with R2 any action for C is now off the equilibrium path and yet everything turns on R's beliefs about C. In particular if R believes that C will play C2, then R2 is not rational because it is not a best response to C2; whereas if R believes that C will play C1 then R2 is a best reply for R.

The issue here is closely related to the earlier one regarding CAB in normal form games. The construction of subgame perfection assumes that no player can believe that someone will play in a way which they actually would not, which is exactly the point of CAB. So an implicit assumption of CAB is at work. The difference here, however, is that this projection from CKR looks rather more controversial in extensive form games when these are beliefs which need not be tested in equilibrium. The comparison with the role of CAB in the construction of the Nash equilibrium concept in normal form games is instructive in this regard. We shall develop this further in section 3.4.2. For now we gauge a part of that difference by considering non-CAB beliefs in the two cases. Should players use non-Nash strategies because they hold inconsistently aligned beliefs in a normal form game, then the inconsistency would be revealed the moment the moves had been made; whereas should R play R2 supported by the belief that C will play C1 in this extensive form game, then this belief is never tested because C is never called upon to play.

One response to both questions comes through the introduction of trembles again. Suppose we assume that we are sometimes off the equilibrium path because of small, random 'mistakes' of one kind or another. Then we have an explanation of how people reach these non-equilibrium positions in the game's tree diagram and it does not upset CKR. So, since deviations have not undermined CKR, players can continue to form beliefs about what happens out of the equilibrium path by assuming the players are rational.

As an illustration of how the idea of trembles is used in game theory to support the concept of an SPNE, consider again the game in Figure 3.4 (in fact every trembling hand perfect equilibrium is subgame perfect). In that game outcome (R1, C2) – the unique SPNE of the game – is the only one compatible with small random trembles in the rationality of the players. Strategy C1 is not a best response to a player R who plays R2 but who may choose R1 mistakenly (i.e. due to a tremble). Instead C2 is the best response to a trembling R player both when they intend to play R1 and when they plan to play R2. Thus in the limit as the trembles go to zero, C1 cannot form part of a trembling hand perfect equilibrium (see section 2.7.1 and notice how C1 is weakly dominated) and the unique trembling hand perfect equilibrium is the SPNE (R1, C2).

Plainly, this is a further useful application of the idea of 'trembles' as it removes at a stroke the worry over how to fix out-of-equilibrium beliefs without undermining CKR. However, it is not without its own problems. For example, consider the game in Figure 3.5 which is called the centipede game. It offers each player a long sequence of alternating choices between ending the game (play down) or continuing it (play across).

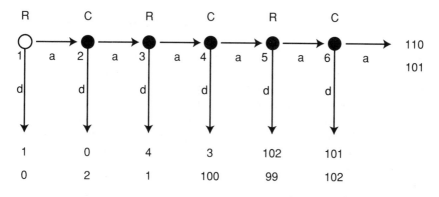

Figure 3.5

The SPNE of this game has player R playing down at the first decision node, thus ending the game straight away. It is derived by Nash backward induction (that is, the blend of backward induction and CKR). The SPNE turns on the thought that, at any point in this game, a rational R would play down. The reason is simple. Consider node number 5. If R plays down she gets pay-off 102. Of course she would prefer 110 but she can see that, given a chance, player C will play down at node 6 (since he prefers pay-off 102 to 101). Similarly at node 3. R will play down because, even though she would dearly like to reach node 5, she believes that player C will end the game at node 4. She believes this because C would rather get 100 at node 4 than 99 at node 5. This would leave R with only pay-off 3 at node 4. Hence she chooses to play down at node 3 where her pay-off equals 4. Lastly, at node 1, player R plays down for exactly the same reason for which she would always play down. Namely, if she plays across, C will end the game immediately (at node 2) fearing that, if he does not, R will do so at node 3 (as we have already concluded). This would yield a zero pay-off for R who, understandably, prefers to get pay-off 1 at node 1.

This SPNE is supported by a long string of out-of-equilibrium beliefs about what would happen at later decision nodes if they were reached. To keep this string consistent with CKR, these stages of the game could only be reached via trembles. But how plausible is it to assume that a sequence of such trembles could take players to the last decision node? Trembles in games like Figure 3.4 are one thing, but to get to the last potential decision node in games like Figure 3.5, it seems that trembles must be a more *systematic* part of the player's behaviour.

3.4.2 Backward induction without CKR or with more than one kind of 'rationality'

This last thought has been at the heart of several critical discussions of the use of backward induction and CKR in game theory (see Binmore, 1987, Pettit and Sugden, 1989, Varoufakis, 1991, 1993, and Reny 1992). If game theory must allow for systematic trembles, would it not be simpler to relax the assumption of CKR and allow for the possibility that a player might be irrational, or might bluff and pretend to be so (and this is why later decision nodes might be reached)? Or, to put the proposition more neutrally, and in a way that conforms with some of the earlier arguments, why not allow for the possibility that two rational agents might not agree on the way that the game is to be played? If this is the case, then CKR does not lead to CAB, and with more than one way for rational players to play the game, it is possible that one type of rational play might involve playing across and so lead them to later decision nodes. Relaxing the CKR assumption in one of

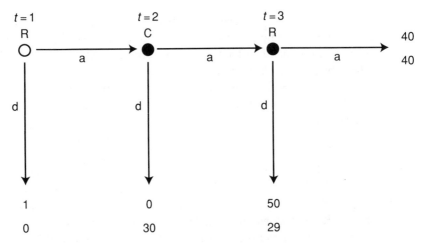

Figure 3.6

these ways may seem simple but it has the immediate effect of opening up many more possible outcomes in such games. Consider for instance a truncated version of a centipede game given by Figure 3.6 when we allow for the possibility of 'irrational' play.

To bring out the difference, we begin with the combination of backward induction and CKR. This means, in effect, that the players would use the following algorithm:

STEP 1 Compute P_3 as your maximum pay-off at $t = 3$ in the following manner: if you are player R, choose P_3 as the largest pay-off; if you are player C, choose P_3 as the pay-off you will collect when player R chooses her largest pay-off

STEP 2 Compute P_2 as your pay-off at $t = 2$ if the game is ended there

STEP 3 If you are player R go to **STEP 6**; otherwise continue

STEP 4 If $P_2 < P_3$ **ACROSS** at $t = 2$; if $P_2 > P_3$ play **DOWN** at $t = 2$

STEP 5 STOP

STEP 6 Compute P_1 as your pay-off at $t = 1$ if the game is ended there

STEP 7 Play **ACROSS** at $t = 1$ if either (a) at **STEP 4** the decision is to play **ACROSS** *and* $P_1 < P_3$, (b) at **STEP 4** the decision is to play **DOWN** *and* $P_1 < P_2$ Otherwise play **DOWN**

When applied to this game, it yields the unique subgame perfect Nash equilibrium with R playing down at the first decision node. Now suppose that CKR is relaxed with the result that player C may believe at some point that there is some chance that R will play across irrationally. Then provided C believes that this chance is sufficiently high (i.e. it is just over $\frac{1}{11}$ in this instance), the best strategy for C at the second decision node is to play across. In turn, R may recognise that playing across at the first decision node could encourage C's belief in her irrationality and so open up the possibility of C playing across with the result that the pay-off of 50 becomes available to R! Provided the chances of this happening are sufficiently high, then playing across by R at the first decision node becomes rational because it is the best thing to do. In effect R would be reasoning like this:

Since playing across deviates from what is prescribed by backward induction and CKR, C will be forced to find an explanation if I play across at the outset. There are two possibilities. One is that he will think that I am irrational for not doing what backward induction plus CKR prescribes. If this is so, he may change his game plan and play **ACROSS** at $t = 2$ expecting a fair chance that my irrationality will overcome my senses yet again so that at $t = 3$ I choose **ACROSS**. Of course, there is the other possibility that I must reckon with. Player C may realise that this is exactly what I am thinking and refuse to believe that I am irrational simply because I have chosen 'irrationally'. Or he may rationalise my weird choice as a tremble. Nevertheless, all I need in order to consider playing **ACROSS** is that C assigns a relatively low probability that I am *systematically* irrational, not that he is convinced of my irrationality. Let p be the non-zero probability that he assigns to this prospect after observing my deviant choice at $t = 2$. If $p > \frac{1}{11}$, then his expected return at $t = 2$ from playing **ACROSS** exceeds that from **DOWN**, therefore giving him a strong incentive to deviate from his equilibrium strategy too, i.e. play **ACROSS** at $t = 2$. So, I conclude that if my defiance of the Nash backward induction logic makes him think with probability at least $\frac{1}{11}$ that I am irrational then it may, after all, make sense for me to play **ACROSS** at $t = 1$ since there is now a realistic chance of getting 50 at $t = 3$ rather than 1 at $t = 1$. More precisely, if there is a probability a shade over $\frac{1}{50}$ that my playing **ACROSS** at $t = 1$ will engender this minimum uncertainty ($p > \frac{1}{11}$) in the mind of C, then it is worth my while doing it!

Thus without CKR, a non-subgame perfect behavioural pattern is possible in this game, with R playing **ACROSS** at $t = 1$, C responding with **ACROSS** at $t = 2$ and R concluding the game with **DOWN** at $t = 3$. Indeed, it may be tempting to conclude that we can even allow for CKR at the beginning of the game because, in effect, we have demonstrated that it has become potentially rational for R to behave irrationally (see Reny, 1992). However, this is not the case. It only becomes rational for R to play irrationally provided this encourages C to think that R is irrational; and this will only be the case if we have not assumed CKR. Perhaps we can assume that players begin the game with CKR if we are happy with the idea that CKR is subverted along the way. Nonetheless, with CKR holding firm throughout player R cannot hope to convince C to do anything other than play **DOWN** at $t = 2$.

The arguments of the last two subsections make clear that there can be difficulties with the use of backward induction in game theory. The attraction of backward induction is undeniable because it can help to narrow the number of admissible equilibria (through the concept of subgame perfection). But as we have seen this will only happen in some games if we also assume CKR. However, the moment we assume CKR, it seems that consistency requires that trembles must be called upon to explain how out-of-equilibrium beliefs are formed. In some games, like the one in Figure 3.6, this seems to require an awful lot of prospective trembles which must be independently distributed. In other words, CKR means that if we observe a 'tremble' in one node (i.e. a deviation from the equilibrium path), this observation should *not* alter our expectations concerning future 'trembles'. Critics of Nash backward induction worry about this because it seems to rule out (by assumption) players trying to bluff or, more generally, to signal something to their opponents by patterning their deviations in a systematic way.

Indeed why should one assume in this way that players cannot (or should not) try to make statements about themselves through patterning their 'trembles'? The question becomes particularly sharp once it is recalled that, on the conventional account, players must expect that there is always some chance of a tremble. Trembles in this sense are part of normal behaviour, and the critics argue that agents may well attempt to use them as a medium for signalling something to each other. Of course, players will not do so if they believe that their chosen pattern is going to be ignored by others. But that is the point: why assume that this is what they will believe from the beginning, especially when agents can see that the generally accepted use of trembles as signals might secure a better outcome for both players (as for example when R plays across or up in the games of Figures 3.5 and 3.6)?

Note that this is not an argument against backward induction *per se*: it is an argument against assuming CKR while working out beliefs via backward induction (i.e. a criticism of Nash backward induction). When agents consider patterning their 'trembles', they project forward about future behaviour given that there are trembles now or in the past. What makes it ambiguous whether they should do this, or stick to Nash backward induction instead, is that there is no uniquely rational way of playing games like Figures 3.5 or 3.6 (unlike the race to 20 game in which there is). In this light, the subgame perfect Nash equilibrium offers one of many possible scenarios of how rational agents will behave.

3.5 SEQUENTIAL EQUILIBRIA

There are some dynamic games where the subgame perfect Nash refinement fails to narrow the number of Nash equilibria. For example, suppose that Gianni can take a third action R3: he can employ someone (a mafioso?) who will punish the relatives if they go to the authorities when he awards himself the fortune. The relatives, however, do not know when Gianni gives the fortune to himself whether he has actually employed someone or not. This is captured in Figure 3.7 by the broken line linking the two decision nodes which C faces (this line defines the **information set** for the stage of the game when C is called upon to move). In effect, when called to play, C does not know which node he is at (that is, where he is in the information set).

C's decision over whether to play C1 or C2 no longer forms a subgame because he does not know in which part of the game he is when called upon to play. Alternatively, there is no unique route from his C1 or C2 decision back to the original decision node of the game and, thus, we

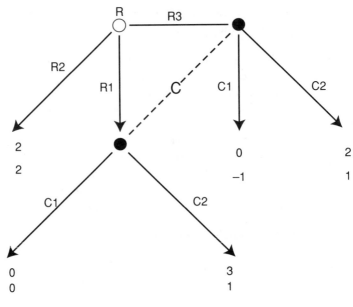

Figure 3.7

cannot solve backwards from this node as we did before. The result is that there is only one subgame for this game: the whole game. This game has two Nash equilibria, (R1, C2) and (R2, C1), and since the game as a whole is a subgame, both Nash equilibria are subgame perfect.

Nevertheless, there is something decidedly fishy about (R2, C1), just as there was before; and it seems we ought to be able to discount it. The strategy for doing this is again to allow for 'trembles' and to notice that there are no beliefs about the likelihood of R trembling to either R1 or R3 which would make C1 an optimal response. In the event of a tremble from R2, C2 is the optimal response and hence R2 cannot be part of a trembling hand perfect equilibrium because it is only a best reply to C1.

Trembles come to the rescue again! In fact, the Nash refinement for extensive games which has enjoyed most prominence is not an extensive form version of trembling hand perfection, but it is the related sequential equilibrium concept (due to Kreps and Wilson, 1982b). (It will become clear how the two are closely related and, in fact, every trembling hand perfect equilibrium is a sequential equilibrium and 'almost every' sequential equilibrium is trembling hand perfect.)

The basic idea behind the sequential equilibrium concept is exactly the same as subgame perfection: strategies should be rational in the sense of being best replies at each stage of the game; so they both use backward induction. The only difference is that the best reply at each stage of the game will depend on where you think you are in the information set which defines that stage of the game. Thus best replies must be conditional upon beliefs about the likelihood of being at one decision node rather than another (i.e. in the example above the likelihood of being at the left hand side of C's information set rather than the right). This explains part (1) of the definition below.

It also means something must be said about the origin of these beliefs; and the sequential equilibrium concept assumes that beliefs should be consistent with the sequentially rational strategies. Hence we have part (2) in the definition below. The sense of consistency is a bit tricky, but the basic idea is that the beliefs which you hold about where you are in an information set should be derived using Bayes's rule and a trembling hand version of the sequentially rational strategies. We shall explain this in more detail.

Definition: sequential equilibria are strategies and beliefs (defined for each decision node) which satisfy the following two conditions.

(1) The strategies must be sequentially rational. That is, they must be best replies given the beliefs held at each information set.

(2) The beliefs at each information set must be consistent in the sense that the probabilities assigned arise from the updating of beliefs using Bayes's rule conditional on a sequence of totally mixed strategies which converge to the strategies in part (1).

The role of trembles will be clear from the example above and it explains the reference in this definition to totally mixed strategies. Totally mixed strategies are strategies where every pure strategy has some (possibly very small but nevertheless) positive probability of being played. Thus when considering whether R2 is sequentially rational above, we assumed that there is always some probability that R will tremble to R1 or R3. This is the basis for C's beliefs about where she is in her information set. Thus we judge that C2 is the best reply and hence R2 is not sequentially rational because R2 is not a best reply to C2. In comparison, when considering R1 and we allow for trembles which take R to R3 or R2 to be the basis for C's beliefs, we find that C2 is the best reply; and since R2 is a best reply to C2, it is a sequential equilibrium.

In this particular example, we did not need to use Bayes's rule to generate the beliefs for C because the prospective sequentially rational strategy, together with the trembles, gives us the likelihood for being at different points in C's information set in a straightforward manner. But in games where there are more stages, the likelihood of being in one part of a later information set will depend on play earlier in the game and so the beliefs

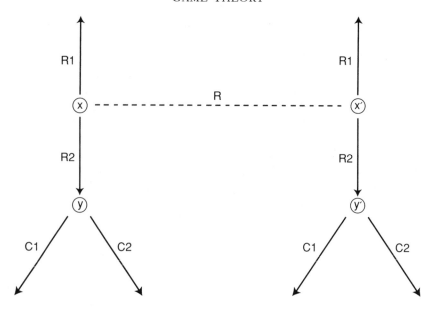

Figure 3.8

have to be linked with the strategies and Bayes's rule provides the mechanism for doing this. We shall develop an extended illustration of this in section 6.5 when we discuss repeated games. To see the connection now, suppose in Figure 3.8, which isolates a part of some larger game, that the sequential equilibrium strategy yields a probability of $\frac{1}{3}$ that R is at x and $\frac{2}{3}$ that she is at x' and a probability of 1 that R will play **UP** in both eventualities. (To explain R's position a bit more, R might expect to find herself at x and x' with these probabilities either because an earlier part of the sequentially rational strategy for C is a mixed strategy which activates x and x' for R with these probabilities; or this could be a game of incomplete information and there may be two types of C player: one moves so as to activate x for R and the other moves so as to activate x' with the respective probabilities of R playing against each type being $\frac{1}{3}$ and $\frac{2}{3}$.)

To complete the construction of the sequential equilibrium, C has to form an assessment as to the likelihood of being at y or y' when deciding whether to play C1 or C2. Since y is reached only by R playing R2 at x, the probability of being at y conditional on the event R2 is given by the probability of R being at x conditional on the event R2. Thus following Bayes's rule:

$$\Pr(y|R2) = \Pr(R2|x)\Pr(x)/[\Pr(R2|x)\Pr(x) + \Pr(R2|x')\Pr(x')]$$

We shall assume that the chance of trembling to R2 is the same at x as it is at x' (i.e. probability ε). Thus,

$$\Pr(y \,|\, R2) = \tfrac{1}{3}\varepsilon / [\tfrac{1}{3}\varepsilon + \tfrac{2}{3}\varepsilon]$$

which tends to $\tfrac{1}{3}$ as ε tends to zero.

The example is useful, not only as a demonstration of how Bayes's rule is used with the strategies to compute sequentially rational beliefs, but also as a further illustration of how the introduction of trembles is crucial for the calculation of out-of-equilibrium beliefs (recall the discussion in sections 3.4.1 and 3.4.2). The information set we have been considering is by construction out of equilibrium because, according to the sequential equilibrium we are considering, R plays R1 with probability 1. Thus without a tremble $\Pr(R2|x)$ equals $\Pr(R2|x') = 0$ and, therefore, Bayes's rule cannot be used to fix the beliefs for C players since the expression above is not defined in these circumstances. In other words, any beliefs might be judged rational in this sense because Bayes's rule cannot be applied to zero probability events. However, once a small tremble is introduced Bayes's rule can be used because R2 is no longer a zero probability event and the expression above can be evaluated. Another way of putting this is to say that the sequentially rational strategies become perturbed by trembles so that they become totally mixed strategies when agents form their beliefs. The fact that they are totally mixed strategies then means that Bayes's rule can always be used to generate beliefs because the perturbed strategies will take you to every possible information set in the game.

3.6 PROPER EQUILIBRIA, FURTHER REFINEMENTS AND FORWARD INDUCTION

Unfortunately even the sequential equilibrium concept often fails to reduce the Nash equilibria. Consider a further variant on the game in Figure 3.4 given by Figure 3.9. In this game the players in the role of R (e.g. the entrant or Gianni or the Warsaw Pact) again have a third strategy.

There are two Nash equilibria here (R1, C2) and (R2, C1) and both are sequential equilibria. (R1, C2) is a sequential equilibrium because a small tremble to R3 will still leave C2 as the best reply for player C. Likewise (R2, C1) is a sequential equilibrium because, whenever the tremble towards R3 is fractionally greater than the tremble to R1, C1 is the best response by player C. The problem really is that the sequential equilibrium concept actually imposes very little on out-of-equilibrium beliefs and so we cannot rule out the possibility that C might think it slightly more likely that R trembles to R3 rather than R1.

One response to these difficulties has been to introduce the concept of **strict perfection** such that the equilibrium does not depend on some arbitrary specification of the trembles (this equilibrium concept is similar to the idea of **strategic stability** in Kohlberg and Mertens, 1986). Unfortunately, there are many games where there are no strictly perfect equilibria.

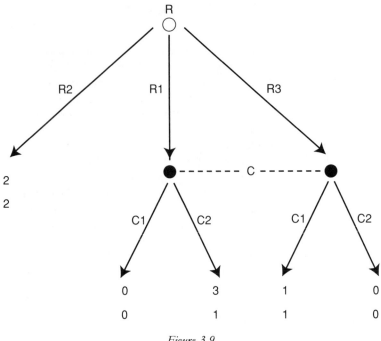

Figure 3.9

Another response has been to consider reasons for placing constraints on the type of trembles which are allowed. Thus, for example, one might argue that a tremble towards R3 is less likely than a tremble to R1 because R3 is dominated by R2, whereas R1 is not. Indeed, if one thinks of trembles occurring because players experiment, there would be no point in experimenting with R3, whereas there is some possibility of a gain from R1. Alternatively Myerson (1978) has suggested that an assessment of the cost of trembles should determine their likelihood. Thus in this example, since R's cost of trembling to R3 is less than that of trembling to R1 when player C plays C1, it is right for C to expect a smaller likelihood of trembles towards R1 when he is considering C1. In Myerson's terminology (R2, C1) is, as a result, a **proper equilibrium**.

All the refinements that have been considered so far work within the tradition of backward induction. There are also those who have argued that this should be supplemented by a principle of *forward induction*. The idea behind forward induction is that players should draw inferences on how future play will proceed on the basis of the past play of the game. This is somewhat in the spirit of the earlier argument regarding R's play of **ACROSS** in the centipede game of Figure 3.5. However, with forward induction, CKR is still maintained. To illustrate how this idea might be used, consider the game given by Figure 3.10.

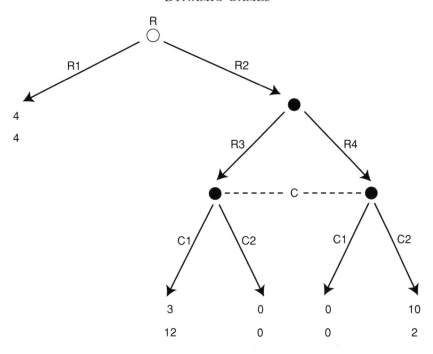

Figure 3.10

In this game, it might be argued that R would only play R2 if she intended to play R4 at her second decision node because playing R3 could only net her a maximum of 3 and she could do better than that by playing R1 in the first place (see Kohlberg and Mertens, 1986). In this way playing R2 acts as a signal to player C courtesy of forward induction. Thus if C gets to play, he should figure that he is on the right hand side of his information set and choose C2. Thus one option for R is to play R2 expecting to get pay-off 10 under the proposed forward inductive interpretation. Under the other option, she plays R1 and collects pay-off 4. So obviously R will choose to play (R2, R4) and C, recognising this logic, will play C2.

Against this view, Harsanyi and Selten (1988) have argued that the strict application of backward induction (together with a principle of risk dominance which we explain below) yields an equilibrium of (R1, R3, C1). Their argument is underpinned by the following claim: *the equilibrium (R3, C1) will be selected in the subgame which begins at R's second decision node.* Why? Notice the broken line joining the two nodes of player C. This broken line indicates that C does not know whether R selected R3 or R4 prior to him having to choose between C1 and C2. R knows that C does not know . . . and so on. If R thought that C expected her to choose R3, she would expect him to play C1. Otherwise she would expect C to play C2. Similarly, if C knew what R expected, then he would know what to do. But neither knows (or can know)! Harsanyi and Selten solve this enigma by means of their assumption of *risk dominance*: with an equal chance of R selecting R3 or R4, C will clearly prefer C1, and so R will prefer R3. Thus the choice, as far as R is concerned, is between R1 yielding 4 and R2 which will shoot play into this subgame with a resulting pay-off of 3. Hence R selects (R1, R3) and C selects C1.

An alternative defence of (R1, R3, C1) using backward induction treats it as a sequential equilibrium where the belief that C holds about the likelihood of where he is in his information set arises from a small tremble to R2. Using Bayes's rule together with the possibility of another small tremble, this time away from R3 towards R4, he will form a small probability assessment that he is at the information node on the right hand side of the tree diagram. Given this assessment that R will have chosen R4 with a vanishingly small probability, he concludes that the chances are that R has chosen R3, in which case his rational response will be C1. Again as far as R is concerned, the best reply to C's choice of C1, and to R's assessment that the probability of C2 is shrinking to zero, is strategy combination (R1, R3).

Intriguingly, in this example backward induction and forward induction pull in opposite directions. Which is to be preferred? Both arguments seem to be internally consistent and so the choice is not an easy one. Perhaps all that can be said is that in playing such games the selection of an equilibrium will turn on which of these extra 'principles' of reason (e.g. backward as opposed to forward induction) agents share.

3.7 CONCLUSION

3.7.1 The status of Nash and Nash refinements

We conclude this chapter by bringing together some of the arguments which have surfaced over the Nash equilibrium concept. Firstly, it is not clear that the consistent alignment of players' beliefs (CAB), which is necessary for Nash, can be justified by appeals to the assumptions of rationality and CKR. This is the same tricky epistemological problem at the foundations of game theory to which we referred in Chapter 1 and which we have followed through various twists and turns in the last two chapters. Something else seems to be required and the best game theory has come up with so far is the Harsanyi doctrine (and its defence by Robert Aumann). This has the effect of making rational players believe that there is a unique rational way to play a game because rational players must draw the same inferences from the same information. Once this is conceded, then indeed it follows from the assumptions of instrumental rationality and CKR that the way to play must constitute a Nash equilibrium. It is the status of the Harsanyi–Aumann argument which is in dispute (recall section 2.2 in Chapter 2).

Even if this controversy is set on one side (and we shall say more about how this might be done below), there remains a difficult question which game theorists in the Nash tradition must answer. How is one Nash equilibrium selected when there are many? Most answers to this question have relied on three components (in varying degrees): the existence of trembles, the use of backward induction (in dynamic games) and a Bayesian consistency between beliefs and strategies chosen (in games of incomplete or asymmetrical information). Refinements in this tradition either explicitly or implicitly require that agents hold mutually consistent beliefs (CAB). Naturally there are reasons for doubting this in the context of refinements of Nash just as there were in connection with the Nash equilibrium concept itself. In addition, there are special reasons for doubting this in dynamic games because of the difficulty of accounting for out-of-equilibrium beliefs by appealing to trembles alone. In some games, it seems more natural to relax CKR and hence CAB. However, this means that we are moving further away from pinpointing a definitive solution (i.e. the problem of equilibrium selection is exacerbated).

Suppose we set this new difficulty on one side as well. Still there are problems. There are, for instance, games with multiple sequential equilibria (the refinement which uses all three elements: trembles, backward induction and a Bayesian consistency between beliefs and strategies). To narrow down the equilibria, yet again something more must be added. In this instance, it seems something more needs to be said about those 'trembles'. The difficulty is to know quite what might be said without relaxing CKR (and thereby recreating the problem with the introduction of further potential equilibria). There have been various attempts at this, but none is especially or generally convincing. Indeed, some of these attempts (like the use of forward induction arguments for instance) are difficult to reconcile with other refinement principles (like backward induction). Perhaps all that can be said is that none of these further ideas regarding trembles can be derived in any obvious way from the assumptions of rationality and CKR. Hence these refinements (e.g. proper equilibria), like the Nash equilibrium project itself, seem to have to appeal to something other than the traditional assumptions of game theory regarding rational action in a social context.

3.7.2 In defence of Nash

The question then is: what sort of other principle needs to be invoked if we are to license Nash (and its refinements)? There are three obvious ways to go. The first is for game theory to become more thoroughly Humean.

The Humean turn

In our introduction (see Chapter 1) we emphasised that game theory adopts a version of David Hume's model of human agency which relies more on the power of reason than Hume did. For example, Hume did not believe that reason offers a complete guide to action. On the contrary, Hume often remarked that, if reason is not provided with sufficient raw materials, it can offer no guide at all. In other words, preferences alone do not necessarily guide action. To use the metaphor of a pair of scales for reason, it is as if we place two equal weights on each side of the scales; we can hardly blame the scales for not telling us which is heavier!

What happens when preferences are such that reason cannot distinguish the uniquely rational action? According to Hume, it is then that custom and habit (or in more modern terms, conventions) fill the vacuum and allow people to act consistently and, with luck, efficiently. If game theory were to become more thoroughly Humean in this sense by allowing for the role of convention, then it might have an answer both to the question of 'why Nash?' and to the question of how to select between Nash equilibria when there are many.

For instance, without enquiring too deeply about how customs and conventions are constituted at this stage, it seems quite plausible to conjecture that they must embody behaviour consistent with the Nash equilibrium. Otherwise at least some people who reflected (in an instrumentally rational fashion) on their custom-guided behaviour would not wish to follow the custom or convention. Thus in the absence of clear advice from reason, if agents appeal to custom as a guide to action then this might underwrite the Nash equilibrium concept. Likewise with the problem of Nash equilibrium selection: if reason cannot tell us which of the many equilibria will materialise, and we come to rely on custom, then we have our explanation. For example, the game in Figure 3.10 can be resolved if we happen to know that as a matter of convention people subscribe, say, to the principle of forward induction *à la* Kohlberg and Mertens.

The introduction of custom and convention can be helpful to game theory in these ways, but it is also a potentially double-edged contribution. Firstly, there is a potentially troubling question regarding the relation between convention following and instrumental rationality. The worry here takes us back to the discussion of section 1.2.3 where for instance it was suggested that conventions might best be understood in the way suggested by Wittgenstein or Hegel. In short, the acceptance of convention may actually require a radical reassessment of the ontological foundations of game theory. Secondly there is a worry that while conventions may answer one set of questions for game theory, they do so only by creating another set of problems since we shall want to know how conventions become established and what causes them to change. There is an ambitious

Humean response to both worries that treats conventions as the products of an evolutionary process and which we shall delay discussing until Chapter 7.

The Kantian move

The second move is to appeal to a part of the Kantian sense of rationality: that part which requires that we should act upon rules which can be acted upon by everyone. In this context, the 'best reply to another's action' rule is one which generalises to form a Nash equilibrium when 'best' is understood in an instrumentally rational fashion. Of course there may be other demands which Kantian reason makes,[2] but taken in isolation, the universalisability condition might provide an alternative foundation for Nash. However, the universalisability requirement will not help with the problem of Nash equilibrium selection because every principle of refinement has the principle of universalisability built into it by construction. To answer this question, it seems that Kantians, like Humeans, will have to appeal to something outside preferences and calculative beliefs (e.g. something like conventions).

For the most part game theorists have not made either move and we examine why this is the case below. For now, it is worth recording that there is a third move which could be made.

Abandon Nash

Why not give up on the Nash concept altogether? This 'giving up' might take on one of two forms. Firstly, game theory could appeal to the concept of rationalisable strategies (recall section 2.4 of Chapter 2) which seem uncontentiously to flow from the assumptions of instrumental rationality and CKR. The difficulty with such a move is that it concedes that game theory is unable to say much about many games (e.g. Figures 2.6, 2.12, etc.). Naturally, modesty of this sort might be entirely appropriate for game theory, although it will diminish its claims as a solid foundation for social science.

What would such an admission mean for social scientists? Either they must make the Humean (or a Kantian) move as discussed above, or alternatively they could opt for a more radical break. Both the Humean and Kantian critiques recognise the ontological value of the essential elements of instrumental rationality. What they do deny is that instrumental rationality is all that governs human action. Many social scientists would want to go further and to reject that a proper analysis of society can have instrumental rationality at its core. In this case, the whole approach of game theory is rejected and the problem of justifying Nash does not arise.

For example, Hegelians evoke an historical perspective from where the observer sees society as a constantly flowing magma: people's passions and beliefs reach violent contradictions; social institutions clash with community or group interests and are reformed as a result; desires remain unfulfilled while others are socially created; everything is caused by something and gives rise, through contradiction, to something else. Yet this is not an anarchic process. The Marxist interpretation of this Hegelian move portrays the reason of men and women maturing as a result of their historical participation. It is an evolving reason, a restless reason, a reason which makes a nonsense of an analysis which starts with fixed preferences and acts like a pair of scales. Unlike the instrumentally rational model, for Hegelians and Marxists action based on preferences feeds back to affect preferences, and so on, in an ever unfolding chain. (See Box 3.1 for a rather feeble attempt to blend desires and beliefs.) Likewise some social psychologists might argue that the key to action lies less with preferences and more with the cognitive processes used by people; and consequently we should address ourselves to understanding these processes.

Box 3.1

BLENDING DESIRES AND BELIEFS

To what extent can game theory transcend its Humean philosophical basis? Some game theorists argue that the theory does not have to be tied down to any particular 'dogma', that it can unify many outlooks and, with a little imagination and skill, cross many boundaries. Consider the major assumption borrowed from David Hume, that agents keep their predictions completely separate from their objectives (or passions). Can it be relaxed?

Suppose you are about to make a choice between acting bravely and beating an ignominious retreat. This could take place at the battlefield, the office (confronted by a nasty boss), the football ground, etc. So far, we have no game in our hands since there is only one party to the decision: you! You act either in one way or in another. What turns this into a genuine 'strategic' game is the interdependence of beliefs and desires. For in this game, your pay-offs depend not only on the outcome but also on what everybody expected the outcome to be. Notice the huge difference between the function of beliefs here and their function in previously discussed games. There, beliefs were mere instruments for satisfying given desires. Here, beliefs are part of the desire structure. John Geanakoplos, David Pearce and Ennio Staccheti create a game out of such a situation in their 1989 paper. We offer a version of it below.

	Your pay-off	Your comrades' pay-offs
You act bravely with probability p	$2 - q'$	$2 + q$
You act cowardly with probability $1-p$	$3(1 - q')$	$1 - q$

where p is chosen by you, q is your comrades' average expectation of p, and q' is your expectation of q.

You are the only active agent in this game. No one else does anything. Your decision variable is probability p, which you alone select. For example, if you set $p = 0$, then you opt for the cowardly behaviour. The opposite happens when $p = 1$. In between you have the option of all sorts of randomisation (i.e. mixed strategies). The problem is that you have an audience of comrades holding expectations of you. Before you act, they expect that you will be brave with a certain probability. Suppose that the average of all their probabilistic expectations (that you will be brave) is q. Notice that their expectation affects their preferences over what you do. If they are convinced you will be brave, that is if $q = 1$, then observing your bravery gives them 3 utils whereas observing cowardice gives them none. If on the other hand they are sure you will disgrace yourself, then they will get 1 util if their expectation is confirmed and 2 if you surprise them. They are always happier to see you perform bravely, but the disappointment if you do not is amplified when they entertain false hopes that you will act bravely.

Let us now scrutinise your character. Your satisfaction (or otherwise) depends on what you think your comrades think of you. Let q' be your estimate of q. That is, when $q' = 0$ ($q' = 1$), you are absolutely convinced they expect you to be cowardly (brave). If $q' = \frac{2}{3}$, you think that they give you a 66.6% chance of being brave. So, what about your preferences? Well, although they are not clear cut, one thing is clear: you are no hero, at least not unconditionally. To see this, suppose you think that your comrades expect you to be cowardly ($q' = 0$). Then you prefer to be cowardly. If, on the contrary, you believe that they expect you to act bravely ($q' = 1$), you prefer to be brave. Unless $q' > \frac{1}{2}$ (that is, unless you think that your comrades give you more than a 50–50 chance of being brave), you are going to be cowardly. This is nice to know, but it still does not tell us what you will do. In reality no reasonable theory can emerge about what expectations (q and q') will emerge. Beliefs feed into desires which then redetermine beliefs; the whole thing becomes thoroughly indeterminate. Not even CKR or CAB can help.

To demonstrate, suppose that some Harsanyian (!) *Deus ex machina* engendered the total alignment of agents' beliefs, that is CAB. There are still three Nash equilibria that may occur. Recalling that CAB means a coincidence of sets of beliefs, in this game the condition for CAB (and thus for the Nash equilibria) is the triple equality $p = q = q'$, that is a situation in which your comrades know exactly the probability with which you will decide to be brave ($q = p$) while you also know exactly the probability that they associate with your bravery ($q = q'$), which of course *is* the true probability. Applying the triple equality, we soon discover the three Nash equilibria:

(a) $p = q = q' = 1$ yielding pay-offs 1 for you and 4 for your comrades
(b) $p = q = q' = 0$ yielding pay-offs 3 for you and 1 for your comrades
(c) $p = q = q' = \frac{1}{2}$ with average pay-offs $\frac{3}{2}$ and $\frac{7}{4}$ for you and for your comrades respectively

Thus with CAB, there are three possibilities. Of these, you prefer (b), that is you prefer to act cowardly when everyone expects you to do just that.

> The worst outcome is to be expected to be brave (case (a)). Then you are trapped in your comrades' high expectations and, in a never ending circle, they are justified in holding them. In between is the equilibrium in which they give you a 50–50 chance of acting bravely (and you act bravely with a 50–50 chance).
>
> The moral of the story is that game theory can allow for beliefs to influence desires (at least in this simple sort of way) at the cost of not being able to predict what will happen even in the simplest of cases.

We divide as two authors at this point. For SHH, there are major difficulties with a purely instrumental account of reason (see Hargreaves Heap, 1989), but it seems undeniable that there are important settings where people do have objectives which they attempt to satisfy best through their actions (i.e. they act instrumentally). In such settings game theory seems potentially useful both when it tells us what might happen and when it reveals that something more must be said about reason before we can know what will happen. YV also recognises this but insists that the social phenomena which *need* to be understood if we are to make sense of our changing social world, cannot be understood in terms of a model of instrumentally rational agents (see Varoufakis, 1991, Chapters 6, 7 and 8). Quite simply, the significant social processes which write history cannot be understood through the lens of instrumental rationality. This destines game theory to a footnote in some future text on the history of social theory. We let the reader decide.[3]

3.7.3 Why has game theory been attracted 'so uncritically' to Nash?

Whatever your view on this last matter, it is a little strange that game theorists have remained so committed to Nash and the minimal philosophical assumptions of instrumental rationality and CKR. It seems that either they should address the difficulties by taking one of the, at least, two positive and more expansive philosophical moves identified above; or they should junk the enterprise and recommence the analysis of social interaction using a different tack. In other words, why has game theory been content to use a series of concepts based on Nash (that is, CAB, the Nash equilibrium, Nash backward induction), which do not seem warranted by their foundational philosophical assumptions (instrumental rationality and CKR)? In a sense, this is a question in intellectual history (or perhaps the sociology of knowledge) and we have no special qualifications to answer it. Nevertheless, we believe that a variety of contributory factors can be identified.

Firstly, one possible way to understand the reluctance of game theory to confront its reliance on the Nash equilibrium concept is to see game theory as essentially a child of its times. Its origins belong firmly in the project of 'modernity' and like all thinking in 'modernity', it has unreflectingly assumed that there is a uniquely rational answer to most questions. This perhaps explains the commitment to Nash and perhaps why the problems with Nash (which actually have a long history in game theoretical discussions) are only now beginning to worry game theorists in a serious way. The critical momentum now is itself part of the new contemporary *zeitgeist* and we can expect a much greater receptivity to the idea of

---

Box 3.2

MODERNITY UNDER A CLOUD: LIVING IN A POST-MODERN WORLD

One of the quests within modernity has been to find ways of resisting the tendency towards the relativisation of all values and claims to power by grounding knowledge and legitimating authority so that they are placed beyond question.

According to the French philosopher, Jean François Lyotard, this legitimation crisis has been solved through the invention of what he calls 'the great meta-narratives' of the modern period. By this he means all those overarching belief systems originating in the Enlightenment – from the belief in rationality, science and causality to the faith in human emancipation, progress and class struggle. These great stories have been used over what he calls the past 'two sanguinary centuries' to legitimate everything from war, revolution, nuclear arsenals and concentration camps to Taylorism, Fordist production models and the gulag. The collapse of faith in these meta-narratives heralds what Lyotard calls the 'post-modern condition'.

(Hebdige, 1989, p. 49)

Post-modern discourses are all *deconstructive* in that they seek to distance us from, and make us sceptical about, the beliefs concerning truth, knowledge, power, the self, and language that are often taken for granted within and serve as legitimation for contemporary Western culture.

Postmodern philosophers seek to throw into radical doubt beliefs still prevalent in (especially American) culture but derived from the Enlightenment, such as:

1) the existence of a stable, coherent self . . .

2) reason and its 'science' – philosophy – can provide an objective, reliable, and universal foundation for knowledge.

3) the knowledge acquired from the right use of reason will be 'True'
. . .

4) Reason itself has transcendental and universal qualities . . .

5) . . .   (Flax, 1987, p. 624)

(See Varoufakis (1993) for a hypothetical attack by post-modernity on Nash backward induction.)

conventions (which can vary with time and place) playing a significant role in social interactions once the ideas of post-modernity have seeped further into the consciousness of economists (see Box 3.2).

Secondly, it is also possible that the strange philosophical moorings of neoclassical economics and game theory have played a part. They are strange in at least two respects. The first is a kind of amnesia or lobotomy which the discipline seems to have suffered regarding most things philosophical during the postwar period. As evidence of this, one need only reflect on the incongruity of the discipline's almost wholesale methodological commitment to one form of empiricism. This was doubly incongruous not only because most philosophers of science have been agreeably sceptical about the claims of such a method during this period, but also because this methodological commitment has been almost completely at odds with the actual practice of economists (see McCloskey, 1983). The second is the utilitarian historical roots of modern economics. This is important because it perhaps helps explain why the full Humean message has not been taken on board by the discipline. Indeed, had Hume unreservedly been the philosophical source for the discipline, then it is more than likely that conventions would have occupied a more central place in economics.

Thirdly, the sociology of the discipline may provide further clues. Two conditions would seem to be essential for the modern development of a discipline within the academy. Firstly the discipline must be intellectually distinguishable from other disciplines. Secondly, there must be some barriers to the amateur pursuit of the discipline. (A third condition which goes without saying is that the discipline must be able to claim that what it does is potentially worth while.) The first condition reduces the competition from within the academy which might come from other disciplines (to do this worthwhile thing) and the second ensures that there is no effective competition from outside the academy. In this context, the rational choice model has served economics very well. It is the distinguishing intellectual feature of economics as a discipline and it is amenable to such formalisation that it keeps most amateurs well at bay. Thus it is plausible to argue that the success of economics as a discipline within the social sciences has been closely related to its championing of the rational choice model.

Consequently, to venture outside the rational choice model by introducing conventions (or, even worse, to make half-disguised invitations to Wittgenstein, Kant or Hegel) is a recipe for undermining the discipline of economics (as distinct from, say, sociology). Of course, intellectual honesty might require such a move but it would be foolish to think that the academy is so constituted as always to promote intellectual development *per se*. It is often more plausible to think of the academy as a battleground between disciplines rather than between ideas and the disciplines which have good survival features (like the barriers to entry identified above) are the ones that prosper. In this vein, the determination of which features help a discipline survive depends less on intellectual criteria and more on the social and political imperatives of the times.

To put the point more concretely, individual economists may find that it is fruitful to explain the economy by recourse to sociological concepts like conventions. Indeed this seems to be happening. But such explanations will only prosper in so far as they are both superior *and* they are not institutionally undermined by the rise of neoclassical economics and the demise of sociology. It is not necessary to see these things conspiratorially to see the point of this argument. All academics have fought their corner in battles over resources and they always use the special qualities of their discipline as ammunition in one way or another. Thus one might explain *in functionalist terms* the mystifying attachment of economics and game theory to Nash.

Box 3.3

FUNCTIONAL EXPLANATIONS

Functional explanations are sometimes regarded as peculiar because they appear to explain something by its beneficial effects. It is the effect of an action rather than intention which lay behind the action which is used to explain why the action was taken. Such explanations have the following form (see Elster, 1983).

(1) Y is an effect of X.
(2) Y is beneficial for some agent Z.
(3) Y is unintended.
(4) The causal relation between X and Y is unrecognised.
(5) Y maintains X by a causal feedback loop through Z.

In this way the behaviour X of some agent Z is explained by its function Y for this agent. Thus one might argue that the rational choice model (X) used by economists (Z) has the unintended consequence of erecting barriers to entry (Y) because it is so amenable to intricate formalisation (e.g. mathematical models) and this keeps amateurs at bay. Of course, this is unintended because most economists believe in the virtue of the rational choice model itself (and not the fact that it can be so readily formalised to keep amateurs out). The existence of barriers to entry (Y) in turn is beneficial for the group of economists (Z) in the competitive battle for resources within the academy and so maintains their position in the academy and their use of the rational choice model (X).

In other words, we might explain in part the apparent reluctance of economists to go beyond Nash by introducing conventions because this threatens a break with the rational choice model and this model holds the key for functional reasons to the success of economics in the academy . . . well, it is only a story!

We have no special reason to prioritise one strand of our proposed explanation. Yet, there is more than a hint of irony in the last suggestion because Jon Elster has often championed game theory and its use of the Nash equilibrium concept as an alternative to functional arguments in social science. Well, if the use of Nash by game theorists is itself to be explained functionally, then . . . !

4

BARGAINING GAMES

4.1 INTRODUCTION

Liberal theorists often explain the State with reference to state of nature. For instance, within the Hobbesian tradition there is a stark choice between a state of nature in which a war of all against all prevails and a peaceful society where the peace is enforced by a State which acts in the interest of all. The legitimacy of the State derives from the fact that people who would otherwise live in Hobbes's state of nature (in which life is 'brutish, nasty and short') can clearly see the advantages of creating a State. Even if a State had not surfaced historically for all sorts of other reasons, it would have to be invented.

Such a hypothesised 'invention' would require a cooperative act of coming together to create a State whose purpose will be to secure rights over life and property. Nevertheless, even if all this were common knowledge, it would not guarantee that the State will be created. There is a tricky further issue which must be resolved. The people must agree to the *precise* property rights which the State will defend and this is tricky because there are typically a variety of possible property rights and the manner in which the benefits of peace will be distributed depends on the precise property rights which are selected (see Box 4.1).

In other words, the common interest in peace cannot be the only element in the liberal explanation of the State, as any well-defined and policed property rights will secure the peace. The missing element is an account of how a particular set of property rights are selected and this would seem to require an analysis of how people resolve conflicts of interest. This is where bargaining theory promises to make an important contribution to the liberal theory of the State because it is concerned precisely with interactions of this sort.

To be specific, the bargaining problem is the simplest, most abstract, ingredient of any situation in which two (or more) agents are able to produce some benefit through cooperating with one another, provided they agree in advance on a division between them. If they fail to agree, the

---

Box 4.1

PROPERTY RIGHTS AND SPARKY TRAINS

How should people decide how to share the use of the 'commons'? This is a classic example where the introduction of some property rights is potentially beneficial to all because without such rights, and even when there is no fighting over use, there is likely to be overgrazing. Dividing the land into little bundles, one for each person, is one solution, but where exactly will boundary lines be drawn? A few feet further in one direction or another will not upset the general advantage any one person has in avoiding overgrazing but it will benefit one person to the detriment of his or her neighbour. Even when the boundary lines have been drawn and the fences have been erected, there are always further tricky issues which property rights do not settle fully. For instance, to quote a rather famous example from economics, the boundary between the farmer and railroad owner might be clear on the map, but when the sparks from the railroad set fire to the farmer's crop, whose fault is it? Is it the railroad owner's because the railroad was the source of sparks or was it the farmer's for planting his or her crops so close to the railway line?

In other words, there are a variety of external effects associated with the economic activity and a full set of property rights will also have to assign liability for those external effects.

---

potential benefit never materialises and both lose out (a case of conflict). State creation in Hobbes's world provides one example (which especially interests us because it suggests that bargaining theory may throw light on some of the claims of liberal political theory with respect to the State), but there are many others.

For instance, there is a gain to both a trade union and an employer from reaching an agreement on more flexible working hours so that production can respond more readily to fluctuations in demand. The question then arises of how the surplus (which will be generated from greater flexibility) is to be distributed between labour and capital in the form of higher wages and/or profits. Likewise, it may benefit a couple if they could rearrange their housework and paid employment to take advantage of new developments (e.g. a new baby, or new employment opportunities for one or both partners). However, the rearrangement would require an 'agreement' on how to distribute the resulting burdens and benefits. Thus the bargaining problem is everywhere in social life and the theory of bargaining promises to tell us something, not only about the terms of State creation in Liberal political theory, but also about how rational people settle a variety of problems in many different social settings. And yet the two examples in this paragraph seem to warn that the study of the bargaining problem cannot be merely a technical affair as it involves issues of social power and justice. Indeed there are many alternative accounts of how conflict is resolved in such settings. For example, Box 4.2 sketches two different approaches to the analysis of State formation which have little in common with the liberal voluntarist conception.

The basic elements of the bargaining problem will remind some readers of the hawk–dove or the chicken game of section 1.4.1 of Chapter 1 as players there have an incentive to cooperate but also an incentive to oppose each other, and this explains why it is often taken to be one of the classic games in social life. In this chapter we discuss two very different approaches which game theorists have adopted in their analysis of the bargaining problem. The first is the so-called axiomatic approach and section 4.3 sets out Nash's original set of axioms. In this tradition, game theorists present a series of principles (encoded in axioms) which they suggest any rule for solving the problem should satisfy and then, through formal analysis, they typically show that only one division of the gains satisfies these principles. It is not always clear how the axiomatic treatment of the bargaining problem is to be interpreted. Indeed, it is sometimes, somewhat misleadingly, referred to as the 'cooperative' approach to the bargaining problem. In fact, we suggest in section 4.5 that it is best understood as a framework which can be used to address certain problems in moral philosophy and we provide some illustrations of how it can be put to work in this way.

The second approach, which is considered in section 4.4, treats the bargaining game non-cooperatively: that is, the bargaining process is modelled step by step as a dynamic non-cooperative game, with one person making an offer and then the other, and so on. At this stage it may be helpful if we recall the basic distinction between cooperative and non-cooperative game theory from Chapter 1. In cooperative games agents can talk to each other and make agreements which are binding on later play. In non-cooperative games, no agreements are binding. Players can say whatever they like, but there is no external agency which will enforce that they do what they have said they will do. Indeed for this reason, and following the practice of most game theorists, we have so far discussed the non-cooperative play of games 'as if' there was no communication, thereby implicitly treating any communication which does take place in the absence of an enforcement agency as so much 'cheap talk'. Since one might suppose that the negotiations associated with bargaining involve quite a bit of talk, it is as well to make the treatment of 'talk' explicit in non-cooperative games and we do this next, in section 4.2.

The reason for focusing on the non-cooperative approach will be obvious. The creation of the institutions for enforcing agreements (like the State) which are presumed by cooperative game theory requires as we have seen that agents first solve the bargaining problem non-cooperatively.

Taken at its face value, the striking result of the non-cooperative analysis of the bargaining problem is that it yields the same solution to the bargaining problem as the axiomatic approach. If this result is robust, then it seems that game theory will have done an extraordinary service by showing that bargaining problems have unique solutions (whichever route is preferred). Thus it will have shown not just what sort of State rational agents might agree to create, but also how rational agents might solve a host of bargaining problems in social life. Unfortunately we have reasons to doubt the robustness of this analysis and it is not difficult to see our grounds for scepticism. If bargaining games resemble the hawk–dove game and the discussion in Chapter 2 is right to point to the existence of multiple equilibria in this game under the standard assumptions of game theory, then how does bargaining theory suddenly manage to generate a unique equilibrium?

Box 4.2

MARXIST AND FEMINIST APPROACHES TO THE STATE

'Hitherto men have constantly made up for themselves false conceptions about themselves, about what they are and what they ought to be' (Preface to the *German Ideology*, p.37). According to Marx and Engels, one of these fictions is the idea that the State under capitalism can be thought of as the product of negotiation between agents under conditions of equality. In reality,

> the State is the form in which individuals of a ruling class assert their common interests . . . . [It] follows that the State mediates in the formation of all common institutions and that the institutions receive a political form. Hence the illusion that law is based on . . . *free will.*
> (p. 80)

Yet 'in the State personal freedom has existed only for the individuals who developed within the relationships of the ruling class, and only insofar as they were individuals of this class' (p. 83). But Marx was not implying that the State is a machine which serves the ruling class directly and unambiguously. Indeed he criticised those on the left and on the right who did not recognise the contradictions within the State. In a famous passage he asserts that the State can act independently of the interests of the ruling class. Indeed the ruling class often benefits when it does not control the State fully: 'in order to save its purse it must forfeit the crown, and the sword that is to safeguard it must at the same time be hung over its own head as the sword of Damocles' ('The Eighteenth Brumaire of Louis Bonaparte' in Marx and Engels, 1979). (Notice that this is a functional argument – see Box 3.3 in Chapter 3.)

Feminists adopt a similarly radical rejection of the fiction of the State as a 'coming together' between free agents. Carole Pateman (1988) contends that the original contract envisaged by liberal theory is both

---

social and sexual. Through it men transform their 'natural' freedom (recall Hobbes's state of nature) into the security of civil freedom. They do this with the help of the implicit sexual contract as they transform their 'natural' right over women into the security of civil patriarchal right. Thus only men 'bargain' and the contract they forge reflects a civil freedom which is masculine and depends upon patriarchal rights. Catharine MacKinnon (1989) takes up this point and applies it to the State. 'Women are oppressed socially, prior to law, without express state acts, often in intimate contexts. The negative (i.e. liberal) state cannot address their situation in any but an equal society – the one in which it is needed least' (p. 165). 'The liberal state coercively and authoritatively constitutes the social order in the interests of men as a gender – through its legitimising norms, forms, relation to society, and substantive policies' (p. 62).

Granted these arguments, it may still be worth reflecting on whether the claim of bargaining theory (to provide an analysis of conflict resolution between individuals with well defined interests) has potential, if more limited, relevance to these non-liberal perspectives. After all, however 'unfree' people may be for one reason or another, they typically still have some choices to make and these often explicitly entail conflicts with other 'unfree' people.

4.2 CREDIBLE AND INCREDIBLE TALK IN SIMPLE BARGAINING GAMES

We begin with two examples.

Example 1 Suppose players R and C (we retain their labels for continuity even though they will not always choose between row and column strategies) are offered a chance of splitting between them $100 in any way they want. We empower player R to make C an offer that C may accept or reject. If he accepts, then we have agreement on a division determined by R's offer. If he rejects the offer, we take away $99 and let them split the remaining $1. Then player C makes an offer on how to do this. If R rejects it, each ends up with nothing. Finally, assume that players' utilities are directly proportional to their pay-offs (that is, no sympathy or envy is allowed and they are risk neutral).

What do you think will happen? What portion of the $100 should R offer C at stage 1? Should C accept? Using backward induction, suppose C rejects R's initial offer. How much can he expect to get during the second stage? Assuming that the smallest division is 1c, and given that the failure to agree immediately loses them $99, the best C can get is 99c (that is, once there is only $1 to split, R will prefer to accept the lowest possible offer of 1c rather than to get nothing). C knows this and R can deduce that C

115

knows this right at the beginning. Therefore, R knows that C cannot expect more than 99c if he rejects her offer during the first stage. It follows that C must accept any offer just above 99c, say $1 or $1.01. Backward induction concludes that, at the outset, R proposes that she keeps $98.99 with C getting a measly $1.01. Since C knows that he will not be in a position to improve upon this terrible offer, he will accept.

Notice that the above case of backward induction requires first-order CKR (so it is a form of Nash backward induction) as it turns on R knowing that C is instrumentally rational. In fact, the equilibrium so derived is subgame perfect (see section 3.3 of the previous chapter).

At this point we must define a notion that we have come across before in the discussion of subgame perfection and which is at the centre of bargaining theory: that of *credibility*. Suppose that agents can talk to each other during the various phases. What if, just before player R issues her offer of $1.01, player C threatens to reject any offer that does not give him at least, say, $40. He may for instance say:

> We have $100 to split. You have a first-offer advantage which, quite naturally, puts you in the driving seat. I recognise this. On the other hand I do not recognise that this advantage should translate into $98.99 for you and $1.01 for me. Thus, I will not accept any offer that does not give me at least $40.

Pretty reasonable, don't you think? No, according to game theorists. For this is a threat that should not be believed by player R. Why not? Because it is a threat that, if carried out, C will lose more from than if it is not. Thus, it is a threat that an instrumentally rational C will not carry out. It is, in other words, an incredible threat.

> **Definition:** A threat or promise which, if carried out, costs more to the agent who issued it than if it is not carried out, is called an **incredible threat or promise**.

Game theory assumes that agents ignore incredible threats; analytically speaking, they resemble the dominated strategies in Chapter 2. Such *cheap talk* should not affect the strategies of rational bargainers. This seems like a good idea in a context where what is and what is not credible is obvious.
Example 2: Consider another simple bargaining case. There are two people R and C to whom we give $7000. We tell them that one of them must get $6000 and the other $1000. However, we will pass the money over only if they agree on who gets the $6000 and who the $1000 (let us assume for argument's sake that they cannot renegotiate and redistribute the money later). If they fail to agree, then neither gets anything. To give some structure to the process, we arrange a meeting for tomorrow morning during which each will submit a sealed envelope to us including a note with either the number 1 or the number 6 on it. (These numbers convey their claims to $1000 and $6000 respectively.) Finally, we tell them that if

both envelopes contain the same number neither gets anything. (Again we assume that the pay-offs are equivalent to utils.)

The two bargainers have all night to come to an agreement as to what they will bid for in tomorrow's meeting. According to standard game theory, whether they talk to each other, make promises or issue threats, or even remain silent, there is no difference. For none of these messages are credible and, thus, it is as if there was no communication. The reason can be found in the following matrix representation of the bidding game, Figure 4.1.

	C1	C6
R6	6, 1	0, 0
R1	0, 0	1, 6

Figure 4.1

Strategy R6 corresponds to R claiming the $6000, R1 to R claiming $1000. Similarly C6 corresponds to C claiming the $6000 etc. Suppose that in the meeting, R declares pompously that she will certainly claim the $6000 (that is, she will play R6). Should C take notice? No, because C ought to know that, when it comes to the crunch, the empty threat does not change anything. It is not that one does not expect the other to go for the $6000, but rather that no one can threaten credibly *always* to do so since it is plain that if R believes C will go for C6 then her best action is to accept R1. Game theory's conclusion is that, if a binding agreement is not reached, it makes no difference whether agents can or cannot communicate with each other prior to playing the game.[1]

What matters here is that it is very difficult to make people believe your intentions when you have an incentive to lie. If so, there is nothing new in the game of Figure 4.1. A brief comparison of this game with that in Figure 2.9 in Chapter 2 shows that the two are identical: add one to everyone's pay-offs in 2.9 and you get 4.1. Once this is noted, we need not go into a great deal of detail concerning the problems that such a game presents when treated non-cooperatively (see section 2.7 for a reminder). The root problem is that this game has no unique Nash equilibrium in pure strategies (each strategy is perfectly rationalisable and both (R1, C1) and (R2, C2) are Nash equilibria).

There is one slightly ironical twist to the bargaining problem. Chapter 2 showed how a unique solution to games such as the one in Figure 4.1 (which is a primitive bargaining problem) can be built on the assumption of CAB (that is, that the beliefs of agents are always consistently aligned): the Nash equilibrium in mixed strategies, NEMS. One might be inclined to think that when bargaining problems do have unique solutions, then either

GAME THEORY

the latent conflict of the situation is never manifest (as in the case of example 1 earlier in this section, where R takes almost $99 and C accepts the remainder) or the conflict does not teach players anything they did not know already. For this is what will happen in example 2 (Figure 4.1) if players follow their NEMS (i.e. claim the $6000 with probability 6/7): even though the probability of conflict (i.e. both claiming the $6000) is high, nothing is learnt after such a conflict since these NEMS-based strategies were compatible with CAB from the beginning.

This line of thought in turn might seem to count against any general assumption that there is a uniquely rational way to play such games since we plainly observe conflict in the real world and, moreover, people do change their views (and positions) afterwards. Of course this can be explained within mainstream theory by the argument that conflict only ever arises when players have different information sets (i.e. a state of asymmetric information). After all, in game theory it is the differences in information which explain (recall the Harsanyi doctrine) how people come to hold different and conflicting expectations about how to play the game. In other words, it seems we are, in effect, asked to think of the 1984 miners' strike in the UK either as the result of irrationality by the bargaining sides, or as the consequence of insufficient information.

However, matters are not so simple. In fact, we doubt that either the NEMS or the asymmetric information explanation of conflict is entirely satisfactory. For example, conflicts often seem to be initiated because matters of honour or principle are at stake and these are not well captured by the instrumental model of action. Moreover, they develop a momentum of their own precisely because actions tend to feed back and effect desires.

4.3 JOHN NASH'S GENERIC BARGAINING PROBLEM AND HIS AXIOMATIC SOLUTION

4.3.1 The bargaining problem

We begin with a warning. When we refer to *Nash's solution to the bargaining problem*, we are talking about something quite different to the Nash equilibrium. So don't confuse the *Nash equilibrium* concept with *Nash's bargaining solution*.

The bargaining problem to be examined here has the simplest possible form. Imagine two persons (R and C) who have the opportunity to split between them a certain sum of money (say, $1) provided they can agree on a distribution (or solution). They have a certain amount of time during which to discuss terms and, at the end of that period, they are asked to submit independently their proposed settlement (say, in a sealed envelope). A bargainer is assumed to care only about the utility he or she will get from the agreed settlement. Considerations such as risk aversion, envy, sympathy,

Box 4.3

UTILITY FUNCTIONS AND RISK AVERSION

Suppose an individual is offered a 50–50 chance of winning $100 in a lottery and a lottery ticket costs $50. We say such persons are risk neutral when they are indifferent between buying the lottery ticket and forsaking the opportunity. If they buy the lottery ticket, then we call them risk lovers; and when they will not buy the ticket, we call them risk averse. The intuition behind these descriptions will be obvious as the expected return from buying the lottery ticket is $50 and so if you positively want to buy this prospect for $50 you must love a gamble. Conversely, if you are indifferent between them, you are neutral to the risk; whereas the risk averse person obviously will not buy the ticket as there is nothing in it for him or her except the risk which they do not like.

When we plot utility as a function of dollars and we assume that the individual is an expected utility maximiser, the curvature of the utility function can be directly linked to these varying attitudes to risk. To see the point consider someone who has a linear utility function in money, as in the figure below.

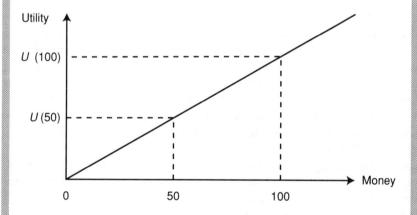

For this person, the utility of $50, $U(50)$ is plainly equal to the expected utility of the lottery ticket $(= 0.5U(0) + 0.5U(100))$. Thus this is the kind of person we have referred to as risk neutral. Now consider another person with a utility function which is convex in money, as in the figure overleaf.

For this person, the utility of $50, $U(50)$ is plainly greater than the expected utility of the lottery ticket $(= 0.5U(0) + 0.5U(100))$ because of the curvature of the utility function. Thus this is the kind of person we have referred to as risk averse. Had the utility curved upwards in the opposite direction, then the result would have been the exact opposite and we would have a person who was a risk lover.

119

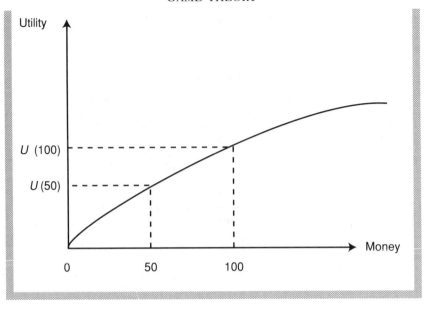

concern for justice, etc., are all supposed to be included within the function that converts pay-offs into utilities (the utility function). Exactly as in the earlier games, bargainers in the present chapter play for utilities rather than for the dollars and cents that generate these utilities. In Figure 4.2(a) we have a simple case in which each player's monetary pay-offs translate linearly into utils (i.e. they are both risk neutral – see Box 4.3). Figure 4.2(b), on the other hand, illustrates the more general problem in which at least one player's utility is a non-linear function of his or her share of the pie. In both cases the origin is labelled *d* and is called the conflict point; it tells us what happens to each player when they cannot agree and in this instance they both get 0. The object of bargaining theory is to find some division which lies on the line AB.

Can we pinpoint a solution? Is a theory which predicts how rational bargainers will split the dollar possible? The general difficulty with supplying an answer can be readily seen because any proposed division will constitute a Nash equilibrium (note: *not* a Nash solution). To see this point, suppose R is *convinced* that C will submit a claim for 80% of the prize. What is her best strategy? It is to submit a claim for 20% (since more than that will result in incompatible claims and zero pay-offs for both). It follows that the strategy 'I will ask for 20%' is rationalisable conditional on the belief 'he will ask for 80%'. Indeed any distribution $(x\%, 100 - x\%)$ is rationalisable given certain beliefs (see the definition of rationalisability in section 2.5, Chapter 2). If it so happens that R's beliefs are identical to

Nash solution N maximises K

Under solution N, x = 1/2

$U_R = x$; $U_C = 1 - x$; x is R's share
(a)

Under solution N, x = 2/3

$U_R = x$; $U_C = (1 - x)^{1/2}$
(b)

Figure 4.2

those of C, then we have a case of Nash equilibrium. The following trains of belief illustrate a Nash equilibrium in a bargaining game:

R thinks: 'I will ask for x% because I think that C expects me to do this and therefore intends to ask for only $100 - x$% for himself.'

C thinks: 'R is convinced that I will ask for $100 - x$% and therefore intends to claim x% for herself. Consequently, my best strategy is to confirm her expectations by claiming $100 - x$%.'

So how do we go about discovering the value of x, i.e. a solution?

4.3.2 Nash's axioms

The Nash axiomatic answer begins by assuming that we are looking for a rule which will identify a particular outcome. (In this way Nash assumes from the beginning that we are only interested in rules which identify unique outcomes. Formally when the conflict point is given by d and the set of available options is given by S then we are looking for a rule R which operates on (d, S) to produce some particular utility combination from the feasible set for R and C.) Nash then suggests that it would be natural for any such rule to satisfy the following four conditions/axioms.

(i) **Individual rationality.** This is an assumption which ensures that the solution lies on the frontier AB; that is, that there will always be an agreement such that no portion of the 'pie' remains unclaimed. (Notice that this is the same as assuming that the outcome will be a Nash equilibrium.)

(ii) **Irrelevance of utility calibrations.** The meaning here is that the solution should be invariant to the choice of cardinal utility function to represent a player's preferences. (Recall from Chapter 1 that the choice of utility function is, by definition, rather arbitrary. Thus it is important to have a solution which is not affected by different calibrations of the utility function, since no one calibration is better than another.)

(iii) **Independence of irrelevant alternatives.**

(iv) **Symmetry.**

We shall say more about these conditions/axioms below. For now we wish only to note that Nash shows that there is only one rule which satisfies these four conditions. This is the so-called Nash solution to the bargaining game:

Definition: The **Nash solution to the bargaining problem** is the distribution $(x\%, 100 - x\%)$ which satisfies axioms (i) to

(iv) above. Furthermore, the value of x which it recommends is such that the product of the utility functions of the two bargaining parties is maximised. In the case of $n > 2$ bargaining parties, the Nash solution specifies a distribution $(x_1\%, x_2\%, \ldots, x_n\%)$ such that $x_1 + x_2 + \ldots x_n = 100$ and the values of $(x_1, x_2, \ldots, x_n)$ maximise the product $f_1(x_1)f_2(x_2) \ldots f_n(x_n)$, where $f_i(x_i)$ is the cardinal utility function of bargainer i $(=1, \ldots, n)$ which relates the utility of player i from having received $x_i\%$ of the 'pie'.

In other words, the Nash solution selects the outcome which maximises the product of the utility gains from the final agreement of the two bargainers relative to the conflict point. The proof of Nash's solution suggests that there is a unique solution to the bargaining problem *once we accept the relevance of these four axioms to the bargaining problem.*

In view of what was said above, it is perhaps worth remarking that Nash did not contrive a unique solution. Although he was looking for rules which specified unique outcomes, he did not assume that there was only one such rule. You only get the unique solution to the bargaining problem when you combine the fact that there is only one rule with the fact that the rule specifies a unique outcome. Had there been many rules, each specifying a unique but different outcome, then there would have been many solutions, one for each rule. Yet Nash showed that there is only one rule that satisfies all four axioms.

In many respects, this is an extraordinary result. Many people are inclined to think that the division of $1 (or whatever sum) involves matters of justice and fairness which in turn are bound to be the source of disagreement; yet here is Nash offering a unique solution, provided the parties accept that these conditions (i.e. his axioms) should apply. But why should we think that bargainers will think that these conditions should apply? Before answering this question, we need to examine the conditions more closely.

The axioms of individual rationality and independence of utility calibrations

With the first axiom Nash assumes that there will be no waste. Individual rationality will ensure that the bargaining process generates an agreement so that no part of the 'pie' goes undistributed. Put differently, there will be no conflict. The second axiom implies that the only relevant information is the strength of preference over outcomes for each person: the manner in which that preference is 'calibrated' does not matter. (For more on this see Box 4.4.)

The axiom of the independence of irrelevant alternatives (IIA)

Imagine the following situation. Bargainer R considers claims x, y and z and she concludes that claim z is the most promising. Now suppose that an external agency (for example, an umpire, a third party with the power to change the conditions of the bargain, the State, etc.) disallows R's claim x. John Nash assumes that nothing will change. Since R would, in any case, not have made claim x, her bargaining behaviour must surely be unaffected by the removal of claim x from her menu. This is the conjecture behind axiom IIA. In effect, the requirement enforces a certain type of relation between the outcome of similar bargaining games, so it is like a consistency requirement.

More generally, IIA asserts that when solutions which agents would not have chosen become infeasible, the outcome is not altered (thus the label *independence of irrelevant alternatives*). Take a hypothetical scenario according to which R and C are about to agree on a 40%–60% split. Suddenly 'legislation' is passed prohibiting any settlement that gives C less than 59%. Nash's IIA means that this piece of 'legislation' has no effect; the initial bargain goes ahead as if the 'legislation' was not introduced (since it rules out alternatives which the two parties would have discarded).

The axiom of symmetry

Symmetry requires that each player should receive an identical amount if the players' valuations of each slice of the 'pie' are identical (that is, if their utility functions are the same). In other words, if you can substitute R for C and vice versa and the description of the game for both players is unaffected, then the solution to the bargaining problem should be the same for both players. Formally if the feasible set S is symmetric around the line $U_R = U_C$ and d lies on this line as well, then the solution must also lie on this line. Notice that this axiom is a version of Harsanyi's doctrine which claimed that people with the same information will come to the same conclusion. Well, if all the relevant information is information on utility valuations (e.g. the diagrams in Figure 4.2), and given that it is commonly known, then the players' strategies will be identical if their utility valuations are identical.

This symmetry axiom/condition means that asymmetries in final payoffs (and thus in the bargainers' demands/offers) can *only* be due to differences in their utility valuations (or functions). For example, in Figure 4.2(b) R demands more than C does only because of differences in their utility functions. We demonstrate this in section 4.3.4.

4.3.3 Do the axioms apply?

Independence axioms like IIA are often thought to be requirements of individually rational choice (see Chapter 1) on the grounds that consistency requires that if you prefer A to B when C is available, then you should still prefer A to B even when C is not available. This may seem more or less plausible to you as a condition of individual rationality. Nevertheless, experimental work on expected utility theory has shown that such consistency may be violated by perfectly rational people (see Hargreaves Heap *et al.*, 1992, Chapter 3). To give a brief flavour of this, imagine that A = croissant, B = bread and C = butter. You may prefer A to B in the absence of C (i.e. you prefer a plain croissant to a piece of plain bread) but your preference may be reversed when C is available (i.e. you prefer a buttered piece of bread to a croissant, buttered or plain). Such complementarities have been used to explain paradoxes like that of Maurice Allais – see Box 1.4.

In the case of bargaining the potential for violations of independence axioms, such as IIA, is enhanced. This is so because it is another person who sets your constraint (through his or her demands). Therefore what you cannot have depends on what the other person thinks you will not ask for. The greater the interaction the more problematic it is to assume independence. Consider for instance the illustration used earlier: imagine that you are R and you were about to settle with C on the basis of a 60%–40% split. Just before you agree, the government legislates that C cannot get anything less than 40%. Will you expect C to see this as an opportunity to up his claim? IIA *assumes* that neither will C do so nor will you expect him to do so.

At best then it seems that IIA is no more than a convention bargainers may or may not accept as a condition which agreements (as well as demands) will satisfy. The problem is that there are other, equally rational, conventions to which bargainers may converge. For example, the convention that when an external agency (such as the State) underpins the bargaining position of one party, this will benefit the pay-off of that party even if the intervention is mild. For example, industrial relations experience shows that the bargaining position of trade unions is improved when a minimum wage is introduced. Moreover, and this is important here, this improvement is not restricted to bargains which involve workers at the bottom of the pay scale; indeed there are spillover effects to other areas in which the minimum wage would not apply and yet the union position (and thus the negotiated wage) improves as a direct repercussion of the minimum wage legislation. This experience contradicts directly the axiom of IIA.

Indeed it is possible to devise explicit alternatives to the IIA axiom. These alternative conventions play the same role as IIA (that is, they

Box 4.4

SOME VIOLATIONS OF NASH'S AXIOMS

Imagine that two bargainers A and B have identical utility functions. They are walking together when A spots a $100 bill lying on the ground. As they are on a Greek island (on holiday), they want to exchange it for drachmas at the local bank. However, A does not have her passport with her, but B does (we assume a passport is required at the Bureau de Change). The Nash solution predicts that they will share the proceeds. Fair enough. What if, however, A and B come from a place where 'finders' are thought to deserve to be 'keepers'. Of course B's passport is important in this instance. Yet both A and B may entertain expectations that the person who found the $100 deserves more than 50% – in which case they might violate the symmetry axiom of John Nash and agree on an asymmetrical distribution (e.g. 60%–40%).

Here is another example. Suppose that A and B have won a sum of drachmas in some local lottery. A is due to fly home hours later while B will stay on for another fortnight. If they split the sum of drachmas in half, then A will be disadvantaged since she will have to change it immediately into her country's currency and will, thus, forfeit a significant amount in bank fees. Nash's axiom of the irrelevance of utility calibrations assumes that the two friends will take this into account and will agree to divide the drachmas in an asymmetrical fashion so that their utility gains are identical. But it seems at least possible that A and B might share the expectation that each would demand an equal division of drachmas.

The point of the above examples is that we cannot rule out the possibility that bargainers will, quite rationally, act on a basis of some convention different to those behind Nash's axioms. One final example: A and B are about to decide that they want to split the drachmas they just won on a 60%–40% basis (perhaps for the reason offered in the previous paragraph). Before they do, they find out that the lottery rules specify that, in the case of joint winning tickets, no partner should get less than 40% of the winnings (some Greek law)! Nash's axiom of the independence of irrelevant alternatives insists that this rule should not change their mind since the 60%–40% split which they were going for is (just) legal. But it is possible that A will not expect B to settle for the bare minimum of his legal entitlement. Equally, it is possible that B (recognising this) will demand more than 40%.

provide a consistent 'link' between the outcomes of different bargaining games), albeit lead to different bargaining solutions. For instance, a 'monotonicity' axiom has been proposed by Kalai and Smorodinsky (1975) whereby when a bargaining game is slightly changed such that the outcomes for one person improve (in the sense that, for any given utility level for the other player, the available utility level for this person is higher than it was before), then this person should do no worse in the new improved game than he or she did before. This might seem more plausible because it embodies a form of natural justice in linking bargaining problems. However, the substitution of this axiom yields a different bargaining solution: one where there is an equal relative concession from the maximum utility gain. Indeed some moral philosophers have argued that this is the result that you should expect from instrumentally rational agents (see Gauthier, 1986).[2]

The axiom of symmetry on the other hand seems more plausible at first. After all, if the two agents are one another's mirror image (that is, they have the same motives, the same personality, etc.), we should expect a totally symmetrical outcome: a 50–50 split. This sounds plausible until we ask the question: 'What does it mean to say that two agents are *identical*?' Can two agents *be* identical? The answer is yes. Once agents are identified only by their utility information, so long as they do not differ in their utility representations, they are identical.

From a normative perspective, this seems unobjectionable. But is it so plausible as a convention which guides bargainers? Utility information actually ignores many features of the situation which plausibly agents might regard as relevant. For example, utility representations are gender blind. A man and a woman with the same utility representations are treated identically by game theory (and so they should be), but is this a plausible assumption about actual behaviour in all settings? In a sexist society, is it not more plausible to assume that the 'convention' operating in that society may actually treat men and women differently even when their utility information is identical?

4.3.4 Nash's solution – a summary

Whatever the doubts about these axioms, they are plainly not completely implausible, and so the result is interesting. Indeed, it is an extraordinary achievement, since it predicts a particular outcome without actually having to say anything about the bargaining process (and remarkably it receives some support from the analysis of bargaining processes, as we shall see in the next section). Thus it is worth spending some time looking at the details of the Nash solution.

Any distribution ($x\%$, $100 - x\%$) can be rationalised as a Nash equilibrium in our bargaining games of Figure 4.2. Nash's bargaining solution selects one out of this plethora of Nash equilibria. The value of x that is picked, say x^*, is the one which maximises the numerical value of *the product of the two agents' cardinal utility gains*. Effectively, the distribution ($x^*\%$, $100 - x^*\%$) maximises this product and is the only distribution that satisfies John Nash's axioms. (A proof can be found in Varoufakis, 1991.)

In the game of Figure 4.2(a), this yields the equal split of the $1 and it is a result which is driven by the fact that players are identical (recall the symmetry axiom). To explore the implications more generally, here is another example.

An example of Nash's solution at work

Suppose that bargainer R 'enjoys' pay-offs in direct proportion to the pay-off. That is, if R's pay-off is doubled, her enjoyment is also doubled because she is risk neutral. In algebraic terms, R's utility function is, simply, x. On the other hand, bargainer C is quite different: he is risk averse so each increment of money yields smaller and smaller increments to his utility. Algebraically, his utility function looks something like $(100 - x)^n$, where n is less than 1 – see Figure 4.2(b) for a graphical representation.

Let us apply the definition of the Nash solution above. Since Nash's solution $(x^*, 100 - x^*)$ is the one that maximises $x(100 - x)^n$, it is easy to see (by setting the first-order derivative of $x(100 - x)^n$, subject to x, equal to zero) that, according to the Nash solution, R's share is $x^*\% = 100 \{1 - [(n + 1)]\}\%$. This means that R's share increases the smaller the value of n. For instance, suppose $n = \frac{1}{2}$; the Nash solution gives bargainer R 66.6% of the total prize, whereas when n is 1 R gets 50%. In other words, given the interpretation that when n is less than 1 C is risk averse, we have the result that the Nash solution gives less to the risk averse player C than the risk neutral player R. Or to put this round the other way, R benefits by playing against a risk averse C.

Many people find this result intuitively plausible as those who are risk averse seem likely to concede more readily in bargains than those who are not; and so this tends to weigh in favour of Nash's solution. However, it is scarcely a decisive point since other solutions (e.g. the Kalai–Smorodinsky solution) exhibit the same property. Instead, the strongest arguments for the Nash solution in recent times have tended to come from the non-cooperative analysis of the bargaining game and we turn to these next.

4.4 ARIEL RUBINSTEIN AND THE BARGAINING PROCESS: THE RETURN OF NASH BACKWARD INDUCTION

4.4.1 Rubinstein's solution to the bargaining problem

In a famed 1982 paper Ariel Rubinstein made a startling claim: when offers and demands are made sequentially in a bargaining game, and if a speedy resolution is preferred to one that takes longer, there is only *one* offer that a rational bargainer will want to make. Moreover, the rational bargainer's opponent (if rational) has no (rational) alternative but to accept it immediately! To cap this extraordinary result, Rubinstein shows that this settlement is approximately the equivalent of Nash's solution. If all this is correct, then John Nash's solution has been vindicated in a most spectacular way.

Before presenting the unabridged story, let us first get a flavour of the argument. We start with the little bargaining game described earlier: bargainers R and C are asked to split $100. R makes an offer. If C accepts, that is the end of the story. If, on the other hand, C rejects it, the $100 shrinks to $1 which they are now called on to split based on an offer by C. Backward induction led to the conclusion that R will demand $98.99 and offer C no more than $1.01 which C will have to accept (since C cannot expect more if he rejects this offer).

Now consider a richer setting. We give R and C the opportunity to split $100. Again we let R make the first proposal as to how they should distribute the money between them. Suppose that C rejects R's initial offer. Then, 15 seconds later, C makes a counter-offer. If R rejects the counter-offer, then after another 15 seconds R makes a counter-counter-offer. And so on. To add urgency to the process, suppose that delay is costly. For example, let us assume that every half hour the prize shrinks (continuously) from $100 initially to $50, to $25, to . . .

How should one play this game? Recall that in all bargaining games, *any* outcome is rationalisable (moreover, any outcome is a Nash equilibrium). If for example R expects C to accept 40% and thus issues a demand for 60%, while C anticipates this, then a 60%–40% split is an equilibrium outcome (as it confirms each bargainer's expectations). And since any outcome is rationalisable, the theory offers no guidance to players. However, backward induction and CKR does help (at least to some extent) weed out some bargaining strategies. Consider the following strategy for player C: 'I will refuse any offer that awards me less than 80%.' This may be rationalisable (and a Nash equilibrium) when we look at the final outcome independently of the bargaining process, but it may not be if we explore the various alternative strategies in the context of the bargaining process. Why? Because such a strategy is based on an *incredible threat* (recall the definition of such threats in section 4.1). This is why:

Suppose R offers C only 79.9%. Were C to stick to his 'always demand 80%' strategy, he would have to reject the offer. However, this rejection would cost bargainer C as the prize shrinks continually until an agreement is reached. Even if his defiant strategy were to bear fruit immediately after the rejection of R's 79.9% offer (i.e. if R were to succumb and accept C's 80% demand 15 seconds after her 79.9% offer was turned down), bargainer C will only get 80% of a smaller prize. To be precise, he will receive $(80\%)(0.5)^{\frac{1}{240}}$ (where $\frac{1}{240}$ represents the 15 second delay as a portion of the half hour during which the prize is halved) times $100, which translates into $79.77, which is less than the 79.9% of the original prize (that is,

$79.99). Thus, C has no incentive to stick to the strategy 'always demand 80%'. If during negotiations bargainer C threatens to reject *any* offer less than 80%, bargainer R should take this threat with a pinch of salt.

The above is an important thought. It discards a very large number of possible negotiating strategies on the basis that they will not work if the agents' rationality is commonly known. Ariel Rubinstein (1982) uses this logic and attempts to show that there exists only one outcome that does not involve use of incredible threats. The brilliance of this thought matches that of John Nash's original idea for solving the bargaining problem and what is even more extraordinary it yields an analytically equivalent solution! Rubinstein's subgame perfect Nash equilibrium of this extensive form bargaining game converges in the limit on the Nash bargaining solution.

The bargaining process examined by Rubinstein is very similar to the preceding example. There is a prize to be distributed and bargainer R kicks the process off by making a proposal. Bargainer C either accepts or rejects. If he rejects, it is his turn to make an offer. If that offer is rejected by R, the onus is on R to offer again. And so on. Every time an offer is rejected, the prize shrinks by a certain proportion which is called the *discount rate*. (Analytically it is very simple to have different discount rates for each bargainer. Agent-specific discount rates give the analyst the opportunity to introduce differences between the bargainers, differences that are equivalent to the differences in the rates of change of utility functions discussed earlier in the context of the Nash solution). Rubinstein's theorem asserts that rational agents will behave as follows: **player R will make an offer that player C will immediately accept.**

Thus, there will be no delay and the prize will be distributed before the passage of time reduces its value. Moreover, the settlement will reflect two things: (a) the first-mover advantage, and (b) the relative discount rates. By (a) we imply that player R (who makes the first, and allegedly, final offer) will retain (other things being equal) a greater portion than C courtesy of the advantage bestowed upon her by the mere fact that she offers first. Note, however, that if offers can be exchanged very quickly, the first-mover advantage disappears (in the limit). By (b) it is meant that eagerness to settle is rewarded with a smaller share. If C is more eager to settle than R, then he must value a small gain now more than R does, as compared with a greater gain later. This result is perfectly compatible with Nash's solution which, as we showed, penalises risk aversion. To the extent that risk aversion and an eagerness to settle are similar, the two solutions (Nash and Rubinstein) are analytically close.

But is Rubinstein's solution conceptually *identical* to that of Nash? The answer is, yes. When agents can exchange offers at the speed of light, and their discount rates reflect their risk aversion, Rubinstein's solution is identical to that of Nash. In this sense, Rubinstein proved that the bargaining process can lead rational agents to the same solution as that deduced axiomatically by John Nash.

A sketch of the proof of Rubinstein's solution

The proof of Rubinstein's theorem is a gem. We propose to sketch it in the following five paragraphs utilising only high-school algebra. However, the logic is quite tortured.

The game starts at $t = 1$ with an offer from R. If this is rejected, it moves to $t = 2$ during which C makes an offer. If this is rejected, R makes her second offer during $t = 3$. Rubinstein wants us to consider what will happen during $t = 3$, if the negotiations last that long. He asserts that the two bargainers at $t = 3$ form an estimate about the final distribution on which there will be agreement. He says, 'let their estimate be that bargainer R will receive proportion k $(0 < k < 1)$ leaving $1 - k$ for bargainer C'. In effect, he assumes that they have common knowledge of the same estimate of the outcome of the bargaining process. Let us call this **the pivotal assumption**. We give it such a grandiose label because it constitutes the foothold that *backward induction* requires in order to unfold right back to the first stage of the game (the stage at which R makes the first offer) and to furnish the subgame perfect Nash equilibrium. The pivotal assumption is of course a reincarnation of CAB (Consistent Alignment of Beliefs), i.e. the assumption that there exists a unique solution which both bargainers must be able accurately to foresee (courtesy of the Harsanyi doctrine). All that Rubinstein added was that their 'visions' of the outcome coincide at exactly the same stage of the 'negotiations'; e.g. at $t = 3$.

Suppose that the discount rate δ $(0 < \delta < 1)$ is the same for each bargainer (that is, assume identical individuals as, although this does not have to be so, it simplifies the exposition). It follows that every time an offer is rejected, the prize loses a proportion given by $1 - \delta$. For example, if $\delta = 0.8$, then, when an offer is rejected, only 80% of the prize is preserved in the next round. Thus at $t = 3$ our players expect a split of $[k, (1 - k)]$ to R and C respectively. However the 'prize' they will split will have 'shrunk' twice: once at the end of round $t = 1$ (following C's rejection of R's opening offer) and again at the end of $t = 2$ (after R's rejection of C's counter-offer). The extent of the 'shrinking' depends on δ.

Rubinstein then puts Nash backward induction to work and takes us back to the earlier stage, $t = 2$, just before C rejected R's offer. He notices that, at $t = 2$, R will reject C's offer at that stage if that offer awards her less than δk (the reason being that if she rejected it she could look forward to k, whose discounted value at $t = 2$ is δk). Equivalently, during $t = 2$ C will offer at most δk, knowing that δk is exactly as satisfying for R as anything she could expect from rejecting this offer and allowing bargaining to enter phase $t = 3$.

Now C faces a dilemma. If at $t = 2$ he offers δk to R, she is bound to accept it, thus leaving him with $(1 - \delta k)$, the value of which, when assessed at the beginning (that is, at $t = 1$ and before the prize started shrinking), is $\delta(1 - \delta k)$. If his offer is lower, it will be rejected and the third stage will commence where he can expect $(1 - k)$, whose value at $t = 1$ is $\delta^2(1 - k)$. Since the latter is less than the former, Rubinstein argues that C, if rational, will want to avoid prolonging the negotiations and will, thus, offer R δk at $t = 2$. You can imagine the next argument. Given the (assumed) common knowledge that R and C have concerning what will happen if the negotiations reach the second stage (that is, C's offer of δk, an offer that a rational R will have to accept), it is easy to find what the rational offer for R to issue at $t = 1$ is. Indeed, by arguments similar to the above, Rubinstein can demonstrate that at $t = 1$ R will offer C $\delta(1 - \delta k)$ because this is greater than C's optimal offer at $t = 2$. Moreover, bargainer C will accept this because it is greater than what he could expect at $t = 1$.

As it turns out, bargainer R's best strategy at $t = 1$ is to demand $[1 - \delta(1 - \delta k)]$ and C's best response is to accept the remainder. But, continues Rubinstein, we have already assumed that the greatest portion of the prize R can expect from this bargaining process is k! Hence, $k = [1 - \delta(1 - \delta k)]$. Solving for k, we get Rubinstein's solution: $k = (1 - \delta)/(1 - \delta^2)$.

In the above proof Rubinstein shows that there is only one rational bargaining strategy that does not involve incredible threats: that is, there is one subgame perfect Nash equilibrium. Of course, there are logical difficulties with the use of backward induction and CKR in the construction of subgame perfect equilibria of this sort which we have discussed in section 3.4 of the previous chapter. Let us rehearse them in this context.

Objections to Rubinstein

Rubinstein's SPNE-based logic insists that C *must* accept R's $k = (1 - \delta)/(1 - \delta^2)$ offer at $t = 1$. Is that necessarily so? What is the basis for what we called the pivotal assumption? Why assume common knowledge of the outcome at $t = 3$? If we can do it then, surely we can do it at $t = 1$, in which case we would be assuming the bargaining problem away. To put this criticism more broadly, suppose that $k = 60\%$, that is C's best strategy (according to Rubinstein's theory) is to accept 40% of the pie instantly. What will happen if C rejects this and counter-claims, say, 60% at $t = 2$? For this bargaining strategy to make sense, two conditions must hold: (a) there must exist a percentage $w\%$ ($> 40\%$) of the pie which at $t = 2$ is worth more than 40% of the pie at $t = 1$; and (b) C must have a rational reason for believing that it is possible to get at least $w\%$ at $t = 2$ if he rejects offer k at $t = 1$.

Condition (a) is easy to satisfy provided the rate at which the pie is shrinking (in the eyes of C) is not too high. Condition (b) is far more tricky. Specifically, it requires that the experience of an unexpected rejection by C *may* be sufficient for R to panic and make a concession not predicted by Rubinstein's model. This development would resemble a tactical retreat by an army which realises that, in spite of its superiority, the enemy may be, after all, determined to die rather than (rationally) to withdraw. If C's rejection of offer k at $t = 1$ inspires this type of fear, then R may indeed make a concession beneficial to C; and if C manages to bring this about purposefully by straying from Rubinstein's SPNE path, then it is not irrational to stray in this manner.

It is obvious that we have returned to the earlier discussion (see sections 2.7 and 3.4) on what beliefs can be held legitimately (and, potentially, rationally) out of equilibrium. Let us rehearse the 'trembling hand' defence of these out-of-equilibrium beliefs.

4.4.2 The (trembling hand) defence of Rubinstein's solution

A sketch of the defence

Suppose $\delta = \frac{1}{2}$. Then Rubinstein's model predicts that R will demand $\frac{2}{3}$ of the pie and C will immediately accept this, settling for the remaining $\frac{1}{3}$. Can C reject Rubinstein's advice and, instead, reason as follows?

> I may do better by rejecting $\frac{1}{3}$ of the pie consistently and always insist on a 50–50 split. In this way R will eventually understand that I am not prepared to accept less than half the pie. Then she will offer me $\frac{1}{2}$ as this is her best response to the signal I will be sending.

According to the theory of subgame perfection (see section 3.3), the above is wishful thinking. The reason is that the theory assumes that any deviations from the subgame perfect equilibrium (i.e. Rubinstein's strategy) must be due to tiny errors, a 'trembling hand'. If this is so, then it is common knowledge that no deviation can be the result of rational reflection; when it *does* occur it is attributed to 'some unspecified psychological mechanism' (Selten, 1975, p.35). Moreover, these lapses are assumed to be uncorrelated with each other. If all this were true, then no bargaining move is unexpected since every move has *some* probability of being chosen (mistakenly) by a bargainer. This means that when C rejects the offer of $\frac{1}{3}$ of the pie, R finds it surprising, but not inexplicable. 'My rival', R thinks, 'must have had one of those lapses. I will ignore it since the probability of a lapse is very small and it is uncorrelated between stages of the process. Next time he will surely accept $\frac{1}{3}$, albeit of a smaller pie.'

If C can predict that R will think this way, then he will have to abandon his plan to reject $\frac{1}{3}$ of the pie as a signal that he means business. The reason, as explained in the previous paragraph, is that he will know that R will not see his rejection as any such signal but only as a random error. Thus Rubinstein (1982) can appeal to Selten's (1975) trembling hand equilibrium in order to show that, provided the assumptions of subgame perfection are in place, the only rational bargaining strategy is for R to demand at the outset a share of the pie equal to $k = (1 - \delta)/(1 - \delta^2)$ and for C to accept the rest, i.e. $1 - k$.

The formal trembling hand defence

The complete trembling hand defence of the Rubinstein solution goes like this. Let x $(0 < x < 1)$ be some share of the pie that goes to R. Consider the pair of strategies in Figure 4.3.

R's strategy In periods 1, 3, 5, . . . propose x.
                 In periods 2, 4, 6, . . . accept C's proposal if and only if it is no less than x.
C's strategy In periods 1, 3, 5, . . . accept any demand by R provided it is not greater than x.
                 In periods 2, 4, 6, . . . propose that R gets x.

Figure 4.3

These strategies are in a Nash equilibrium (regardless of the value of x) since they are best replies to one another. Underlying them is the threat that any demand by R for more than x will be rejected, and that any attempt by C to reduce R's share to a value below x will be resisted. The question is: *Are these threats credible?*

Rubinstein defends his solution by showing that all other x values (even though they are potential Nash equilibria) are not credible. To see this, suppose that the pair of strategies above are in place but that some 'lapse' at $t = 1$ makes R propose $x + \varepsilon$ (where ε is some very small positive number) instead of x. If the pair of strategies in Figure 4.3 are in a trembling hand equilibrium, this means that they can survive small trembles (i.e. small values of ε), in which case C will stick to his guns and will not concede to R's $x + \varepsilon$ demand. But if the strategies are not in a trembling hand equilibrium, they will break down (and be abandoned by bargainers) the moment the possibility of lapses (i.e. ε) makes an appearance. Rubinstein argues that a 'good' bargaining solution must be in a trembling hand equilibrium and shows that his is the only one that is!

To demonstrate this, following R's demand for $x + \varepsilon$ (when she intended to demand only x), C can reject it hoping that in the next round ($t = 2$) C will accept R's offer of exactly x. Indeed C has a good reason to expect this, since the probability of another lapse in R's rationality (i.e. of ε being greater than 0) is tiny and independent of what happened at $t = 1$. But then again, even if this happens, C values $(1 - x)$ at $t = 2$ less than he values $(1 - x - \varepsilon)$ at $t = 1$ – recall that after he rejects R's proposal at $t = 1$

the pie shrinks. Thus if ε is sufficiently small, C's best reply is to *accept* R's slightly inflamed demand at $t = 1$. Thus C's strategy in Figure 4.3, which is to threaten that any demand by R exceeding x will be categorically rejected, is not credible. Thus the strategies in Figure 4.3 are not in a trembling hand equilibrium. Rubinstein's defence concludes by showing that the only pair of strategies that *are* in a trembling hand equilibrium is the one his bargaining solution recommends, i.e. $x = k = (1 - \delta)/(1 - \delta^2)$.

Objections to the trembling hand defence of Rubinstein

In summary, rejection by C at $t = 1$ of the unique Rubinstein demand[3] of $k = (1 - \delta)/(1 - \delta^2)$ can only have a rational basis if: (a) there exists some alternative distribution to k, say w, which is valued by C at $t = 2$ more than k was at $t = 1$[4] and (b) C has a rational reason for believing that it is possible to get R to agree to w at $t = 2$ if he rejects R's demand for k at $t = 1$.

The trembling hand argument rules out (b) and, in so doing, removes any basis for a rational rejection of Rubinstein's k by player C at $t = 1$. This 'removal' is due to the assumption that any deviation from an equilibrium strategy will necessarily be interpreted by other players as (i) due to a lapse of rationality by C, and (ii) as an error/lapse whose occurrence at $t = 1$ does not make a similar lapse/error at $t = 2$ more or less likely (i.e. the probability of ε exceeding zero by a certain amount at $t = 2$ is not affected at all by the value of ε at $t = 1$; errors across stages are uncorrelated). Sure enough, if *any* deviation from the SPNE (e.g. rejection of demand k by C at $t = 1$) is bound to be interpreted by R as the manifestation of a random error which has nothing to tell R about the future behaviour of C, then R will take no notice of this rejection. And if it is common knowledge that R will take no notice of such a deviation from the SPNE at $t = 1$, then C cannot entertain rational hopes that by rejecting k at $t = 1$ he will bring about a better deal (e.g. w) for himself.

The question is, 'Why is it uniquely rational for R to see nothing in C's rejection at $t = 1$ which can inform her about his future behaviour?' And 'Why does C have to accept that R will necessarily treat his rejection as the result of a random tremble rather than as a signal of a defiant, purposeful, stance?' The answer is that there can be no answer. The trembling hand argument above refuses to answer these questions. Instead it assumes them away by imposing a particular, narrow view on out-of-equilibrium beliefs (that is, the beliefs that agents form when they observe others stepping out of the equilibrium path).

On the one hand, there is no doubt that it is entirely possible that R will not 'read' anything meaningful in C's resistance to k at $t = 1$. It is equally possible that C will have anticipated this, in which case he will not reject k. If this happens, then Rubinstein's solution applies and the trembling hand explanation of deviations from equilibrium makes sense. On the other hand, it is not at all irrational for R to take notice of C's rejection of k at $t = 1$ and to see in it evidence of a 'patterned' deviation from the Rubinstein (subgame perfect) equilibrium. If this happens, she may rationally choose to concede more to C. And if C has anticipated this, he will have rationally rejected k at $t = 1$. In conclusion, an SPNE solution (like that by Rubinstein) may or may not hold – rationally.

A final word on Nash, trembling hands and Rubinstein's bargaining solution

In Chapter 3, at the end of section 3.4.1, we wrote:

> This SPNE is supported by a long string of out-of-equilibrium beliefs about what would happen at later decision nodes if they were reached. To keep this string consistent with CKR (Common Knowledge Rationality), these stages of the game could only be reached via trembles. But how plausible is it to assume that a sequence of such trembles could take players to the last decision node? Trembles in games like Figure 3.4 are one thing, but to get to the last potential decision node in games like Figure 3.5, it seems that trembles must be a more *systematic* part of the player's behaviour.

The same criticism applies equally well here. Bargaining (in Rubinstein's game) will only reach a later stage (e.g. $t = 3$) via trembles. But how plausible is it to build a theory of what offers will be made at $t = 1$ on what we think will happen at $t = 3$ (or more) when we assume that bargainers can only get that far as a result of improbable, tiny, errors? How reasonable is it to assume that it will be common knowledge that these 'errors' are not a systematic part of bargainers' strategy?

To put the same objection differently, there is no doubt that if rational bargainers *must* choose strategies that are in some trembling hand equilibrium with one another, Rubinstein is correct to show that his version of the bargaining problem has a uniquely rational solution. But this is not crucial: the crucial question is, why should rational players *necessarily* choose strategies that are in a trembling hand equilibrium? Indeed, why should they be expected always to choose bargaining strategies that are best replies to one another as in Figure 4.3 (that is, in a Nash equilibrium)? The only way to be certain that they *will* choose strategies which are best replies to one another is if we accept the following assumption.

Uniqueness assumption: If players start with the same information about the nature of the (bargaining) game they are about to play, then any expectations they form about one another must be common knowledge.

Notice that the above is a restatement of the Harsanyi doctrine, or the CAB assumption, from previous chapters. Notice also that before we make the above assumption we must be confident that all games have uniquely rational solutions.

In Chapters 2 and 3 we concluded that *if* games are to have a unique solution, then it must be a Nash equilibrium solution. Similarly, in this chapter, we have seen that *if* the bargaining problem is to have a unique solution, then bargaining strategies must be best replies to one another (i.e. they must be part of some Nash equilibrium). Bacharach (1987) and Sugden (1991a) acknowledge this. However, they go further (in contrast to other game theorists like John Harsanyi, Robert Aumann and Ariel Rubinstein, who stay with the CAB or the uniqueness assumption above). Bacharach (1987) for instance (after acknowledging that a unique solution to a game must be in a Nash equilibrium) rejects the implication that rational players *must* choose Nash equilibrium strategies, even if a unique Nash equilibrium exists (see also Bernheim, 1984).[5] Some games simply do not have uniquely rational solutions. The bargaining problem seems a good case in point.

Finally, consider the trembling hand equilibrium idea once more. Does it offer a good defence of Rubinstein? What it does is to narrow down the number of Nash equilibrium bargaining strategies through the introduction of random strategic errors. So, if we introduce these trembles, and if we accept the particular (and very narrow) theory of trembles in Selten (1975), and if we allow the probability of trembles to tend to zero, then we will inevitably conclude that the only defensible Nash equilibrium set of strategies is one compatible with the trembling hand equilibrium (and therefore Rubinstein's bargaining solution). But even if we are happy to do all this, all we have shown is that the trembling hand equilibrium is a 'natural' refinement of the Nash equilibrium. Yet this will only matter if we are convinced that bargaining games have uniquely rational solutions. Thus, as Sugden (1992a) puts it, the only thing that Rubinstein's analysis of bargaining can do is to: 'show us what the uniquely rational solution to a bargaining game would be, were such a solution to exist. But we still have no proof that a uniquely rational solution exists' (p. 308).

4.5 JUSTICE IN POLITICAL AND MORAL PHILOSOPHY

So far, we have argued against the claim that Nash's solution is the unique solution to the bargaining problem. Neither the axioms of the axiomatic approach nor the CAB assumption of the non-cooperative approach seem to us beyond reproach. As we remarked at the beginning of the chapter, this should not come as much of a surprise because at root elements of the hawk–dove game are found in most bargaining problems and it seems difficult to escape the conclusion that this game has multiple Nash equilibria. Moreover, there is not even a guarantee that the chosen strategies will be in some Nash equilibrium (that is, there may be conflict which destroys, or prevents the creation of, a part of the pie).

If the Nash solution were unique, then game theory would have answered an important question at the heart of liberal theory over the type of State which rational agents might agree to create. In addition, it would have solved a question in moral philosophy over what justice might demand in this and a variety of social interactions. After all, how to divide the benefits from social cooperation seems at first sight to involve a tricky question in moral philosophy concerning what is just, but if rational agents will only ever agree on the Nash division then there is only one outcome for rational agents. Whether we want to think of this as just seems optional. But if we do or if we think that justice is involved, then we will know, and for once unambiguously, what justice apparently demands between instrumentally rational agents.

Unfortunately, though, it seems we cannot draw these inferences because the Nash solution is not the unique outcome. Accepting this conclusion, we are concerned in this section with what bargaining theory then contributes to the liberal project of examining the State as if it were the result of rational negotiations between people.

4.5.1 The negative result and the opening to Rawls and Nozick

Our conclusion is negative in the sense that we do not believe that the Nash solution is the unique outcome to the bargaining game when played between instrumentally rational agents who have CKR and this means that game theory is unable to predict what happens in such games. However, this failure to predict should be welcomed by John Rawls and Robert Nozick as it provides an opening to their contrasting views of what counts as justice between rational agents.

Nozick (1974) and entitlements

Nozick argues against *end state theories of justice*, that is theories of justice which are concerned with the attributes or patterns of the outcomes found in society. He prefers instead a *procedural theory of justice*, that is one which judges the justice of an outcome by the procedure which generated it. Thus he argues against theories of justice which are concerned, for instance, with equality (a classic example of an end state or patterned theory) and suggests that any outcome which has emerged from a process that respects the 'right' of individuals to possess what they are 'entitled' to is fine. The two types of theory are like chalk and cheese since an intervention to create a pattern must undermine a respect for outcomes which have been generated by voluntary exchange. You can only have one and Nozick thinks that justice comes from a procedural respect for people's entitlements. And, in his view, you are entitled to anything you can get from voluntary exchange (i.e. at the market place). Furthermore, Nozick equates a respect for such entitlements with a respect for a person's liberty.[6]

The importance of the negative result for Nozick's defence of procedural in preference to end state theories will now be obvious. If each bargain between 'free' and rational agents yielded the Nash solution then it *would* be a matter of indifference whether we held an end state theory or Nozick's procedural theory because there would be an end state criterion which uniquely told us what we should expect from Nozick's procedure: the Nash solution.

Rawls (1971) and justice

Rawls is concerned with the agreements which rational agents with what he calls 'moral personalities' will come to about the fundamental institutions of their society. The introduction of 'moral personalities' is important for his argument because he suggests that they want their institutions to be impartial in the way that they operate with regard to each person. In turn, it is the fact that we value impartiality which explains Rawls' particular view on the make-up of our agreements about social arrangements.

Consider how we might guarantee that our institutions are impartial. The problem, of course, is that we are liable (quite unconsciously sometimes) to favour those institutional arrangements which favour us. So Rawls suggests that we should conduct the following thought experiment to avoid this obvious source of partiality: we should consider which institutional arrangement we would prefer if we were forced to make the decision without knowing what position we will occupy under each arrangement. This is known as the *veil of ignorance* device: we make our choice between alternative social outcomes as if we were behind a veil which prevented us from knowing which position we would get personally in each outcome.

He then argues that we should all agree on a social outcome based on the principle of rational choice called *maximin*. Maximin implies the following procedure: imagine that you are considering *n* alternative social outcomes (e.g. types of societal organisation, or income distribution). You look at each of these *n* potential social outcomes on offer and observe the person who is worst off in each. Thus you mark *n* persons. Then you make a note of how badly off each of these *n* persons is. Finally, you support the social outcome which corresponds to the most fortunate of these *n* unfortunate persons. That is, you select the social outcome (or, more broadly, the society) in which the well-being of the most unfortunate is highest.[7] (The principle is therefore called maximin because it maximises the minimum outcome.)

Rawls carefully constructs his argument that maximin (or the 'difference principle' as it is also called) is the principle that rational agents would want to use behind the veil of ignorance. It is not just that they ought to choose it; they will also have a preference for it. In other words, we would all choose the social arrangement which secured the highest utility level for the person (whoever it actually turns out to be) who will have the lowest utility level in the chosen society. Thus inequality in a society will only be agreed to (behind the veil of ignorance) in so far as it makes the worst-off person better off than this person would have been under a more equal regime (see the adjacent box).

Box 4.5

BEHIND THE VEIL OF IGNORANCE

Let us suppose there are three people (A, B and C) in some society. They wish to design the institutions for that society and there are four possible options (I, II, III and IV). They decide in Rawlsian fashion to go behind the 'veil of ignorance' in order to select one of these arrangements. Each arrangement gives the following utility triple for the three possible positions in that society:

	Arrangement I	Arrangement II	Arrangement III	Arrangement IV
A	5	3	4	1
B	6	5	4	6
C	7	12	4	12

Behind the veil of ignorance, no person knows which position they will occupy under any arrangement, so for instance under arrangement I, each person simply knows they could end up with a '5' or a '6' or a '7' util level. Rawls argues that each person will select arrangement I in these circumstances because it generates the highest utility for the worst-off member of society – Rawls' maximin principle (5 is better than 3, 4 and 1, which are the values received by the poorest member under the other arrangements). You will notice this rule does not simply pick out the egalitarian solution (III). This is because by construction, it has been assumed that some inequality in society, by providing incentives, makes the society as a whole more productive. So arrangement I yields a total of 18 utils while arrangement III only yields 12 utils.

The arrangement with the highest total utils is II (= 20 utils). It is also the one which would be chosen if the people behind the veil of ignorance, rather than using the maximin rule, selected the arrangement which offered the highest expected (or average) utility (since the expected utility level under this arrangement with an equi-probability of occupying each position is 6.66 compared with 6 under arrangement I). For this reason a (19th century) utilitarian social philosopher would have recommended arrangement II, as opposed to Rawls' choice of arrangement I. It will also be clear from this example how justice and self-interest need not coincide. If people knew which position they were to occupy, then the middle and best-off people would in all likelihood band together and vote for arrangement IV and this is the arrangement that neither Rawls nor the utilitarians think justice singles out.

This is an interesting and controversial result in a variety of respects. We will mention just two before returning to the theme of bargaining theory. Firstly you will notice that the thought experiment requires us to be able to make what are, in effect, interpersonal comparisons of utility. We have to be able to imagine what it would be like to be the poorest person under each arrangement even though we do not know who that person is (or indeed whether we will be that person). In general we might have to weigh this possibility up with all the other possibilities of occupying the position of each of the other people under some arrangement (although, in fact, the maximin rule means we can ignore the latter types of comparisons).

In other words, in general, we have to be able to assign utility numbers to each possible position under each possible arrangement and make a judgement by comparing these utility numbers across arrangements and across positions. As a result, there is a troubling question about where we get these apparently (interpersonally) comparable utility numbers from and why we should assume that all people from behind the veil of ignorance will work with the same numbers for the same positions under the same arrangements. It is perhaps interesting to note that the Harsanyi doctrine has been used by some game theorists (see Binmore, 1987) to paper over this problem. The point you will recall is that, according to the Harsanyi doctrine, rational agents faced by the same information must draw the same conclusions, and this includes assessments of various arrangements from behind the veil of ignorance. Thus given the same information about the institutional arrangements, all rational agents are bound to come up with the same arrays of utility numbers.

Secondly, the maximin principle for decision making is controversial because it is not what economists take to be the general principle of instrumentally rational choice under conditions of uncertainty. The general principle for this purpose in game theory and neoclassical economics is expected utility maximisation (see Boxes 1.3 and 1.4 in Chapter 1). This has an interesting implication. In so far as people behind the veil of ignorance attach an equal probability to occupation of each position under each arrangement, if they select an arrangement on the basis of expected utility maximisation, then they will select the arrangement which generates the highest average utility level for that society (see Box 4.5 again). So, expected utility maximisation behind Rawls' veil of ignorance would return us to 19th century utilitarianism; that is, to the principle that the good society is the one which maximises average utility (see Box 1.2 in Chapter 1). Of course Rawls rejects expected utility maximisation and argues strongly that rational agents will be using his maximin principle behind the veil.

This is enough of the parenthetic comments on Rawls' theory. The general point is that the whole apparatus of the 'veil of ignorance' only fits smoothly into this argument once we accept that there is no unique solution to the bargaining problem. After all, if rational agents always reached the Nash agreement, then why do we need to worry about what justice demands when agents contract with each other over their basic institutions? In short, the introduction of 'moral personalities' and the concern with impartiality is a way of selecting arrangements (by appealing in this sense to justice), and this presumes there is a problem of selection. Otherwise why do we need to bring justice into the discussion? Of course, even if Nash's solution was the unique outcome to the bargaining game between instrumentally rational agents, then we might still believe that justice has a part to play in the discussion (because we are not simply instrumentally rational as we have 'moral personalities' too). But this does not avoid a difficulty. It simply recasts the problem in a slightly different form. The problem then becomes one of elucidating the relationship between instrumental reason and the dictates of our 'moral personalities' when they potentially pull in different directions. Whichever way the problem is construed, it is plain that Rawls' argument is made easier when there is no unique solution to the bargaining problem.

4.5.2 Procedures and outcomes (or 'means' and ends) and axiomatic bargaining theory

One of the difficulties in moral philosophy is that our moral intuitions attach both to the patterns, or attributes, of outcomes (our *ends*) and to the processes (or the *means*) which generate them. These different types of intuition can pull in opposite directions. A classic example is the conflict which is sometimes felt between the competing claims of freedom from interference and equality. We have already referred to this problem when discussing Nozick (who simply finesses it by prioritising freedom from interference, which he identifies with liberty). Another example in moral philosophy is revealed by the problem of torture for utilitarians. For instance, a utilitarian calculation focuses on outcomes by summing the individual utilities found in society. In so doing it does not enquire about the fairness or otherwise of the processes responsible for generating those utilities with the result that it could sanction torture when the utility gain of the torturer exceeds the loss of the person being tortured. Yet most people would feel uncomfortable with a society which sanctioned torture on these grounds because it unfairly transgresses the 'rights' of the tortured.

To explore the nature of these conflicts between *means* and *ends*, and advance our understanding of what is at stake when such conflicts occur, it would be extremely helpful if we could somehow compare these otherwise contrasting intuitions by, for instance, seeing how constraints on means feed through to affect the range of possible outcomes. This is one place where axiomatic bargaining theory might be useful. In effect, the rule for selecting a utility pair under this approach is like a procedure because it shows how to move from an unresolved bargain to a resolution, or an outcome. The axioms then become a way of placing constraints upon these procedures which we select because we find them morally appealing and the theory tells us how these moral intuitions with respect to procedures constrain the outcomes. We may or may not find that the outcomes so derived accord with our moral intuitions about outcomes, but at least we will then be in a position to explore our competing moral intuitions in search of what some moral philosophers call a 'reflective equilibrium'.

But even those who have little time for moral philosophy or for liberal political theory may still find it interesting to ask: 'Granted that society (and the State) are *not* the result of some living-room negotiation, what kind of "axioms" would have generated the social outcomes which we observe in a given society?' That is, even if we reject the preceding fictions (i.e. of the State as a massive resolution of an *n*-person bargaining game, or of the veil of ignorance) as theoretically and politically misleading, we may still pinpoint certain axioms which *would* have generated the observed income distributions (or distributions of opportunities, social roles, property rights, etc.) as a result of an (utterly) hypothetical bargaining game. By studying these axioms, we may come to understand the existing society better.

The reader may wish to think about axiomatic bargaining solutions such as the Nash or Kalai–Smorodinsky solutions, and the axioms on which they are based, in this light. Do they embody any moral or political intuitions about procedures? And if so, how do the Nash or Kalai–Smorodinsky solutions fare when set against any moral or political intuitions that we have about social outcomes? Rather than pursue these questions here, we shall conclude this chapter with an example based on a different set of axioms.

Roemer (1988) considers a problem faced by an international agency charged with distributing some resources with the aim of improving health (say lowering infant mortality rates). How should the authority distribute those resources? This is a particularly tricky issue because different countries in the world doubtless subscribe to some very different principles which they would regard as relevant to this problem; and so agreement on a particular rule seems unlikely. Nevertheless, he suggests that we approach the problem by considering the following constraints (axioms) which we might want to apply to the decision rule because they might be the object of significant agreement.

(1) The rule should be *efficient* in the sense that there should be no way of reallocating resources so as to raise infant survival rates in one country without lowering them in another.

(2) The rule should be *fair* in the sense (a) of monotonicity (that an increase in the agency's resources should not lead to a lower survival rate for any one country) and (b) of symmetry (that for countries which have identical resources and technologies for processing

resources into survival rates, then the resources should be distributed in proportion to their populations).

(3) The rule should be *neutral* in the sense that it operates only on information which is relevant to infant survival (the population and the technology and resources available for raising infant survival).

(4) Suppose there are two types of resources the agency can provide: x and y. The rule should be *consistent* in the sense that if the rule specifies an allocation $[\mathbf{x}', \mathbf{y}']$, then when it must decide how much of x to allocate to countries which already have an allocation of y given by $\mathbf{y}'$, the rule should select the allocation $\mathbf{x}'$. (This means the agency having decided on how to allocate resources can distribute the resources to countries as they become available and it will never need to revise its plan.)

(5) The rule should be applicable in *scope* so that it can be used in any possible situation (that is, budget, technologies, etc.).

Each constraint cashes in a plausible moral, pragmatic or political intuition and Roemer shows that only one rule will satisfy all five conditions. It is a leximin rule which allocates resources in such a way as to raise the country with the lowest infant survival rate to that of the second lowest, and then if the budget has not been exhausted, it allocates resources to these two countries until they reach the survival rate of the third lowest country, and so on until the budget is exhausted.

4.6 CONCLUSION

The solution to bargaining games is important in life and in political theory. To put the point baldly, if these games have unique solutions, then there are few grounds for conflict either in practice (for example, there will never be a genuinely good reason for any industrial strike[8]) or in theory (when we come to reflect on whether particular social institutions might be justified as products of rational negotiations between individuals). In this context, the claim that the Nash solution is a unique solution for a bargaining game between rational agents is crucial.

Is the claim right? It is at its strongest when it emerges from a non-cooperative analysis of the bargaining process (as in Rubinstein, 1982). The problem with its justification is, however, the same whether we are looking at its axiomatic (cooperative) version or its non-cooperative incarnation: it relies on the contentious assumptions which support the Nash equilibrium concept, as well as on the extensions of these assumptions which are necessary for the refinements of the Nash equilibrium. In brief, we must assume that there is a uniquely rational way to play all games and it is not obvious that this can be justified by appeals to the assumptions of rationality and common knowledge of rationality (see sections 2.5 and 3.7 of the last two chapters). With respect to solutions based on refinements to the Nash equilibrium, what seems to be missing is a generally acceptable theory of mistakes, or trembles, and of how they can be sensibly distinguished from bluffing. Without such an authoritative account, it seems possible to adopt a different view of behaviour which deviates from Nash behaviour, with the result that many potential alternative outcomes to those proposed by the Nash theoretical project remain plausible.

5

THE PRISONERS' DILEMMA

5.1 INTRODUCTION: THE DILEMMA AND THE STATE

The prisoners' dilemma fascinates social scientists because it is an interaction where the individual pursuit of what seems rational produces a collectively self-defeating result. Each person does what appears best to them and yet the outcome is painfully inferior for all. Even though there is nothing obviously faulty with their logic, their attempt to improve their prospects makes everyone worse off. The paradoxical quality of this result helps explain part of the fascination. But the major reason for the interest is purely practical. Outcomes in social life are often less than we might hope and the prisoners' dilemma provides one possible key to their understanding.

The name comes from a particular illustration of the interaction which is credited to Albert Tucker in the 1950s. In this example, two people are picked up by the police for a robbery and placed in separate cells. They both have the option to confess to the crime or not, and the district attorney tells each of them what is likely to happen and makes each an offer. Figure 5.1 sets out the likely consequences presented by the district attorney in terms of years in prison.

		Player B	
		Not confess	Confess
Player A	Not confess	1, 1	5, 0
	Confess	0, 5	3, 3

Figure 5.1

The rationale behind these (negative) pay-offs is something like this. If both 'confess' then the judge, being in no doubt over their guilt, will give them 3 years each in prison. Whereas if they both 'don't confess' then conviction is still likely, but the doubts in the case make the judge err on the side of leniency with a sentence of 1 year each. In addition, the DA points out that he or she can intercede with the judge on behalf of one prisoner when that prisoner confesses and the other does not. The judge looks kindly on such action because a confession helps to make the prosecution case and it earns the confessing prisoner a suspended sentence (i.e. 0 years in prison now). In contrast, the judge feels that an exemplary punishment (5 years) is required for the prisoner who does not confess in these circumstances because his or her plea of not guilty has wasted court time. Of course, the DA cannot intercede with the judge when both prisoners confess because then there is no trial and no prosecution case to be made as both have accepted their guilt.

The structure of the pay-offs in Figure 5.1 is the same as those used in Figure 2.3 to illustrate the concept of dominance. Once it is assumed that each prisoner cares only to avoid spending time in prison, 'confess' is similarly the dominant strategy for each player. Thus we expect an equilibrium where each spends 3 years in prison; and there is no need in arriving at this conclusion for either player to get entangled in thoughts about CKR. Each knows the best thing to do is 'confess' and yet it yields a paradoxical result of making each worse off than they might have been had they each chosen 'don't confess' and so spent only 1 year in prison.

Box 5.1

TOSCA'S DILEMMA

In Puccini's opera *Tosca*, there is a police chief called Scarpia who lusts after Tosca. He has an opportunity to pursue this lust because Tosca's lover is arrested and condemned to death. This enables Scarpia to offer to fake the execution of Tosca's lover if she will agree to submit to his advances. Tosca agrees and Scarpia orders blanks to be substituted for the bullets of the firing squad. However, as they embrace, Tosca stabs and kills Scarpia. Unfortunately, Scarpia has also defected on the arrangement as the bullets were real. Thus an elated Tosca, expecting to find her lover and make good their escape, actually discovers that he has been executed; and in one of opera's classic tragic conclusions, she leaps to her death.

It is tempting to think that the problem only arises here because the prisoners cannot communicate with one another. If they could get together they would quickly see that the best for both comes from 'not confessing'. But as we saw in the previous chapter, communication is not all that is needed. Each still faces the choice of whether to hold to an agreement that they have struck over 'not confessing'. Is it in the interest of either party to keep to such an agreement? No, a quick inspection reveals that the best action in terms of pay-offs is still to 'confess'. As Thomas Hobbes remarked in *Leviathan* when studying a similar problem, 'covenants struck without the sword are but words'. The prisoners may trumpet the virtue of 'not confessing' but if they are only motivated instrumentally by the pay-offs, then it is only so much hot air because each will 'confess' when the time comes for a decision.

What seems to be required to avoid this outcome is a mechanism which allows for joint or collective decision making, thus ensuring that both actually do 'not confess'. In other words, there is a need for a mechanism for enforcing an agreement—Hobbes's 'sword', if you like. And it is this recognition which lies at the heart of a traditional liberal argument dating back to Hobbes for the creation of the State which is seen as the ultimate enforcement agency. (Notice, however, that such an argument applies equally to some other institutions which have the capacity to enforce agreements, for example the Mafia.) In Hobbes's story, each individual in the state of nature can behave peacefully or in a war-like fashion. Since peace allows everyone to go about their normal business with the result that they prosper and enjoy a more 'commodious' living (as Hobbes phrased it), choosing strategy 'peace' is like 'not confessing' above; when everyone behaves in this manner it is much better than when they all choose 'war' ('confess'). However, and in spite of wide ranging recognition that peace is better than war, the same prisoners' dilemma problem surfaces and leads to war.

The reason is that the individually perceived best action is 'war', since bellicosity is a best response to those who are bellicose (the worst fate awaits those who treat aggressors kindly) but also to those who are peaceful (because of the lure presented by the thought of dominating them). The recognition of this predicament helps explain why individuals might rationally submit to the authority of a State, which can enforce an agreement for 'peace'. They voluntarily relinquish some of their freedom that they enjoy in the (hypothesised) state of nature to the State because it unlocks the prisoners' dilemma. (It should be added perhaps that this is not to be taken as a literal account of how all States or enforcement agencies arise. The point of the argument is to demonstrate the conditions under which a State or enforcement agency would enjoy legitimacy among a population even though it restricted individual freedoms.)

While Hobbes thought that the authority of the State should be absolute so as to discourage any cheating on 'peace', he also thought the scope of its interventions in this regard would be quite minimal. In contrast much of the modern fascination with the prisoners' dilemma stems from the fact that the prisoners' dilemma seems to be a ubiquitous feature of social life. For instance, it plausibly lies at the heart of many problems which groups of individuals (for instance, the household, a class, or a nation) encounter when they attempt a collective action.

The next section provides some illustrations of how easy it is to uncover interactions which resemble prisoners' dilemmas. The following four sections and the next chapter, on repeated games, discuss some of the developments in the social science literature which have been concerned with how the dilemma might be unlocked without the services of the State. In other words, the later sections focus on the question of whether the widespread nature of this type of interaction necessarily points to the (legitimate in liberal terms) creation of an activist State. Are there other solutions which can be implemented without involving the State or any public institution? Since the scope of the State's activities has become one of the most contested issues in contemporary politics, it will come as no surprise to discover that the discussions around alternative solutions to the dilemma have assumed a central importance in recent political (and especially in liberal and neoliberal) theory.

5.2 EXAMPLES OF HIDDEN PRISONERS' DILEMMAS IN SOCIAL LIFE

The prisoners' dilemma may seem contrived (by the cunning of the DA's office) but it is not difficult to find other examples. Indeed, it is not uncommon to find the dilemma treated as the essential model of social life (see Taylor (1976) and Stinchcombe (1978) for a critical review). Here are some examples to convey its potential significance.

It arises as a problem of **trust** in every elemental economic exchange because it is rare for the delivery of a good to be perfectly synchronised with the payment for it and this affords the opportunity to cheat on the deal. For instance, you may buy a good through the mail and the supplier is naturally attracted by the opportunity of cashing the cheque and not posting the goods (or sending you a 'lemon'). You have to trust that the supplier will not do such a thing before you are willing to engage in the transaction. A moment's reflection may suggest that what makes this unlikely is precisely the intervention of the State to overcome the dilemma through the laws of contract, the police and the courts. Without such laws and enforcement agencies, individuals who were solely motivated by their own returns would surely be tempted to take such actions (particularly when these were one-off interactions). And each agent realising the temptation to the other would, as a result, not be willing to enter into the transaction even though there is the potential for mutual benefit.

This version of the dilemma has been central to much recent discussion in industrial economics because there are many goods where payment and supply cannot be perfectly synchronised not only for the reasons mentioned above but also because of imperfect information. For example, you may make the payment for a second-hand car at the same time as you take delivery, but it will only be over a period of time after purchase that you discover the quality of the car (so, you will not know what you have really purchased until some time after you have paid for it, just as in the example of the mail order purchase). This is particularly worrying because the second-hand car dealer often has a much better idea than you about the respective qualities of his or her cars and what is to stop him or her selling you a 'lemon'? Likewise, the problem has attracted much attention in labour economics because the typical exchange specifies that a worker be paid $x an hour for being on the factory premises; it rarely details the performance which is expected during those hours. What then prevents the worker goofing-off during working hours, or the employer forcing the pace?

These are two-person examples of the dilemma, but it is probably the '*n*-person' version of the dilemma (usually called the *free rider problem*) which has attracted most attention. It creates a collective action problem among groups of individuals. Again the examples are legion. Here are a few.

The free rider problem

Suppose you would like to see a less polluted environment and there is an attachment that can be made to cars which is capable, when used by a large number of drivers, of both improving local air quality (thus helping with a number of local ailments like bronchitis and asthma) and of mitigating the problem of global warming. Of course, the device is costly, but you think it worth the cost if it reduces the ill-effects on the environment. The difficulty is that the improvement to the environment only comes when large numbers of people attach the device; the application of the device to a single car makes no difference. Consider your decision (attach = C, not attach = D) under two possible settings: one where other people do not attach (D) the device and another where other people do attach (C) the device. Your ranking of the outcomes is given by the 'utils' (the arbitrary assignation of utility numbers to your preferences) in Figure 5.2. They are plausible given what has already been said, taken together with the reflection that when others attach and you do not, you get all the benefits to the environment without any of the cost.

		Others	
		Cooperate (C)	Defect (D)
You	Cooperate (C)	3	1
	Defect (D)	4	2

Figure 5.2

The instrumentally rational individual will recognise that the best action is 'do not attach' (i.e. defection) whatever the others do. This means that in a population of like-minded individuals, all will decide similarly with the result that each individual gains 2 utils. This is plainly an inferior outcome for all because everyone could have attached the device and if they all had done so each would have enjoyed 3 utils.

In these circumstances the individuals in this economy might agree to the State enforcing attachment of the device. Alternatively, it is easy to see how another popular intervention by the State would also do the trick. The State could tax each individual who did not attach the device a sum equivalent to 2 utils and this would turn 'attach' (C) into the dominant strategy.

Domestic labour

A similar predicament arises within the household. Every member of the household may prefer a clean kitchen to a dirty one (even though it is costly to clean up one's mess, the individual effort is worth it when you get a clean kitchen). But unfortunately, no individual decision to clean up one's own mess will have a significant influence on the state of the kitchen when the household is large because it depends mostly on what others do and not on what a single person does. Accordingly, since it is also costly to clean up one's mess after a visit to the kitchen, each individual leaves the mess they have created and the result is a dirty kitchen. There is nothing like the State which can enforce contracts within the household to keep a kitchen clean, but interestingly within a family household one often observes the exercise of patriarchal or paternal power instead. Of course, the potential difficulty with such an arrangement is that the patriarch may rule in a partial manner with the result that the kitchen is clean but with no help from the hands of the patriarch! The role of the State has in such cases been captured, so to speak, by an interested party determined by gender. Then gender becomes the determinant of who bears the burden and who has the more privileged role. Social power which 'solves' prisoners' dilemmas can be thus exercised without the direct involvement of the State (even though the State often enshrines such power in its own institutions).

In fact all public goods set up forms of the free rider problem (see Olson (1965) for an extended discussion). To see why, notice that these are goods which by definition cannot be easily restricted to those who have paid for the service (for instance, like the defence of a nation which, once it is there, is enjoyed by everyone). Thus there is always an incentive for an individual not to purchase this good because it can be enjoyed without paying for it provided others do; and if others do not pay, it is likely to be prohibitively expensive for a single individual to purchase the good.

151

Disarmament

Hobbes's state of nature discussion is also often thought to apply to the community of nations (see Richardson, 1960). Each nation faces a choice between arming (= D) or disarming (= C). Each would prefer a world where everyone 'disarmed' to one where everyone was 'armed'. But the problem is that a nation which is instrumentally rational and is only motivated by its own welfare might plausibly prefer best of all a world where it alone is armed because then it can extract benefits from all other nations (in the form of 'tributes' of one kind or another). Since it is also better to be armed than unarmed if all other nations are armed (so as to avoid subjugation), this turns 'arming' into the dominant strategy – thus yielding the now familiar inferior result. This has sometimes been taken as the basis of an argument for some form of world government, at least for the purposes of monitoring disarmament.

Joining a trade union

Suppose you have no ideological feelings about unions and you treat membership of your local union purely instrumentally: that is, you are concerned solely with whether membership improves your take-home pay. Further let us suppose that a union can extract a high wage from your employer only when a large number of employees belong to the union (say because only then will the threat of industrial action by the union worry the employer). Now consider your decision regarding membership under two scenarios: one where everyone else joins and the other when nobody else joins. To join looks like C and not joining is the equivalent of D (see Figure 5.2) because the benefits of the higher wage when everyone joins the union could outweigh the costs of union membership (outcome CC is better than DD) and when everyone joins and you do not, you enjoy the higher wage and avoid paying the union dues (and possibly the ire of the employer at having joined the union). Perhaps not unsurprisingly, the recognition that this might be a feature of the membership decision has sometimes led to calls for a closed shop. Alternatively it might be thought to reveal that ideological commitment is an essential constituent of trade union formation.

The shared interest that workers have here is a class interest because workers as a group stand to gain from unionisation while their employers do not. There are many further examples of this type: Boxes 5.2 and 5.3 give two famous ones. Hence the prisoners' dilemma/free rider might plausibly lie at the distinction which is widely attributed to Marx in the discussion of class consciousness between a class 'of itself' and 'for itself' (see Elster, 1986b). On such a view a class transforms itself into a 'class for itself', or a society avoids deficient demand, by unlocking the dilemma.

Box 5.2

THE STRUGGLE OVER THE WORKING DAY

The first Statute of Labourers was passed in England in 1349 under the pretext that the plague had so decimated the population that everyone had to do more work. The Act of 1833 created a normal working day in the four textile industries: from 5.30 am to 8.30 pm (the only restriction being that children between 9 and 13 years of age could only be employed for 8 hours). Since the formation of unions the length of the working day has been a source of industrial conflict. Marx offers the following perspective based on the free rider problem:

> History further shows that the *isolated* 'free' labourer is defenceless against the capitalist and succumbs . . . . Thus the labourer comes out of the production process quite different than he entered. The labour contract was not an act of a *free-agent*; the time for which he *is free* to sell his labour power is the time for which he is *forced* to sell it, and only the *mass* opposition of workers win for them the *passing of a law* that shall prevent the workers from selling, by voluntary contract with capital, themselves and their generation into slavery and death. In place of the pompous catalogue of the inalienable rights of man comes the modest *Magna Charta* of the Factory Act.
>
> *Das Kapital*, Vol. 1, Chapter 3, section iv

Adam Smith and the invisible hand

Adam Smith's account of how the self-interest of sellers combines with the presence of many sellers to frustrate their designs and to keep prices low might also fit this model of interaction. If you are the seller choosing from the two row strategies C and D, then imagine that C and D translate into 'charge a high price' and 'charge a low price' respectively. Figure 5.2 could reflect your preference ordering as high prices for all might be better than low prices for all and charging a low price when all others charge a high might be the best option because you scoop market share. Presumably the same applies to your competitors. Thus even though all sellers would be happier with a high level of prices, their joint interest is subverted because each acting individually quite rationally charges a low price. It is as if an invisible hand was at work on behalf of the consumers.

Corruption

The prisoners' dilemma might also lie behind a worry that the pursuit of short term gain may undermine the long term interest of a group or individual. For instance, it is sometimes argued that every member of a

---

Box 5.3

THE PARADOX OF UNDERCONSUMPTION

In both Marxist and Keynesian economics there is a prediction that the capitalist economy has a natural tendency towards underconsumption, or inadequate aggregate demand. In Joan Robinson's description, it is 'an essential paradox of capitalism that each capitalist wants low wages for his own workers, since this makes for high profits, yet high wages for the workers employed by other capitalists, since this makes for high demand for his products' (see Elster, 1986b, p.26). Marx's original formulation was:

> Every capitalist knows this about his worker, that he does not relate to him as a producer to a consumer, and he therefore wishes to restrict his consumption, ie. his ability to exchange, his wage, as much as possible. Of course he would like the workers of other capitalists to be the greatest consumers possible of his own commodity. But the relation of every capitalist to his own workers is the relation as such of capital and labour, the essential relation.

> (Marx, 1972, p. 420)

---

government faces a choice between a 'corrupt' and an 'upstanding' exercise of office ('corruption' here might range from serious 'kickbacks' to the favouring of departmental policies which benefit the minister's local constituents when alternatives would secure greater advantage for the party nationally). Corruption by all reduces the chances of re-election for the government and this undermines the long term returns from holding office (including the ability to form policy over a long period as well as the receipt/exercise of minor, undetectable bribes or local biases). Thus, it is probably inferior to a situation where all are 'upstanding' and long term rule is secured. Nevertheless, each member of the government may act 'corruptly' in the short run because it is the best action both when others are 'upstanding' and when others behave corruptly (since a single act of corruption will not affect the party's chance of re-election and it will enrich the individual). Thus each individual finds it in their own interest to pursue the short run strategy of corrupt practice in government and this undermines the long term interests of all by shortening the period in office.

Why do we stand when we can all sit?

To end on a lighter note, consider the choice between standing and sitting at a sporting event. Each person's view of the action is the same when either everyone stands or everyone sits; the only difference between these two outcomes is that sitting is less tiring and so is preferred. However, when you stand and everyone else sits, the view is so improved that the cost of standing is worth bearing. Of course, the worst outcome is when everyone stands and you sit because you see nothing. Thus standing can be associated with D and sitting with C, and the strict application of instrumental logic predicts that we should all stand. Interestingly this is far from what always happens at sporting events and since there is nothing like the State (or a patriarch) which taxes standers (or enforces a closed shop of standers), it suggests that people must be able to solvie the dilemma in other ways. We turn to these possibilities now.

5.3 KANT AND MORALITY: IS IT RATIONAL TO DEFECT?

In the prisoners' dilemma and free rider interactions, there is a cooperative outcome (CC) yielding high benefits for all and yet it is not achieved because every individual has the incentive to defect (D) from such an arrangement. This seems strange because the resulting mutual defection (DD) produces low benefits for all. Perhaps there is something faulty with our model of rational action if it predicts such perverse behaviour. For instance, we might have wrongly assumed earlier that there is no honour among thieves because acting honourably could be connected to acting rationally in some full account of rationality in which case the dilemma might be unlocked without the intervention of the State (or some such agency). This general idea of linking a richer notion of rational agency with the spontaneous solution of the dilemma has been variously pursued in the social science literature and this section and the following three consider four of the more prominent suggestions.

The first connects rationality with morality and Kant provides a ready reference. His practical reason demands that we should undertake those actions which when generalised yield the best outcomes. It does not matter whether others perform the same calculation and actually undertake the same action as you. The morality is deontological and it is rational for the agent to be guided by a categorical imperative (see Chapter 1). Consequently, in the free rider problem, the application of the categorical imperative will instruct Kantian agents to follow the cooperative action (C), thus enabling 'rationality' to solve the problem when there are sufficient numbers of Kantian agents.

This is perhaps the most radical departure from the conventional instrumental understanding of what is entailed by rationality because, while accepting the pay-offs, it suggests that agents should act in a different way upon them. The notion of rationality is no longer understood in the means–end framework as the selection of the means most likely to satisfy given ends. Instead, rationality is conceived more as an expression of what is possible: it has become an end in its own right. This is not only radical, it is also controversial. Deontological moral philosophy is controversial for the obvious reason that it is not concerned with the actual consequences of an action, as well as for the move to connect it with rationality. (Nevertheless, O'Neill (1989) presents a recent argument and provides an extended discussion of this moral psychology and how it might be applied.)

Kant's morality may seem rather demanding for these reasons, but there are weaker or vaguer types of moral motivation which also seem capable of unlocking the prisoners' dilemma. For example, a general altruistic concern for the welfare of others may provide a sufficient reason for people not to defect on the cooperative arrangement. Certainly this seems to be the case in a study of the voluntary blood donation system found in the UK. Titmuss (1970) is the source. He argues that the voluntary blood donation system functions better than commercially based systems and he explores the reasons for blood donation. The reasons are puzzling from an instrumentally rational perspective because at first glance a voluntary system seems to be prone to a free rider problem – since donation is costly to the individual and is unlikely to affect the viability of the system and hence the likelihood of the individual obtaining future benefits from the system. Why do individuals donate in these circumstances? Titmuss reports that 'a desire to help others' is the single most important reason given by donors.

The very emergence of trade unions in the face of the extreme losses to the pioneers who started them, points to an overcoming of the workers' free rider problem on the basis of a sense of duty, an ideology. Similarly, with the observation that most people actually vote even when voting is not compulsory. If voting is somewhat inconvenient (that is, costly) and the chances that *your* vote will determine the outcome of the election minuscule, then a free rider problem emerges which should reduce the turnout to zero. This does not happen because of people's apparent commitment to exercising a 'right'. Likewise, Hardin (1982) suggests that the existence of environmental and other voluntary organisations usually entails overcoming a free rider problem and in the USA this may be explained in part by an American commitment to a form of contractarianism whereby 'people play fair if enough others do'. Thus it seems a sense of fairness demands for some people that they contribute if others do and they will benefit from the activity. Plainly not everyone is motivated by such a sense, but sufficient numbers are to fund a large number of voluntary organisations in North America and other countries. Similarly partisans in occupied Europe during the Second World War risked their lives even when it was not clear that it was instrumentally rational to confront the Nazis. In such cases, it seems people act on a sense of what is right.

Box 5.4

ADAM SMITH'S MORAL SENTIMENTS

How selfish soever man may be supposed, there are evidently some principles in his nature, which interest him in the fortunes of others, and render their happiness necessary to him, though he derives nothing from it except the pleasure of seeing it.

(Smith, 1795, p.1)

Of course, there is a tricky issue concerning whether these rather weaker or vaguer moral motivations (like altruism, acting on what is fair or what is right) mark a deep breach with the instrumental model of action. It might be argued that such ethical concerns can be represented in this model by introducing the concept of ethical preferences. Thus the influence of ethical preferences transforms the pay-offs in the game. So even though people still act instrumentally, the game ceases to be a prisoners' dilemma after the transformation. On the other hand, given the well-known difficulties associated with any coherent system of ethics (like utilitarianism), it seems quite likely that a person's ethical concerns will not be captured by a well-behaved set of preferences (see for instance Sen (1970) on the problems of being a Paretian Liberal). Indeed rational agents may well base their actions on reasons which are external to their preferences. This is not the place to pursue the issue (see Hollis (1987) and Sen (1989), for a discussion) and it is sufficient to conclude that there is some evidence that the prisoners' dilemma can be unlocked when individuals are suitably morally motivated. We revisit this discussion in Chapter 7.

5.4 WITTGENSTEIN AND NORMS: IS IT REALLY RATIONAL TO DEFECT?

Another departure from the strict instrumental model of rational action comes when individuals make decisions in a context of norms and these norms are capable of overriding considerations of what is instrumentally rational. Thus a norm of truth telling or promise keeping might lead each prisoner to keep an agreement 'not to confess'.

There is plenty of evidence to attest to the influence of norms in this regard. The anthropological literature is full of examples where norms operate in this fashion as a constraint upon self-interested action. Turnbull (1963), for instance, tells the story of how the Forest People (the Pygmies of the Congo) hunt with nets in the Ituri Forest. It is a cooperative enterprise in the sense that it requires each person to form a ring with their nets to catch the animals which are being beaten in their direction. In addition, it is tempting for each individual to move forward from their allotted position because they thereby get a first shot at the prey with their own net. Such action is, of course, disastrous for the others because it creates a gap in the ring through which the prey can escape and so lowers the overall catch for the group.

Hunting among the Pygmies, therefore, has all the elements of a free rider problem and yet, almost without exception, the norm of hunting in a particular way defeats the problem. Interestingly Turnbull witnessed a rare occasion when someone (Cephu) ignored the norm. He slipped away from his allotted position and obtained a 'first bite' at the prey to his advantage. He was spotted (which is not always easy, given the density of the forest) and Turnbull describes what happened that evening.

> Cephu had committed what is probably one of the most heinous crimes in Pygmy eyes, and one that rarely occurs. Yet the case was settled simply and effectively, *without any evident legal system* being brought into force. It cannot be said that Cephu went unpunished, because for those few hours when nobody would speak to him he must have suffered the equivalent of as many days solitary confinement for anyone else. To have been refused a chair by a mere youth, not even one of the great hunters; to have been laughed at by women and children; to have been ignored by men – none of these would be quickly forgotten. Without any formal process of law Cephu had been put in his place.
>
> (pp. 109–10; emphasis added)

The description is a classic account of how the norms in a group are informally policed. A related issue is currently debated in Australia. Disputes within Aboriginal society are neither perceived as simply between two individuals nor subject to some established community tribunal. It is for this reason that the resolution of a major conflict will involve a significant amount of negotiation between the parties. Yet the informal laws which govern the contents of the negotiations are well entrenched in the tribal culture. For example, it is not uncommon for family members of the perpetrator to be asked to accept 'punishment' if the individual offender is in prison and therefore unavailable. And it is not uncommon for such requests to be accepted. This has led to a very interesting debate on how the norms of Aboriginal society (and the ensuing punishment) ought to be taken into consideration by judges who are obviously tuned into another set of cultural norms: western criminal law.

There are also examples of norms which have operated in the most unlikely conditions. For instance, Axelrod (1984) building on Ashworth (1980) gives a detailed account of the 'live and let live' norm which developed during the First World War. This was a war of unprecedented carnage both at the beginning and the end. Yet during a middle period, non-aggression between the two opposing trenches emerged spontaneously in the form of a 'live and let live' norm. Christmas fraternisation is one well-known example, but the 'live and let live' norm was applied much more widely. Snipers would not shoot during meal times and so both sides could go about their business 'talking and laughing' at these hours. Artillery was predictably used both at certain times and at certain locations. So both sides could appear to demonstrate aggression by venturing out at certain times and to certain locations, knowing that the shells would fall predictably close to, but not on, their chosen route. Likewise, it was not considered 'etiquette' to fire on working parties who had been sent out to repair a position or collect the dead and so on.

Of course, both sides (that is, the troops, not the top-brass) gained from such a norm; and yet it was surprising that a norm was adhered to because there was an incentive for every individual to behave differently. After all, each individual was under extreme pressure to demonstrate aggression (through, for instance, the threat of court martial if you were caught being less than fully bellicose) and no individual infraction of the norm was likely to undermine the existence of the norm itself. Thus, the pressure of norm compliance itself must have provided a sufficient counterweight in this period to solve what seems, in key respects, to be a free rider problem which otherwise would have yielded an outcome of maximum aggression.

Likewise there are examples in economics where norms have been invoked to explain economic performance. For instance, it is sometimes argued that the norms of Confucian societies enable those economies to solve the prisoners' dilemma/free rider problems within companies without costly contracting and monitoring activity and that this explains, in part, the economic success of those economies (see Hargreaves Heap, 1991, Casson, 1991, North, 1991). Akerlof's (1983) discussion of loyalty filters, where he explains the relative success of Quaker groups in North America by their respect for the norm of honesty, is another example – as Hardin (1982) puts it: 'they came to do good and they did well'. And in the management literature, the best seller by Peters and Waterman (1982) argues that the culture of a company is central to its performance (for this and other reasons).

It is tempting to think that norms operate simply as an extraneous force modifying the pay-offs. In such cases defecting when there is a norm counselling against such action is not the dominant strategy it used to be in the absence of such a norm. Thus the game itself is transformed by the presence of the norms and the model of instrumental rational action does not seem to require modification in order to explain cooperation. Matters, though, are somewhat more complex. There is a teasing question with respect to the relation between instrumental rationality and the following of norms which we have touched upon before (see section 1.2.3). Two further observations are worth making in this context.

The first draws on the observation that norms often seem to embody a moral or a quasi-moral obligation (see, for instance, Ashworth's (1980) account of the 'live and let live' norm at the front). Even a norm like driving on the right that would seem to command respect on straightforward instrumental grounds (namely that it would be downright foolish to drive on the left when others drive on the right) nevertheless seems also to have a quasi-moral character. For instance, when people drive in the wrong direction on the opposing carriageway of a motorway because their direction has been blocked (a depressingly frequent occurrence), there is a tendency to think that they are not only foolish but also, in some degree, morally defective. Thus, the earlier question arises concerning the relation between a moral and an instrumental motivation. We consider next Gauthier's (1986) attempt to reduce morality to instrumental rationality and we shall have more to say in Chapter 7 about Hume's view that morality arises out of conventions which serve individual interests.

The second doubt surfaces over whether norms can be simply reduced to devices which serve instrumental rationality. Hume plainly wants to answer yes, but others answer no. Their contrary position holds that the individual interests, upon which instrumental rationality goes to work, cannot be defined independently of norms. Indeed our preferences, beliefs and ideas are at the very least co-authored by our social environment. So it can make no sense to interpret norms as derivatives of instrumentally rational agents who have some pre-norm (i.e. pre-social) interests (desires or preferences) which they wish to see satisfied. As we have seen in section 1.2.2 the Wittgenstein of *Philosophical Investigations*[1] is an obvious source for this view because he would deny that the meaning of something like a person's interests or desires can be divorced from a social setting; and this is a useful opportunity to take that argument further. The attribution of meaning requires language rules and it is impossible to have a private language. There is a long argument around the possibility or otherwise of private languages and it may be worth pursuing the point in a slightly different way by asking how agents have knowledge of what action will satisfy the condition of being instrumentally rational. Any claim to knowledge involves a first unquestioned premise: I know this because I accept x. Otherwise an infinite regress is inevitable: I accept x because I accept y and I accept y because . . . and so on. Accordingly, if each person's knowledge of what is rational is to be accessible to one another, then they must share the same first premises. It was Wittgenstein's point that people must share some practices if they are to attach meaning to words and so avoid the problem of infinite redescription which comes with any attempt to specify the rules for applying the rules of a language.

There are interesting parallels between this argument and the earlier discussion of the Harsanyi doctrine because a similar claim seems to underpin that doctrine. Namely that all rational individuals must come to the same conclusion when faced by the same evidence. Wittgenstein would agree to the extent that some such shared basis of interpretation must be present if communication is to be possible. But he would deny that all societies and peoples will share the same basis for interpretations. The source of the sharing for Wittgenstein is not some universal 'rationality', as it is for Harsanyi; rather it is the practices of the community in which the people live, and these will vary considerably across time and space.

There is another similarity and difference which might also be usefully marked. To make it very crudely one might draw an analogy between the difficulty which Wittgenstein encounters over knowledge claims and a similar difficulty which Simon (1982) addresses. (Herbert Simon is well known in economics for his claim that agents are procedurally rational, or boundedly rational, because they do not have the computing capacity to work out what is the best to do in complex settings.) To be sure, Wittgenstein finds the problem in an infinite regress of first principles while Simon finds the difficulty in the finite computing capacity of the brain. Nevertheless, both turn to 'procedures', 'practices' or 'rules of thumb' to explain how individuals operate.[2] In the context of game theory where the 'procedures' must supply a key to understanding the behaviour of others (and not the complexity of nature), it is difficult to see how they could do the job unless Wittgenstein was right in his claim that they must be shared in some degree.

Box 5.5

THE PROPENSITY 'TO BARTER, TRUCK AND EXCHANGE'

No less thinker than Adam Smith suggested that the division of labour in society was dependent upon the existence of markets, or, as he put it, upon man's 'propensity to barter, to truck and exchange one thing for another'. This phrase was later to yield the economic concept of the Economic Man. In retrospect it can be said that no misreading of the past ever proved more prophetic of the future.
(Polanyi, 1945, p. 53)

The outstanding discovery of recent historical and anthropological research is that man's economy, as a rule, is submerged in his social relationships. He does not act so as to safeguard his individual interest in the possession of material goods; he acts so as to safe-guard his social standing, his social claims, his social assets. He values material goods only in so far as they serve this end.
(Polanyi, 1945, p. 53)

To conclude this section, let us make the view inspired by Wittgenstein very concrete. The suggestion is that what is instrumentally rational is not well defined unless one appeals to the prevailing norms of behaviour. This may seem a little strange in the context of a prisoners' dilemma where the demands of instrumental rationality seem plain for all to see: defect! But, in reply, those radically inspired by Wittgenstein would complain that the norms have already been at work in the definition of the matrix and its pay-offs because it is rare for any social setting to throw up unvarnished pay-offs. A social setting requires interpretation before the pay-offs can be assigned and norms are implicated in those interpretations. (See for example Polanyi (1945) who argues, in his celebrated discussion of the rise of industrial society, that the incentives of the market system are only effective when the norms of society place value on private material advance.)

5.5 GAUTHIER: IS IT INSTRUMENTALLY RATIONAL TO DEFECT?

The last reflection on rationality comes from David Gauthier. He remains firmly in the instrumental camp and ambitiously argues that its dictates have been wrongly understood in the prisoners' dilemma game. *Instrumental rationality demands cooperation and not defection!* To make his argument he distinguishes between two sorts of maximisers: a straightforward maximiser (SM) and a constrained maximiser (CM). A straightforward maximiser defects (D) following the same logic that we have used so far. The constrained maximiser uses a conditional strategy of cooperating (C) with fellow constrained maximisers and defecting with straightforward maximisers. He then asks: which disposition (straightforward or constrained) should an instrumentally rational person choose to have? (The decision can be usefully compared with a similar one confronting Ulysses in connection with listening to the Sirens, see Box 5.6. Also see Smith (1994) on deciding on which rule one ought to use in order to reach a decision.)

The calculation is easy. Consider first the case where the disposition of the other player is transparent and where the pay-offs are given by Figure 5.2. Let us assume that the probability of encountering a constrained maximiser is p.

$$E(\text{return from CM}) = p.3 + (1 - p).2$$
$$E(\text{return from SM}) = 2$$

For any $p > 0$, this clearly gives a better return from being a CM. The reason is simple. CMs when they meet each other generate a pay-off of 3 and they get 2 when they meet an SM, while SMs only ever get 2. So provided there is some chance ($p > 0$) that a CM will meet another CM,

---

Box 5.6

ULYSSES AND THE SIRENS

Homer tells the story of Ulysses who, on his way home from Troy, came across the Sirens' island. He knew of their magnificent songs. But he knew also of the effect of their beautiful music on people: mesmerised by the melody, no one could resist approaching the island, whereby a terrible end awaited. Not wishing to risk his life, he instructed his crew to tie him tightly to the ship's mast, plug their ears with wax, and ignore his protests until the ship was miles away from the island. Thus he enjoyed the Sirens' song without falling into their trap. (A modern example of Ulysses' strategy: have you ever gone to a bookshop intending only to browse yet, to be certain, you left your wallet at home?) Gauthier (1986) asks us to do something similar: to find a way of being constrained maximisers in social interactions, and by so doing to escape the trap of the prisoners' dilemma. The problem is that, in most cases, there is no crew to obey our orders, and no mast robust enough to 'constrain' us. Some ontological change *in* us is necessary so that, if the rope becomes loose, we will not rush headlong towards the Sirens' trap.

---

then it will always make sense to be a CM. (Notice that in undertaking this calculation we have implicitly assumed something further about the utility numbers which represent the person's preferences: they can be represented by a cardinal utility function, see section 1.2.1.)

Of course, the disposition of each agent may not be transparent and so CMs may fail to achieve mutual recognition. A CM may mistakenly believe a player is a CM when they are not and an SM will benefit from the mistake. To cover such eventualities, let us assume now that p is the probability that CMs achieve mutual recognition when they meet; let q be the probability that a CM fails to recognise an SM; and let r be the probability of encountering a CM.

$$E(\text{return CM}) = rp.3 + r(1 - p).2 + (1 - r)q.1 + (1 - r)(1 - q).2$$
$$= 2 + rp - (1 - r)q.2$$

$$E(\text{return SM}) = r(1 - q).2 + rq.4 + (1 - r).2$$
$$= 2(1 + rq)$$

Thus the instrumentally rational agent will choose a CM disposition when

$$p/q > 2 + [(1 - r).2]/r$$

The result makes perfect intuitive sense. It suggests that provided the probability p of CMs achieving mutual recognition is sufficiently greater than the probability q of failing to recognise an SM (which means that the

163

CM gets 'zapped', thus lowering their pay-offs while boosting the return to an SM), then it will pay to be a CM. How much is 'sufficiently greater'? This depends (inversely) on how often you encounter a CM. To put some figures on this, suppose the probability of encountering a CM is 0.5; then the probability of achieving mutual recognition must be four times greater than the probability of failing to recognise an SM.

Hence it is perfectly possible that the disposition of agents will be sufficiently transparent for instrumentally rational agents to choose CM with the result that on those occasions when they achieve mutual recognition, the cooperative outcome is achieved. Hence it becomes rational to be 'moral' and the prisoners' dilemma has been defeated!

It is an ambitious argument, and if successful it would connect rationality to morality in a way which Kant had not imagined. (It has been attempted before in a similar way by Howard (1971); see Varoufakis, 1991.) However, there is a difficulty. The problem is: what motivates the CM to behave in a cooperative manner once mutual recognition has been achieved with another CM? The point is that if instrumental rationality is what motivates the CM in the prisoners' dilemma, then a CM must want to defect once mutual recognition has been achieved. There is no equivalent of the rope which ties Ulysses hands and the *best* response in the prisoners' dilemma remains 'defect' no matter what the other person does and this resurfaces in Gauthier's analysis as an incentive for the CM to cheat on what being a CM is supposed to entail. In other words, being a CM may be better than being an SM, but the best strategy of all is to label yourself a CM and then cheat on the deal. And, of course, when people do this, we are back in a world where everyone defects.

5.6 TIT-FOR-TAT IN AXELROD'S TOURNAMENTS

The obvious response to this worry over the credibility of constrained maximisation in Gauthier's world is to point to the gains which come from being a true CM once the game is repeated. Surely, this line of argument goes, it pays not to 'zap' a fellow CM because your reputation as a CM is thereby preserved and this enables you to interact more fruitfully with fellow CMs in the future. Should you zap a fellow CM now, then everyone will know that you are a rogue and so in your future interactions, you will be treated as an SM. In short, in a repeated setting, it pays to forgo the short run gain from defecting because this ensures the benefits of cooperation over the long run. Thus instrumental calculation can make true CM behaviour the best course of action.

This is a tempting line of argument, but it is not one that Gauthier can use because he wants to claim that his analysis holds in one-shot versions of the game. Nevertheless, it is a line we shall want to pursue, especially in the next chapter, because it provides a potentially simple explanation of how the dilemma can be defeated without the intervention of a collective agency like the State – that is, provided the interaction is repeated sufficiently often to make the long term benefits outweigh the short gains. We conclude the current chapter with a report on some experimental evidence which reinforces this line of argument.

Axelrod invited professional game theorists (especially those who had written on the prisoners' dilemma) to enter programs for playing a computer-based repeated, round robin, version of the prisoners' dilemma game. Under the tournament rules, each entrant (program) was paired with another once in a random ordering, and in each of these contests the game was repeated 200 times. In fact 14 people responded and the round robin tournament was actually played five times to produce an average score for each program.

Tit-for-Tat, submitted by Anatol Rapoport, won the tournament. The program starts with a cooperative move and then does whatever the opponent did on the previous move. It was, as Axelrod points out, not only the simplest program, it was also the best! Moreover, it achieved a remarkable degree of cooperation. Under the tournament rules, you obtained 3 points for a jointly cooperative move and the average score per contest for Tit-for-Tat was 504 points. In fact, it was one of a group of programs which did noticeably better than the rest and they shared the property of being 'nice'; that is, of not being the first to defect. A number of more sophisticated variants on the principle of Tit-for-Tat were entered but they did not perform as well as the simple Tit-for-Tat which forgives a defection after a one-period punishment.

A second version of the tournament was announced after the publication of the results of the first one. The rules were basically the same. The only change came with the introduction of a random end to the sequence of plays between two players (i.e. rather than fixing the number at 200). This time 62 programs were entered.

Tit-for-Tat was again the simplest submission to the second round; and again it was the most successful! (And again only one person submitted it, Anatol Rapoport.) The results were also qualitatively similar in other regards: for instance, being 'nice' was again closely correlated with the final score. Interestingly, it was known that a strategy which was not entered in the first version, Tit-for-two-tats, would have performed better in that tournament than the simple tit-for-tat rule. Not unsurprisingly, it was entered in the second version of the tournament, but this time it came in 24th.

Thus, matters do seem, at least in experiments involving computer programs (rather than people), to be rather different when this game is repeated. A simple 'nice' and forgiving strategy of tit-for-tat emerges as the best and it achieves the cooperative outcome with other players/programs on a remarkable number of occasions.

5.7 CONCLUSION

Stinchcombe provocatively asks: 'Is the Prisoners' dilemma all of sociology?' Of course, it is not, he answers. Nevertheless, it has fascinated social scientists and proved extremely difficult to unlock in one-shot plays of the game – at least, without the creation of a coercive agency like the State which is capable of enforcing a collective action or without the introduction of norms or some suitable form of moral motivation on the part of the individuals playing the game. Of course, many interactions are repeated and so this stark conclusion may be modified by the discussion of the next chapter.

6

REPEATED GAMES AND REPUTATIONS

6.1 INTRODUCTION

Many social interactions are repeated either with the same person or with people who are drawn from the same social group. Indeed, since one-off encounters typically occur only between strangers, the analysis of repeated games promises to extend the scope of game theory considerably.

In addition, when the same game is played repeatedly the strategic options for players expand significantly, becoming in the process more life-like in a number of respects. For instance, it becomes possible to condition what you do on what your opponent has done in previous rounds. Thus you can punish or reward your opponent depending on what they have done in the past. By definition, this cannot be done when the game is played only once. Likewise players learn things about their opponents from the way they have behaved in the past. Such learning can be exploited by players behaving in particular ways to develop reputations for playing the game in particular ways. Therefore the analysis of repeated games also promises further insights regarding the types of behaviour which we might expect from instrumentally rational players.

This chapter considers repeated games in various settings. We begin with the *finitely* repeated prisoners' dilemma game in section 6.2 and make use of backward induction and the subgame perfect Nash equilibrium concept from section 3.3. Perhaps somewhat surprisingly, mutual defection remains the only Nash equilibrium. The following two sections discuss, respectively, *indefinitely* repeated prisoners' dilemma and the related free rider games. We show (section 6.4) that mutual cooperation is a possible Nash equilibrium outcome in these games provided there is a 'sufficient' degree of uncertainty over when the repetition will cease. There are some significant implications here both for liberal political theory and for the explanatory power of game theory. We notice that this result means that mutual cooperation might be achieved without the intervention of a collective agency like the State and/or without appealing to some expanded notion of rational agency (see Chapter 5). In other words cooperation could emerge between interacting instrumentally rational players provided they cannot accurately pinpoint the moment in the future when their interaction (or relation) will end. This is the good news. The bad news is that, even though cooperation may have become possible, this is so because almost anything goes once the game is repeated (we show this in section 6.3). By this we mean that repetition generates so many Nash equilibria that it is impossible to know what will happen. This realisation reinforces the earlier critical discussion (see Chapters 2 and 3) regarding the absence of a theory of equilibrium selection.

Section 6.5 investigates finitely repeated games when there is uncertainty of a different type. Here the identity of players is not known with certainty and this connects with the earlier discussion of games of incomplete information (see section 2.6) and the sequential equilibrium concept (section 3.5).

The special role of reputations in repeated games arises because early plays of the game can be used to secure a reputation in later plays of the game. However, the opportunities for reputation building behaviour may also arise outside the particular game which is being played (whether it is played once or repeatedly). For instance, an individual may be able to take some 'extraneous' action (that is, an action which is unrelated to the game in question) which tells the opponent something about his or her character. We discuss such 'signalling' behaviour in section 6.6.

In the final section, we return to the discussion of the status of the Nash equilibrium concept (in sections 2.5 and 3.7) and reflect on whether its foundations are any more secure in repeated games than in those where games are played only once.

6.2 THE FINITELY REPEATED PRISONERS' DILEMMA

One of the main reasons for looking at repeated games is to explore the intuition in section 5.6 linking repetition with cooperation. According to this line of thought, individuals might want to secure a reputation for cooperation in a repeated version of the game, even if this required some sacrifice in the short run, because the returns over the long run from mutual cooperation would outweigh these costs. In fact, conventional game theoretical wisdom (e.g. the assumptions of CKR and backward induction) does not agree with intuition when the game is repeated a finite number of times (finite repetitions often occur when the interaction has a fixed time horizon, as when a second-term President interacts with Congress on a known number of bills before his or her office expires).

To appreciate the conventional wisdom, notice that no player will care about their reputation for cooperation in the last play of the game as there is no further play of the game in which the players can benefit from a good reputation. Accordingly, in the finitely repeated prisoners' dilemma both players will defect in the last play – the last play is, after all, just a one-shot version of the game and the logic of defection for instrumentally rational agents in these circumstances seems impeccable. Now consider the penultimate play of the game. Since it is known that both players will defect in the last play, neither player has any need to carry a reputation for cooperation into that last play of the game. Hence neither player need nurture future reputation when they play the penultimate round of the game. But, when neither party cares about their reputation, the logic of defection as the dominant strategy re-emerges and so both players will defect in the penultimate play. Now turn to the pre-penultimate play: since neither player needs a reputation in the penultimate round . . . and so on.

Thus the application of the Nash backward induction logic (see Chapter 3) to the finitely repeated game yields the clear prediction that both players will defect in every round of the game. Consequently the intuition regarding the influence of repetition seems to be wrong (to the extent of course that we accept Nash backward induction). However, cooperation early on in the finitely repeated game can be induced *with* Nash backward induction in place provided some uncertainty is injected into the game.

The Nash backward induction argument for defection rests on two pieces of certain knowledge. One is that the players will know, when they play the last play, that it is the last play. This enables each to project forward and argue that when the last play is reached both will decide to defect. This established, they can work backwards. But if the players do not know for certain when the last play is, then the argument has no starting point. Indeed they cannot say for certain that defection will occur in any play of the game without begging the question of what strategy is rational. And without the sure knowledge that defection occurs in some future play of the game, then it is not possible to argue backwards to the present that defection will happen in all the intervening rounds. Instead the players are forced to engage in a different type of calculation. They must look wholly forward and evaluate each strategy in terms of its current and future returns, taking into account the various likelihoods that the game will be repeated into the future. Not unsurprisingly, in the absence of any clear, dominant strategy, these calculations become quite complicated and the results are less clear cut. They form the material of the next two sections.

The other piece of certain knowledge that is necessary for the Nash backward induction argument is common knowledge of instrumental rationality (CKR). Of course, this is a standard assumption of game theory and so, perhaps, it hardly needs restating. However, there is a difference between the repeated and one-shot versions of the prisoners' dilemma in this regard that makes it worth drawing out. It will be recalled that CKR is not necessary in a one-shot prisoners' dilemma because defection is the dominant strategy and so it does not matter what motivates the other player: your best strategy is to defect. Without CKR, the same cannot be said with complete confidence in a finitely repeated prisoners' dilemma because it seems possible that an instrumentally rational player may be able to exploit some idiosyncrasy on the part of the other player so as to achieve the cooperative outcome (and hence superior returns over the long run) by playing some strategy which does not defect in all plays. We consider this possibility in section 6.5 (see also Pettit and Sugden, 1989).

6.3 THE FOLK THEOREM AND THE INDEFINITELY REPEATED PRISONERS' DILEMMA

In this section we shall demonstrate that almost anything goes in the indefinitely repeated prisoners' dilemma game. For instance, that a pair of tit-for-tat strategies is one of (many) strategy pair(s) which can form a Nash equilibrium in the indefinitely repeated prisoners' dilemma game. This is an important result for several reasons which we discuss now. The proof is given at the end.

Cooperation without collective agencies

Firstly, it provides a theoretical warrant for the belief that cooperation in the prisoners' dilemma can be rationally sustained without the intervention of some collective agency like the State, provided there is sufficient (to be defined later) doubt over when the repeated game will end. Thus the presence of a prisoners' dilemma interaction does not *necessarily* entail either a poor social outcome or the institutions of formal collective decision making. The third alternative is for players to adopt a tit-for-tat strategy rationally.[1] If they adopt this third alternative the socially inferior outcome of mutual defection will be avoided without the interfering presence of the State or some other formal (coercive) institution.

In a way this result is quite un-mysterious. Recall that the problem in one-shot games arose because the obvious remedy of making an agreement to cooperate failed in the absence of an enforcement mechanism. The point, then, about repetition is that it allows the players themselves to enforce an agreement. Players are able to do this, quite simply, by being able to threaten to punish their opponents in future plays of the game if they transgress now. The tit-for-tat strategy embodies precisely this type of behaviour. It offers implicitly to cooperate by cooperating first and it enforces cooperation by threatening to punish an opponent who defects on cooperation by defecting until that person cooperates again. (Or to put this slightly differently, playing tit-for-tat allows your opponent to develop a reputation for cooperation simply by playing cooperatively in the previous play of the game.)

Implicit agreements

Secondly (as we mentioned in Chapter 5), the result appears to have direct applicability to the social world because there seem to be many examples of social interaction where this type of threat could explain how cooperation is achieved. Plainly it might explain the 'live and let live' norm which developed during the First World War since the interaction was repeated and each side could punish another's transgression. Equally, it is probable that both prisoners in the original example may think twice about 'confessing' because each knows that they are likely to encounter one another again (if not in prison, at least outside) and so there are likely to be opportunities for exacting 'punishment' at a later date.

Also consider the role of internal career ladders in companies in enforcing agreements between employers and employees. The point is that a career ladder both encourages repetition of the interaction (because you advance up the ladder by staying with the firm) and it provides a system of reward which is capable of being used to punish those who do not perform adequately. Alternatively, to reinforce the potential use of this insight for understanding social interactions, why do many of us find it difficult to 'trust' second-hand car sellers? Perhaps it is because we do *not* interact with sufficient frequency with them to develop the informal mechanisms for enforcing an implicit agreement not to supply a 'lemon'.

Having said all this, some obvious mysteries remain with our earlier examples of cooperation. For instance, how is it that battalions who were about to leave a particular front (thus discontinuing their long term relationship with the enemy on the other side of their trench) continued to 'cooperate' until the very last moment?

Defection: an ever present threat

Thirdly, the result turns on the fact that tit-for-tat strategies are not the only pairs of Nash equilibrium strategies in the indefinitely repeated game. This will be obvious in the sense that 'always defect' will still be the best response to 'always defect' and so this pair must also form another Nash equilibrium in the repeated game. Moreover, it will also be apparent from the discussion of how cooperation works under the tit-for-tat strategy pair that the simple tit-for-tat cannot be the only other Nash equilibrium strategy. Indeed there is any number of potentially more complicated forms of punishment strategies which can also be utilised to produce a variety of different patterns of cooperation (and defection). Indeed, there is a formal result in game theory, known as the *Folk theorem* (so called because it was widely known in game theory circles before it was written up), which demonstrates that in infinitely and indefinitely repeated games any of the

171

potential pay-off pairs in these repeated games can be obtained as a Nash equilibrium with a suitable choice of strategies by the players!

This is an extremely important result for the social sciences because it means that there are *always* multiple Nash equilibria in such indefinitely repeated games. Hence, even if Nash is accepted as the appropriate equilibrium concept for games with individuals who are instrumentally rational and who have common knowledge of that rationality, it will not explain how individuals select their strategies because there are many strategy pairs which form Nash equilibria in these repeated games. Of course, we have encountered this problem in some one-shot games before, but the importance of this result is that it means the problem is always there in indefinitely repeated games. Even worse, it is amplified by repetition. In other words, game theory needs to be supplemented by a theory of equilibrium selection if it is to explain action in these indefinitely repeated games, especially if it is to explain how cooperation actually arises spontaneously in indefinitely repeated prisoners' dilemma games.

We turn now to the formal proof of the proposition in the game given by Figure 6.1.

	Player B		
		C	D
Player A	C	3, 3	1, 4
	D	4, 1	2, 2

Figure 6.1

Proposition: Tit-for-tat (τ) **is** a Nash equilibrium strategy in the indefinitely repeated prisoners' dilemma of Figure 6.1 provided the chances that the game will be repeated in the next round exceed 50%.

Proof We shall capture the uncertainty over the end of the game by assuming that in any play of the game both players believe that there is a probability p that the game will be repeated again. Consequently a strategy which specifies (possibly conditionally) a move for each possible play of the game will generate a stream of pay-offs whose value will be weighted by the appropriate probabilities.

Box 6.1

COOPERATION IN SMALL GROUPS AND THE OPTIMAL SIZE OF A GROUP

It is commonly observed that small groups seem better able to cooperate amongst themselves than do large groups. For example, Olson (1965, 1982) has made much of the role of small groups in this regard when explaining why nations rise and fall. The result in section 6.3 regarding the possibility of cooperation through a tit-for-tat Nash equilibrium provides a potential explanation of this apparent phenomenon. Suppose individuals randomly interact with members of their group in a manner which has the structure of a prisoners' dilemma. By definition the larger the group, the smaller the probability that any one individual will interact with the same member of the group again. Hence the smaller the group the greater the likelihood that the 'greater than 50%' chance of future interaction, which is necessary for the tit-for-tat Nash equilibrium, will be satisfied.

When the observation regarding cooperation is taken together with the opposing thought that larger groups permit greater specialisation, it seems likely that groups might have some optimal size: one which exploits a division of labour without undermining the capacity for trust and cooperation in individual relationships. And indeed there seem to be examples of this. For instance, most modern armies have evolved to a form with companies consisting of three platoons of 30–40 people each; and it is a conventional rule of thumb in the management literature that 100–150 people is the maximum size for a firm run on a person-to-person basis (thereafter, some kind of hierarchic form of management becomes necessary).

Step 1: There are only three types of response to someone playing τ

The proof proceeds by showing that under certain conditions τ is a best response to someone who is playing τ and it turns on the recognition that there are only three broad types of best response strategies to someone who is playing τ (see Axelrod, 1984, and Sugden, 1986). They are those: (a) which cooperate in all future plays; (b) which alternate cooperation with defection; and (c) which defect in all plays.

To see why all the best possible responses will fit into one or other of these three types, notice first that in any round your opponent will either (i) cooperate now or (ii) defect (depending on what you did in the last round under your best reply strategy) and in each case your best strategy will either specify that (α) you cooperate now or (β) that you defect.

So consider the possible best response case given by (iα), where your opponent will cooperate and your best strategy involves cooperation also. If

173

this is the case then in the following round your opponent will cooperate under τ and so you will face exactly the same situation. If your best strategy specified cooperation before it will do so again. Thus your best reply strategy will specify cooperation in all periods – case (a).

Alternatively suppose your best strategy response is to defect when your opponent cooperates (case (iβ)); then your opponent will defect in the following round and what happens next can be studied under case (ii). So consider case (iiα), where the best reply involves cooperating in response to a defection. Then your opponent will cooperate in the subsequent round and since you defect in response to cooperation, a pattern of alternate defection and cooperation will have been established as the best response – thus case (b). The alternative possibility with case (ii) is that you defect (β). In this instance, there is defection thereafter – case (c). This exhausts all possible types of best replies to τ: they cooperate always or they alternate or they always defect.

Step 2: Proving that τ can be best response to τ

If both play according to strategy τ, then each is looking forward to expected returns:

$$E(\tau, \tau) = 3(1 + p + p^2 + p^3 + \ldots) = 3/(1 - p) \tag{6.1}$$

where p^k is the probability that the game will be repeated exactly k rounds. Now compare this with the expected return to the alternate (λ) type of strategy:

$$E(\lambda, \tau) = 4 + 1p + 4p^2 + 1p^3 + \ldots = (4 - p)/(1 - p^2) \tag{6.2}$$

Finally there is the third possible type of best reply which defects always (say, δ) yielding

$$E(\delta, \tau) = 4 + 2p + 2p^2 + \ldots = 4 + 2p/(1 - p) \tag{6.3}$$

Through inspection, it can be seen that the alternate strategy λ is always inferior as a response to τ than the δ (obsessive defection) strategy; and τ is a better response than $p > \frac{1}{2}$. Accordingly, we can conclude that (τ, τ) is a Nash equilibrium when $p > \frac{1}{2}$. QED.

6.4 INDEFINITELY REPEATED FREE RIDER GAMES

6.4.1 Spontaneous public good provision

We generalise the result of the previous section here to the n-person prisoners' dilemma game which is known in the literature as a free rider problem. Our example is borrowed from Sugden (1986).

Assume that a group of individuals live in an environment which exposes them to danger (it could be robbery or illness or some such negatively valued event). The danger is valued at $-d$ by each person and it occurs with a known frequency. It affects one person randomly in any period: so with n people the chance of falling 'ill' is $1/n$. In this environment, each individual faces a choice between 'cooperating' (that is, helping a member of the group who falls 'ill') which costs c and 'defecting' (that is, not helping a member of the group who falls 'ill') which costs nothing. These choices have consequences for the person who is 'ill'. In particular the 'ill' or 'robbed' person obtains a benefit bN from the N group members who contribute. We assume that $b > c$ as help is more highly valued by someone who receives it, when 'ill', than someone who gives it, when 'healthy'. The free rider character of the interaction will be plain. Everyone has an interest in a collective fund for 'health care'. But no one will wish to pay: when others contribute you enjoy all the benefits without the cost and when others do not you will be helping others more often than you help yourself.

Now consider a tit-for-tat strategy in this group which works in the following way. The strategy partitions the group into those who are in 'good standing' and those who are in 'no standing' based on whether the individual contributed to the collective fund in the last time period. Those in 'good standing' are eligible for the receipt of help from the group if they fall 'ill' this time period, whereas those who are in 'no standing' are not eligible for help. Thus tit-for-tat specifies cooperation and puts you in 'good standing' for the receipt of a benefit if you fall 'ill' (alternatively, to connect with the earlier discussion, one might think of cooperating as securing a 'reputation' which puts one in 'good standing').

To demonstrate that cooperating (to secure a reputation) could be a Nash equilibrium in the indefinitely repeated game, consider the case where everyone is playing tit-for-tat and so is in 'good standing' with each other. You must decide whether to act 'cooperatively' (that is, follow a strategy like tit-for-tat as well) or 'defect' by not making a contribution to the collective fund. Notice your decision now will determine whether you are in 'good standing' from now until the next opportunity that you get to make this decision (which will be the next period if you do not fall 'ill' or the period after that if you fall 'ill'). So we focus on the returns from your choice now until you next get the opportunity to choose.

We assume that the game will be repeated next period with probability p

(for instance, because you might die this period or migrate to a different group). So, there is a probability p/n that you will fall 'ill' next period in this group and a probability $(p/n)^2$ that you will remain 'ill' for the time period after and so on. Consequently the expected return from 'defecting' now is that you will not be in 'good standing' **and** that you will fall 'ill' next period with probability p/n. Moreover, there is a further probability $(p/n)^2$ that you remain 'ill' the period after while still in 'no standing' and so on. Thus the expected return from 'defecting' now is $(-d)[p/n + (p/n)^2 + \ldots]$ i.e. these are the expected returns from putting yourself in 'no standing' (by declining to contribute to the collective health fund) until you next get a chance to decide whether to contribute.

By the same kind of argument, if you decide to cooperate now, then the expected returns are given by $-c + [(n - 1)b - d][p/n + (p/n)^2 + \ldots]$. Through inspection cooperating is more profitable when $p > nc/[(n - 1)b + d]$. The intuition behind this result is simple. You have more to lose from losing your reputation when there is a high chance of the game being repeated and when the benefit (b) exceeds the cost (c) of contribution significantly. To demonstrate the connection with earlier insights from the repeated prisoners' dilemma, suppose $n = 2$, $b = 3$ and $c = 1$: cooperation becomes possible as long as $p > \frac{1}{2}$. (The proof is the same as that of the earlier proposition that tit-for-tat is a Nash equilibrium provided the game will be repeated with probability at least $\frac{1}{2}$.)

6.4.2 Who needs the State?

Box 6.2 on the power of prophecy explores one possible implication of the result we have just proved. Here we pick up threads of the Hobbesian argument for the State and see what the result holds for this argument. At first glance, the argument for the State seems to be weakened because it appears that a group can overcome the free rider problem without recourse to the State for contract enforcement. So long as the group can punish free riders by excluding them from the benefits of cooperation (as for instance the Pygmies punished Cephu – see Chapter 5), then there is the possibility of 'spontaneous' public good provision through the generalisation of the tit-for-tat strategy. Having noted this, nevertheless, the point seems almost immediately to be blunted since the difference between a Hobbesian State which enforces collective agreements and the generalised tit-for-tat arrangement is not altogether clear and so in proving one we are hardly undermining the other. After all, the State merely codifies and implements the policies of 'punishment' on behalf of others in a very public way (with the rituals of police stations, courts and the like). But, is this any different from the golf club which excludes a member from the greens when the dues have not been paid or the Pygmies' behaviour towards Cephu? Or the gang which excludes people who have not contributed 'booty' to the

Box 6.2

THE POWER OF PROPHECY

The result in this section suggests that groups that have some degree of permanency will be more likely to achieve cooperation than those which are transient because the probability of repetition is greater in the former than the latter. Indeed, perhaps this explains why cowpokes are notorious law breakers in Westerns while the barber and the Sunday school teacher are upstanding members of the community. On this account, there is nothing morally defective, after all, about the cowpokes. They simply interact with other members of the town with less frequency than do the permanent residents and so their assessments of the probability of future interactions with members of the town are correspondingly lower. In turn, this suggests a further interesting implication for the power of prophesy when group membership is made endogenous.

Suppose people join a group and stay with it when it is successful, but they leave when it fails because it cannot secure cooperation among its members. In these circumstances, an initial belief regarding the likely success/permanence of the group is liable to be self-fulfilling. Since when people expect permanence rather than transience, the equivalent probability condition above is more likely to be satisfied and so it is more likely that cooperation is achieved with the result that the group keeps its members (i.e. achieves permanence). By contrast, when transience is expected rather than permanence, the probability of repetition is expected to be lower and so the probability condition is less likely to be satisfied. Thus when the group's members are pessimistic about the possibility of cooperation, their pessimism feeds into the constituents of their decision making and often confirms their expectations. The unfortunate aspect of such a confirmation is that it does not mean that, objectively, cooperation (and thus the success of the group) was impossible or 'irrational'. It becomes impossible or irrational for individuals to cooperate because of the cloud of pessimism; and so perhaps the sort of inspirational rhetoric which encourages optimism among a group does play an important part in the success of groups.

Of course, this capacity for beliefs to become self-fulfilling makes the source of the original beliefs quite crucial; and perhaps in turn this provides a key to our understanding of why cooperation is often achieved among a group which has 'other reasons' for being together. For instance, the fact that there is a family relationship or a shared ethnicity or shared gender often seems to provide 'other reasons' for being together and these might be just enough to tilt the original expectation with respect to likely repetition in an optimistic direction. Thereafter the self-fulfilling character of any belief does the rest. Likewise, perhaps this helps explain why revolutionary change is so difficult to achieve. By definition revolution involves overthrowing traditional sources of allegiance within the group and, unless it can offer a new reason for the group to exist as a group, it will not be able to create the beliefs of new permanence which secure cooperation within the group on new terms.

common fund? Is it really very different if you pay the State in the form of taxes or the Mafia in the form of tribute?

Instead the result seems important because it demythologises the State. Firstly the State *qua* State (that is, the State with its police force, its courts and the like) is not required to intrude into every social interaction which suffers from a free rider problem. There are many practices and institutions which are surrogates for the State in this regard. Indeed, the Mafia has plausibly displaced the State in certain areas precisely because it provides the services of a State. Likewise, during the long civil war years inhabitants of Beirut somehow still managed to maintain services which required the overcoming of free rider problems.

Secondly since something like the State as contract enforcer might well arise 'spontaneously' through the playing of free rider games repeatedly, it need not require any grand design. There need be no constitutional conventions. In this way the result counts strongly for what Hayek (1962) refers to as the English as opposed to the European continental Enlightenment tradition. The latter stresses the power of reason to construct institutions that overcome problems like those of the free rider. (It also often presupposes – recall Rousseau's social contract – that the creation of the State by the individual also helps shape a superior individual.) Hayek, however, prefers the 'English tradition' because he doubts (a) that the formation of the State is part of a process which liberates (and moulds) the social agent and (b) that there is the knowledge to inform some central design so that it can perform the task of resolving free riding better than spontaneously generated solutions (like tit-for-tat). In other words, reason should know its limits and this is what informs Hayek's support for English pragmatism and its suspicion of the State.

Of course there is a big 'if' in Hayek's argument. Although Beirut still managed to function without a grand design, most of its citizens prayed for one. In short, the spontaneous solution is not always the best. Indeed, as we have seen, the cooperative solution is just one among many Nash equilibria in repeated games, so in the absence of some machinery of collective decision making, there seems no guarantee it will be selected. Against this, however, it is sometimes argued that evolution will favour practices which generate the cooperative outcome since societies that achieve cooperation in these games will prosper as compared with those which are locked in mutual defection. This is the cue for a discussion of evolutionary game theory and we shall leave further discussion of the State until we turn to evolutionary game theory in the next chapter.

6.5 REPUTATION IN FINITELY REPEATED GAMES

In the last section, one might plausibly associate a person's reputation with whether they were in 'good standing'. In this section, we consider a different sense of reputation and a different reason for caring about it. In this instance both arise because there is some uncertainty over the types of player playing the game.

6.5.1 Relaxing the assumption of common knowledge instrumental rationality

Suppose that two players A and B (once more female and male respectively) are to play the prisoners' dilemma game in Figure 5.2 three times. We will refer to these three instances as $t = 1, 2$ and 3. If A and B are convinced that Nash backward induction will determine the thoughts of each, as we saw in section 6.2, the result will be that neither will cooperate at any stage of the game. Suppose, however, that CKR does not hold and each faces only one certainty: at $t = 3$ 'defect' is their dominant strategy. If they know that their opponent is instrumentally rational, they will expect him or her to choose strategy D. But this is exactly what we do not wish to build in. Instead we suppose that player B thinks there is a chance that A is a tit-for-tat kind of person who initially cooperates and continues to cooperate without fail as long as the other player cooperated in the previous round. If A were such a backward looking, stubborn follower of tit-for-tat, she would cooperate even at $t = 3$ provided, of course, that B cooperated at t = 2.

Let the probability that A is a tit-for-tatter be given by p. What should player B do? The tree diagram in Figure 6.2 describes the six possible outcomes.

$t = 3$:At the last play of the game, an instrumentally rational B will always defect. Even if he expects A to cooperate, he will not reciprocate.

$t = 2$: If at $t = 1$ he cooperated, then there is a chance that player A will cooperate at $t = 2$. This is so because there is a chance (given by probability p) that A is a tit-for-tat 'cooperator' who plays at time $t = k$ the same strategy her opponent chose $t = k - 1$. Thus, assuming that cooperation was achieved (for some reason which we will investigate later) at $t = 1$, player B's expected returns from cooperating at $t = 2$ are

$$ER^B(\text{from cooperating at } t = 2 \mid \text{cooperation occurred at } t = 1) =$$
$$3p + (1 - p) + 4p + 2(1 - p) \tag{6.4}$$

An explanation: at $t = 2$ cooperation will lead to further cooperation with probability p (yielding pay-off 3) or to defection (with probability $1 - p$) by a player A who was never really a tit-for-tat person (yielding pay-off 1 for B). In addition, it will lead to pay-off 4 at $t = 3$ (again with probability p) if B gets a chance to 'zap' a tit-for-tat A in that round. If not, then at $t = 3$

	A	B	A	B	A	B		Subjective probabilistic expectations for each outcome by B at $t = 0$	Pay-offs A	Pay-offs B	Notes
	C	C	C	C	C	D	1	p	7	10	1 Player B will *not* choose D at $t = 2$ if both he and A choose C at $t = 1$. For B to have chosen C at $t = 1$, he must have thought that the chances A is a tit-for-tat person are good enough to risk playing C at $t = 1$. So if at $t = 1$ A does play C, this observation *cannot* reduce B's confidence that A is a tit-for-tat person. Thus B will also choose C at $t = 2$.
		D	D	D	D	D	2	p	5	8	
			D	C	D	D	3	$(1 - p)r$	9	6	
		D	D	D	D	D	4	$(1 - p)r$	5	8	
			D	D	D	D	5	$(1 - p)(1 - r)$	8	5	2 An instrumentally rational A will *never* play C beyond the first round
		C	D	D	D	D	6	$(1 - p)(1 - r)$	6	6	

Tit-for-tat person (p)

Instrumentally rational $(1 - p)$

C (r)

D $(1 - r)$

A ●

$t = 0$ $t = 1$ $t = 2$ $t = 3$

Probabilities in brackets under arrows. In each round players choose without knowing the choice/strategy of their opponent in that round. All they know is how their opponent played in previous rounds.

Figure 6.2

player B can expect pay-off 2 (with probability $1 - p$) since both he and A will defect. Similarly, the expected returns to B from defecting at $t = 2$ are

ER^B(from defecting at $t = 2$ | cooperation occurred at $t = 1$) =
$4p + 2(1 - p) + 2$ (6.5)

An explanation: if B defects at $t = 2$ when A is a genuine tit-for-tat follower, then he gets pay-off 4. The probability of this happening is p. However, there is always a chance $(1 - p)$ that A will also defect (that is, if she is not a tit-for-tat player) in which case A receives pay-off 2. At $t = 3$, if B has defected at $t = 2$, then mutual defection will follow (a sure pay-off of 2).

When B selects the strategy with the greatest expected return, it follows that at $t = 2$ B will cooperate if $p > \frac{1}{2}$ (that is, when (6.4) > (6.5)). As for player A, if she is a tit-for-tat player then, provided B cooperated at $t = 1$, she will cooperate at $t = 2$. If she is not, then she will defect at $t = 2$ hoping that B will cooperate (knowing that B will defect at $t = 3$ and so defect is best then *and* at $t = 2$). Condition (6.6) specifies the condition for B to cooperate at $t = 2$:

B will cooperate if and only if $p > \frac{1}{2}$ (6.6)

$t = 1$: We have arrived at the most interesting part of the game. At $t = 2$ player B may or may not cooperate depending on A's reputation as a player who follows the norm of tit-for-tat. Player A, if not that sort of player, will always defect at $t = 2$. Things are, however, quite different at $t = 1$. Indeed, even a player in A's position who is *not* a tit-for-tat type may choose to start this game by cooperating! This is why:

An instrumentally rational player A has a reason to pretend to follow a tit-for-tat strategy at $t = 1$ (that is, to cooperate) if this is what is needed to make B expect further cooperation in rounds 2 and 3. If it works, then she will collect the fruits of cooperation at $t = 1$ (pay-off 3) and at $t = 2$ will defect thus claiming pay-off 4. Once she has revealed that she is not following a tit-for-tat strategy, at $t = 3$ she will receive pay-off 2 (as both will defect). Her overall pay-offs from all three rounds would be $3 + 4 + 2 = 9$ – the maximum possible. Thus, at $t = 1$ there are two reasons why player A may cooperate: (a) she is genuinely a tit-for-tat type, and (b) she is pretending to be cooperative in order to create (or to retain) a reputation for being a tit-for-tat type. Suppose that ρ is the probability that (b) is the case and let B's estimate of ρ be given by probability r. Then B's expectation that player A will cooperate at $t = 1$ equals $p + r(1 - p)$. His expected returns are

ER^B(from cooperating at $t = 1$) = $p(3 + 3 + 4) + (1 - p)r(3 + 1 + 2) + [1 - p - r(1 - p)](1 + 2 + 2)$ (6.7)

181

ER^B(from defecting at $t = 1$) $= p(4 + 2 + 2) + (1 - p)r(4 + 2 + 2)$
$+ [1 - p - r(1 - p)](2 + 2 + 2)$ (6.8)

The simplest explanation of the above is to be had from a tree-like representation of all potentialities – see Figure 6.2. Note that if B co-operates he will receive the string of pay-offs 3, 3, 4 (at $t = 1, 2, 3$) if A is playing tit-for-tat, or string 3, 1, 2 if A was simply pretending at $t = 1$, or string 1, 2, 2 if B defects in each of the three rounds. The probabilities of these strings are p, $r(1 - p)$ and $1 - p - r(1-p)$ respectively. Similarly, the strings which are possible (with the same probabilities) when B defects at $t = 1$ are: 4, 2, 2; 4, 2, 2; and 2, 2, 2.

Summing up, player B will cooperate at $t = 1$ if (6.7) > (6.8), or if

$$r < (3p - 1)/(1 - p)$$ (6.9)

Suppose that $p = \frac{1}{2}$ at $t = 1$. Then (6.9) always holds and, thus, player B will cooperate whatever his expectations about the behaviour of an A who is contemplating bluffing. In effect, as long as there is a 50–50 chance that player A follows a tit-for-tat strategy, player B will want to take the risk of cooperating at the very beginning: A's reputation for cooperation is suffi-ciently high. Now suppose that $p = \frac{1}{3}$ or less. Then, nothing (i.e. even if $r = 0$) can make B cooperate at $t = 1$: A's reputation as a genuine tit-for-tat follower is too low for B to risk it. This means that player A will not rationally cooperate at $t = 1$ as part of a bluff (provided of course she knows the values of r and p). Interestingly, if player A *does* cooperate at $t = 1$, she must be a genuine tit-for-tat follower. This is a case of a *revealing equilibrium* (as it is known in the literature). By behaving in a manner that would not be in the interest of a 'non-cooperator', the tit-for-tat follower reveals her identity.

Example Let $r = \frac{1}{2}$ and $p = \frac{2}{5}$. From (6.9) it follows that player B will not cooperate at $t = 1$. If A knows the values of r and p, then she will not cooperate either unless she is a genuine tit-for-tat follower. If, on the other hand, $r = \frac{1}{4}$ and $p = \frac{2}{5}$, then B would risk cooperation at $t = 1$. For this reason (provided again we make the assumption that the values of r and p are common knowledge), even a player A who is not committed to tit-for-tat will cooperate at $t = 1$ in order to play along with B's expectations of her. Her reason is that, in this way, she will receive the cooperative pay-off (3) at $t = 1$ and at $t = 2$ will get an opportunity to zap player B thus receiving pay-off 4. At this stage, we should not really feel sorry for player B – his motivation for cooperating at $t = 1$ is to play along (with what he believes to be A's tit-for-tat idiosyncratic behaviour) in order to zap her at $t = 3$. It all boils down to who is going to get the other one first. The interesting bit is that, in spite of the pervasive unpleasantness of their motives, in the end they may end up cooperating at $t = 1$. *Indeed it can be demonstrated that, the greater the number of repetitions of this game, the longer they may cooperate before they try to zap each other.* Thus what looks like moral behaviour is actually underpinned by sophisticated selfishness.

6.5.2 Learning

Let us now connect the initial beliefs of player B before the play of the prisoners' dilemma at $t = 1$ with what he believes after $t = 1$. Suppose for instance that he observes cooperation by player A. How should he filter that information? To be more precise, suppose that before $t = 1$ his expectation that A is a genuine tit-for-tat person is p_1. What should p_2 be – i.e. what should the level of p be just before $t = 2$ once player A has chosen cooperatively at $t = 1$?

Notice that p_2 is a conditional probability with the event 'A chose cooperatively at $t = 1$' doing the conditioning. A simple probability theorem referred to as **Bayes's rule** (see Chapter 1) offers an easy answer to our problem. Suppose there exist two events: X and Y. Recalling the explanation of how Bayes's rule works in Chapter 1, suppose you have just observed Y. What is then the probability of X also occurring? According to Bayes's rule, the conditional probability of X given Y $[\Pr(X|Y)]$ is

$$\Pr(XY) = \{\Pr(Y|X)\Pr(X)\}/[\{\Pr(Y|X)\Pr(X)\}+ \{\Pr(Y|\text{not } X)\Pr(\text{not } X)\}] \tag{6.10}$$

As an example consider the case where X is 'cloud in the morning' and Y is 'rain in the afternoon'. If we have just observed a cloudy morning sky, what is the chance of rain in the afternoon? Suppose we know that the probabilities of (i) cloud in the morning when it rains in the afternoon, (ii) cloud in the morning, (iii) rain following a sunny morning are $\frac{3}{4}$, $\frac{1}{3}$ and $\frac{1}{4}$ respectively. Substitution in (6.10) yields a conditional probability of $\frac{3}{5}$. This means that, following the observation that the morning was cloudy, the probability with which one should expect rain in the afternoon is $\frac{3}{5}$. Learning here takes the form of using observation in order to form a better probability estimate of the uncertain phenomenon one is interested in. In Bayesian language this is referred to as converting, by means of empirical evidence, prior beliefs into posterior beliefs.

We shall apply (6.10) to our example. If we think of Y as the event 'player A is a genuine follower of tit-for-tat' and event X as 'player A cooperated a $t = 1$', how can player B use the observation of the latter in order to update his probabilistic (prior) belief about the former? Equation (6.10) can be used directly. The numerator of the right hand side equals p_1 – notice that the probability of a tit-for-tat player cooperating at $t = 1$ equals one. The denominator equals $p_1 + (1 - p_1)r$ – since the probability that a player A is not genuinely cooperative but still cooperates equals $(1 - p_1)r$. Thus,

$$p_2 = p_1/[p_1 + (1 - p_1)r] \qquad\qquad (6.11)$$

Example Using numerical values from the previous example, suppose $p_1 = \frac{2}{5}$ and $r = \frac{1}{4}$. If player A cooperates at $t = 1$, equation (6.11) suggests that her reputation as a tit-for-tatter will jump from $\frac{2}{5}$ to $\frac{8}{11}$. Surely this will not escape an unscrupulous A who wants to lead B to expect cooperation from her in both rounds $t = 2$ and $t = 3$. Nevertheless, there are limits for this type of 'learning' imposed by the structure of the game. As we saw already, if p_1 is more than $\frac{1}{2}$ or less than $\frac{1}{3}$, then player A cannot do anything to change B's beliefs in the subtle manner of equation (6.10) since even an uncooperative A is expected to cooperate in order to retain her high reputation.

When $p_1 < \frac{1}{3}$, nothing A can do will ever convince B to give cooperation a chance. We conclude that the type of learning offered by (6.10) is possible only when A's initial reputation lies in the region $(\frac{1}{3}, \frac{1}{2})$. If it is greater than that cooperation will take place regardless; if it is lower it will never take place. In either case, learning will have to be abrupt. For instance, if $p_1 < \frac{1}{3}$ and A cooperates at $t = 1$, B will immediately conclude that he was wrong about A and that she was indeed a tit-for-tatter. Of course, by that time, he will have lost the opportunity to take advantage of this. If $p_1 > \frac{1}{2}$ (B cooperates) and A defects at $t = 1$, he will again realise he was wrong, only this time he will have suffered a serious loss.

6.5.3 The return of common knowledge and the sequential equilibrium

In order to tell a more particular story as to what will happen, many game theorists make the assumption that the probabilistic thoughts of one agent are known by the other accurately. To be more precise, they assume (in exactly the same way as in the case of Nash equilibrium mixed strategies, see sections 2.7.2–2.7.4) that agents' subjective probabilities are common knowledge. We have already explained in Chapter 2 our reservation with respect to this type of application of common knowledge rationality and so we shall not rehearse the arguments again. At first glance, though, it may seem that the introduction of CKR and CAB raises particular difficulties here. After all, the point of the analysis is to understand what might happen when we relax CKR and allow for the possibility of tit-for-tat behaviour. However, there need be no inconsistency on this matter. We can assume CKR and still allow for the possibility of tit-for-tat behaviour by turning the

→ Common Knowledge ≠ instrumental rationality

game into one of incomplete information by allowing for uncertainty over the types of player playing the game. Thus we could allow for a type of player whose pay-offs are such that, when acting instrumentally rationally, his or her behaviour corresponds to tit-for-tat. In this way doubt over whether a player will play tit-for-tat is to be understood as doubt over whether he or she is that type of player and not doubt over whether he or she is instrumentally rational.

Recall that ρ was the probability with which a non-cooperative player A will cooperate at $t = 1$. Probability r captured player B's estimate of ρ. It is assumed now that $r = \rho$. Moreover, in a CAB logic identical to the one underpinning Nash equilibrium mixed strategies, it is assumed that each agent's expected returns from strategies 'defect' and 'cooperate' at $t = 1$ must be equal. Hence (6.9) converts into an equality.

Substitution of the equality version of (6.9) in (6.11) simplifies the belief updating mechanism to

$$p_2 = p_1/(4p_1 - 1) \tag{6.12}$$

In the example where $p_1 = \frac{2}{5}$ this means that $p_2 = \frac{2}{3}$. The suggestion here is that if, at the beginning, B thinks that the probability of A being a tit-for-tat follower is $\frac{2}{5}$, then if A actually cooperates at $t = 1$ that belief is updated and A's cooperative reputation rises (in the eyes of B) to $p_2 = \frac{2}{3}$. Notice that in this version of the game the value of r is immaterial because it is assumed to be commonly known and exactly equal to the value that would make B indifferent between cooperating and defecting at $t = 1$. In terms of the analysis in section 3.5, equation (6.11) delineates a sequential equilibrium.

6.5.4 Two illustrations: predatory pricing and political manoeuvring

Figure 6.3 offers two examples of the ways in which reputation games can be applied in a variety of contexts. The first example comes from strategic decisions by the legislature when the Executive is trying to push through Parliament a series of bills that the latter is unsympathetic towards. The second example is borrowed from the large literature on price wars instigated by incumbent firms which willingly choose to incur losses battling entrants in their market. As the pay-offs are identical, a common analysis of the two situations follows.

In the first example, the President proposes legislation. The Congress is not in sympathy with the proposal and must decide whether to make amendments. If it decides to make an amendment, then the President must decide whether to fight the amendment or acquiesce. Looking at the President's pay-offs it is obvious that, even though he or she prefers that the Congress does not amend the legislation, if it does, he or she would

Congress/ President			Entrant/ incumbent		
Congress does not amend	0	3	Entrant stays out	0	3
Congress amends and President acquiesces	$\frac{1}{2}$	2	Entrant enters and incumbent submits	$\frac{1}{2}$	2
Congress amends and President fights	$-\frac{1}{2}$	1	Entrant enters and incumbent fights	$-\frac{1}{2}$	1

Figure 6.3

not want to fight on the floor of the House. In the second example, an incumbent firm with the assigned pay-offs will wish that the entrant stays out of its market but, if the entrant enters, fighting a price war would be the worst possible outcome for the incumbent. The equilibrium solution in the one-shot version of this game is simple enough: the Congress amends and the President gives in, while the entrant enters without facing a price war.

Suppose now that these games are repeated. If they are infinitely repeated, then all sorts of outcomes are possible – the Folk theorem ensures that an infinity of war/acquiescence patterns are compatible with instrumental rationality. Nevertheless, the duration of such games is usually finite and sometimes their length is definite – e.g. US Presidents have a fixed term and incumbents have only a fixed number of local markets that they wish to defend. What happens then? Would it make sense for the President or the incumbent to put on a show of strength early on (e.g. by fighting the Congress or unleashing a price war) in order to create a reputation for belligerence that would make the Congress and the entrant think that, in future rounds, they will end up with pay-off $-\frac{1}{2}$ if they dare them?

In the finitely repeated version of the game Nash backward induction argues against this conclusion. Just as in the case of the prisoners' dilemma in the previous subsection, it suggests that, since there will be no fighting at the last play of the game, the reputation of the President/incumbent will unravel to the first stage and no fighting will occur (rationally). The conclusion changes again once we drop CKR (or allow for different types of players).

Recall the reason why tit-for-tat-like cooperative behaviour was possible: it became instrumentally rational the moment some doubt was introduced in the mind of player B about A's motivation. Similarly, in the examples of Figure 6.3 such reputation effects can play a role once we allow for some uncertainty. For instance, suppose that there is a small chance the President is unbending and that once he or she is committed to a policy he or she is prepared to fight doggedly for it (perhaps irrationally) *irrespective of his or her pay-offs*. Or, that an incumbent may be conditioned to waging price wars regardless of their effect on the bottom line (alternatively, imagine that there is a chance that the incumbent has already built up sufficient excess capacity to make low prices profitable in the presence of competition). Let the probability of these events be (as before) equal to p.

It is easy to see that as long as $p > \frac{1}{2}$, then in the last play of the game the Congress/entrant will hesitate. (Compare this to condition (6.6) above.) Moreover, one can see how the rest of the analysis of tit-for-tat reputation building from the previous subsection carries over. What are the expected pay-offs for the Congress/entrant if they amend/enter in the penultimate round? The potential pay-offs are $\frac{1}{2}$ and $-\frac{1}{2}$ and the probability of conflict with the President/incumbent equals $p + (1 - p)r$, where p is the probability that the latter is belligerent and r is the probability that a 'soft' President/incumbent will act 'tough' in order to cultivate a suitable reputation for the next round. The expected returns from amending/entering are, therefore, $(\frac{1}{2})[p + (1 - p)r] - (\frac{1}{2})[1 - p - (1 - p)r]$ and the expected returns from staying put are zero. Thus, the equivalent of inequality (6.9) above is

$$r > (\tfrac{1}{2} - p)/(1 - p) \tag{6.13}$$

Just as (6.9) was the condition for cooperation by B at $t = 2$, (6.13) is the condition that must hold during any round prior to the last one so that the Congress/entrant refrains from challenging the President/incumbent in that round.

Finally, when a President/incumbent fights an amendment/entry, the opposition learns by using exactly the same belief updating mechanism as that in (6.11). Indeed clever Presidents and incumbents will want to use (6.11) in order to build a propitious reputation. And, the more often the game is repeated, the more room the agent whose character is cloaked in mystery will have to indulge in demonstrations of his or her aggression. Thus relatively small doubt in the minds of Congress early on in a President's term can deter amendment. Nevertheless it becomes increasingly likely that, as time goes by, the Congress will make amendments and that the President will be turned into a lame duck (see the adjacent box).

Box 6.3

SMALL DOUBTS AND LAME DUCK PRESIDENTS

Suppose the last play of the game between the Congress and the President occurs in time T. We know that if the Congress entertains probabilistic doubt of p greater than, or equal to, $\frac{1}{2}$ (p being the probabilistic expectation that the President is dogmatically unbending) in the last play then it is no longer certain that the Congress will amend the legislation in that period. This, then, is the condition which must be satisfied if we are to avoid the logic of backward induction taking hold to produce an equilibrium with amendments and acquiescence in all time periods.

The interesting feature of this game is that the doubt in the Congress's mind can be considerably less than this in earlier plays of the game and yet the Congress can still believe that this terminal value of $p = \frac{1}{2}$ could be reached in time T. This thought provides the key to constructing a sequential equilibrium where amendments do not necessarily occur, at least in early plays of the game. The reason behind this result is that the President can exploit Bayes's rule to build a reputation for being dogmatic by acting dogmatically in earlier plays of the game. This means there may be some early plays of the game when the Congress will decide there is no point in amending legislation because the President will always fight these amendments.

In formal terms you can see from the expressions for Bayes's rule in (6.10) and (6.11) that the President can boost his or her reputation (increase the value of p) by selecting a value for r between zero and one in earlier rounds of the game: that is, by behaving dogmatically with some positive probability. You will also note that building a reputation in this way is risky, in the sense that the President cannot simply always fight amendments (i.e. $r = 1$); there must be some positive chance that he or she will acquiesce. This is so because, when the ordinary President always fights, there is a difference between the behaviour of a dogged and an ordinary President in this regard and so the evidence of a fight would not provide a reason for revising beliefs about the type of President. It is only when a President fights and there is some chance that an ordinary President will not fight that there is a reason for updating beliefs about the type of President. But this is risky because it means there is always some chance that an ordinary President does not fight an amendment and the moment this happens, the doubt vanishes because only ordinary Presidents do not fight amendments.

Let us now trace the values of r and p in earlier periods which are *just* consistent with building a reputation of $p = \frac{1}{2}$ by time T and with leaving the Congress indifferent in each time period between amending and not-amending. Consider the penultimate play in $T - 1$. We know from (6.13) that the Congress will be indifferent between amending and not amending when

$$r_{T-1} = (0.5 - p_{T-1})/(1 - p_{T-1})$$

and we know from Bayes's rule in (6.11) that to achieve $p = \frac{1}{2}$ by time T, the following relationship must hold between r and p in $T - 1$:

$$0.5 = p_{T-1}/[p_{T-1} + (1 - p_{T-1})r_{T-1}]$$

Solving these two expressions, we obtain the result that when r is selected in this way, the value of p in $T - 1$ which makes the Congress *just* indifferent is $(\frac{1}{2})^2$. This analysis can be repeated identically for all periods and we obtain the locus drawn in the figure below for the values of p in each time period which will make the Congress indifferent when the President selects r in order to maintain the possibility of just building the terminal reputation in T to $p = \frac{1}{2}$.

We shall suppose that the President is elected in time 0 and that the initial doubt in the Congress's mind at this time about how dogmatic the President is, is given by p_0. In this game, there is a sequential equilibrium which has the President proposing pieces of legislation which are not amended until time k. The reason is that the Congress realises that the President does not have to start building a reputation for doggedness in these early periods as the current doubt (p_0) exceeds the crucial value in each time period which must be achieved to keep on a possible course for achieving the terminal value of $p = \frac{1}{2}$ in time T. Furthermore since reputation building is risky (i.e. there must be some chance that the President does not fight an amendment and so reveal his or her true character), the President will delay as long as possible. Thus, he or she can always afford to fight an amendment before time k with certainty. Realising this, the Congress will definitely not propose amendments until time k. Thereafter the President proposes legislation and there is always the chance that it will be amended (since at time k with $p = p_0$, the Congress is indifferent between amending and not amending) and once amended there is always a chance that the President will acquiesce (since r is less than one during the reputation building phase). If he or she fights then the reputation advances up the locus depicted and the game repeats itself. If he or she acquiesces, then his or her identity is revealed and thereafter the Congress always amends and the President always acquiesces.

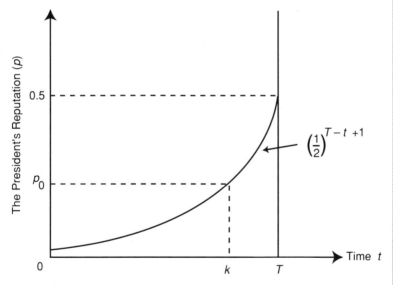

In other words, there is a period when the President gets his or her way, early in office. This gives way to a period where the Congress tests the President and it becomes increasingly likely, the closer you get to the last period, that the identity of the President will have been revealed by these tests (for the same reason that the probability of tossing two consecutive heads is less than tossing one). At this point, he or she will have become a lame duck, acquiescing in all legislative amendments.

6.6 SIGNALLING BEHAVIOUR

The reputation creating behaviours in previous sections are one of a kind. In each case a person plays the game now in a particular way in order to create an expectation of future play which will encourage the other player to play in a particular way in that future. Of course, there may be actions that can be taken outside the game and which have a similar effect on the beliefs of others. Such 'signalling' behaviour is considered briefly in this section to round out the discussion of reputations. It is of potential relevance not only to repeated, but also to one-shot games.

A famous illustration comes from Spence (1974). Let us suppose that out of n people who apply for managerial positions, half of them are of high ability while the rest are of low ability. Suppose that employers have no direct way of identifying worker quality as this only becomes apparent after a number of months on the job. Suppose also each employee has the option to undertake a Masters in Business Administration (MBA) at considerable personal cost. Spence shows that it may make sense to do the course because it signals that the employee is of high quality *even if the MBA is useless from an educational point of view and employers are fully aware of this!*

To simplify the problem, suppose that:

(i)   High ability employees generate 5 units of output per period.
(ii) Low ability employees generate 3 units of output per period.
(iii) Doing the MBA course costs high quality employees less than low quality employees (1.25 as opposed to 2.5 units). (The assumption here is that high quality is correlated with the capacity to survive more easily the strains of an MBA course.)
(iv) Competition between employers drives their profits to zero (this is a convenient and inessential assumption; we could have equally well argued that competition forces profits to, say, x units per period for each employer).

One Nash equilibrium in this labour market has all employers offering a wage equal to 4 units of output per period to all employees and no employee enrolling on an MBA course. An MBA is known to be useless and will have no effect on salaries since the employer does not think that an MBA is indicative of high or low ability. The probability remains 0.5 for each type. This is referred to as a *pooling* (or non-revealing) Nash equilibrium because there is no distinction between employees. To see why it is a Nash equilibrium, first notice that the zero-profit assumption in (iv) above is satisfied because the expected benefits from one employee [0.5(3) + 0.5(5)] equal the wage cost [4]. Further, there is no incentive for either type of employee to acquire an MBA because it is costly and it does not affect the wage. Hence the employers have no incentive to make the wage conditionally vary with an MBA given their beliefs. (Notice that these

---

Box 6.4

SELF-FULFILLING SEXIST BELIEFS AND LOW PAY FOR WOMEN

Suppose employers are sexist and think that an MBA is a stronger signal of high ability in men than in women. We also suppose, not implausibly, that high ability women find it more costly to acquire MBAs than high ability men because they live in a world where they are expected to do more in the household than men: so it costs them 1.75 units (compared with 1.25 for high quality men). Further we assume that men are as likely to be highly able as women and that half the labour pool is men and half is women. With the earlier assumption that half the labour pool has high ability, we have a new separating (or revealing) Nash equilibrium.

Men with high ability acquire MBAs and are paid 5 and all others do not acquire education and are paid 3.5. To check that this is a Nash equilibrium, first notice that the zero expected profit condition holds (let q = the proportion of MBA holding men employed; then expected profits = $q(5 - 5) + (1 - q)([0.75][3] + [0.25][5] - 3.5) = 0$). There is only an incentive for high ability male employees to acquire an MBA because the wage gain of 1.5 exceeds the cost (1.25). Notice in particular that there is no incentive for high ability women to do likewise because the expected wage gain does not exceed the cost (and this holds even when women mistakenly believe they would get the higher wage of 5 which men with MBAs get). *Consequently, the sexist belief of employers that holding an MBA denotes high ability in men but not in women is never tested.* In this instance, the character of the employers' beliefs would help explain why high ability women are paid less than high ability men.

---

beliefs are never tested (in this equilibrium) because no one acquires an MBA.)

Suppose, however, that employers (for some reason) believe that an MBA signals high ability. Then another Nash equilibrium exists which is referred to as *separating* (or revealing): it is called this because it separates employees between those who receive a high and those who receive a low wage on the basis of a signal. In particular, those who hold an MBA are paid 5 and those without are paid 3. Moreover, the high ability employees will enrol at their nearest business school on an MBA course while low ability ones will not. Again it is easy to check that this is a Nash equilibrium because with those wages only the high ability employees have the incentive to do an MBA course: the wage gain from an MBA is 2 whereas the cost of doing an MBA is 2.5 for low ability workers but only 1.25 for high ability workers. Thus the employers' beliefs are confirmed by the actual behaviour of employees even though undertaking an MBA degree has no positive effect on productivity; and with these behaviours the wages offered will always satisfy the zero-profit condition as the wage exactly covers each worker's productivity. The loop is complete. We start with the assumption that employers (somehow) have come to think that an MBA is a signal of ability. Once this belief is in place *it* sets into motion a set of actions which confirm it!

The example is interesting for at least two reasons. Firstly it reveals yet again the importance of *which* beliefs agents are assumed to hold; and there is no obvious reason for preferring one set to another. After all, what is wrong with the employers' belief that an MBA has no effect on ability? By assumption in the model, this type of education really does not have any effect on ability. Secondly, it provides an interesting explanation of the recent trend of a high correlation between managerial salaries and MBAs. The normal explanation revolves around business education making people more productive (an investment in human capital, no less). Against this, we now see that business schools need not contribute to productivity and yet their qualifications may be associated with high earnings. Perhaps they signal something which is valuable given the beliefs of the employers. The latter are plainly crucial as we have seen and it is not difficult to construct more complicated beliefs which could also explain other aspects of income distribution (see Box 6.4 on self-fulfilling sexist beliefs).

6.7 REPETITION, STABILITY AND A FINAL WORD ON THE NASH EQUILIBRIUM CONCEPT

We have doubted earlier whether we should expect the Nash equilibrium in one-shot games, even when the game has a unique Nash equilibrium (see sections 2.3–2.5). In such games, there is no obvious reason for supposing that everyone's *ex ante* and *ex post* beliefs are aligned. However, when the game is repeated and there is a unique Nash equilibrium things change. The Nash equilibrium is attractive because as time goes by and agents adjust their expectations of what others will do in the light of experience, then they will seem naturally drawn to the Nash equilibrium because it is the only resting place for beliefs. Any other set of beliefs will upset itself.

Nevertheless, there is still no guarantee that a Nash equilibrium will surface even if it exists and it is unique. Recall the game in Figure 2.6 of Chapter 2 which features a unique Nash equilibrium pair of strategies: (R2, C2). Suppose during the first round, R chooses R1 and C chooses C3. From the analysis in Chapter 2 it is clear that player R will be disappointed since her choice of R1 must have been preceded by the expectation that C would play C1. Player C, on the other hand, had his expectation confirmed (since his C3 choice must have been based on the expectation that R would choose R1; which is exactly what she did). Thus one of our players has just realised she made a mistake. What will she choose next time? To answer this, we must make assumptions about the way in which forecasting errors feed into behaviour.

Let us make the simple assumption that players who realise they were wrong change their behaviour, while those who were right do not. Then, in our example, next time the game is played our players will choose R3 and C3 (notice that R3 is the best response by R to C3). However, this time player C will be frustrated as he realises that he was mistaken to assume that R would again choose R1. In the next round, he will play C1 (which is the best response to R1) and, by assumption, player R will stick to R3 (since during the last round her prediction was correct). It is easy to see that this type of *adaptive* learning will never lead the players to the Nash equilibrium outcome (R2, C2). Instead, they will be oscillating between outcomes (R1, C1), (R1, C3), (R3, C1) and (R3, C3).

Can they break away from this never ending cycle and hit the Nash equilibrium? They can provided they converge onto a common forward looking train of thought. For instance, after the first round in which outcome (R1, C3) materialised, player C may anticipate that R will be unhappy by what has happened. Thus C may not expect R to play R1 again (even though he had previously predicted R1 and R1 occurred), in which case he will not play C3 again as he no longer expects R to repeat her R1 choice. In that case anything goes. The strength of the Nash equilibrium is that forward looking agents may realise that (R2, C2) is the only outcome that does not engender such thoughts. We just saw that adaptive (or backward looking) expectations will not do the trick. If, however, after having been around the pay-off matrix a few times players ask themselves the question 'How can we reach a stable outcome?', they may very well conclude that the only such outcome is the Nash equilibrium (R2, C2).

But why would they want to ask such a question? What is so wrong with instability (and disequilibrium) after all? Indeed in the case of Figure 2.6 our players have an incentive to *avoid* a stable outcome (observe that on average the cycle which takes them from one extremity of the pay-off matrix to another yields a much higher pay-off than the Nash equilibrium result). If, on the other hand, pay-offs were as in Figure 6.4 below, they would be strongly motivated to reach the Nash equilibrium.

The structure of the above game may be identical to that in Figure 2.6

	C1	C2	C3
R1	$^+1, 0$	0, 0	0, 1^-
R2	0, 0	$^+100, 100^-$	0, 0
R3	0, 2^-	0, 0	$^+1, 0$

Figure 6.4

193

but there is a real difference in that here our players have a reason to focus their minds on ways of getting to the Nash equilibrium since cycling is not profitable. Thus we conclude that whether repetition makes the Nash equilibrium more or less likely when it is unique must depend on the contingencies of how people learn and the precise pay-offs from non-Nash behaviour.

6.8 CONCLUSION

This chapter has considered games which are repeated under a variety of conditions. This usefully expands the scope of game theory, not only by adding to its domain of application but also because it introduces the idea of endogenous reputation creation. However, it also has the effect of highlighting the weaknesses of game theory which have already been noted in the discussion of one-shot games. Namely, the difficulty with explaining prior beliefs which agents hold when these beliefs affect the character of the equilibrium and the difficulty with explaining how agents select one Nash equilibrium when there are many.

Broadly put, this is one and the same problem. It is a problem with specifying how agents come to hold beliefs which are extraneous to the game (in the sense that they cannot be generated endogenously through the application of the assumptions of instrumental rationality and common knowledge of instrumental rationality) and which nevertheless profoundly affect behaviour in the game. (For instance, in this sense, recall the importance of the prior beliefs about the likelihood that a player is a follower of tit-for-tat or the beliefs of employers about the value of an MBA.) To take the argument forward on this point we need to say something about the source of extraneous beliefs; and this is the challenge of evolutionary game theory.

7

EVOLUTIONARY GAMES

7.1 INTRODUCTION: SPONTANEOUS ORDER VERSUS POLITICAL RATIONALISM

Evolutionary game theory is central to a number of themes of this book. Firstly it addresses our concerns over the rationality and·common knowledge of rationality (CKR) assumptions used by mainstream game theory. It does this by introducing a more modest assumption that has people adjusting their behaviour on a trial and error basis towards the action which yields the highest pay-off. Many find this more plausible than the pyrotechnics which conventional game theory often seems to demand from its agents under the guise of 'being rational' (see the discussion of CKR and CAB in Chapter 2). Secondly it potentially helps with the problem of equilibrium selection (which, as we have seen, has come to haunt the mainstream) by offering an account of the origin of conventions. Finally, the insights of evolutionary game theory are crucial material for many political and philosophical debates, especially those around the State.

To appreciate this last contribution, recall where we left the discussion of collective action agencies like the State in section 6.4. The argument for such an agency turns on the general problem of equilibrium selection and on the particular difficulty of overcoming the prisoners' dilemma. When there are multiple equilibria, the State can, through suitable action on its own part, guide the outcomes towards one equilibrium rather than another. Thus the problem of equilibrium selection is solved by bringing it within the ambit of conscious political decision making. Likewise, with the prisoners' dilemma/ free rider problem, the State can provide the services of enforcement. Alternatively when the game is repeated sufficiently and the issue again becomes one of equilibrium selection, then the State can guide the outcomes towards the cooperative Nash equilibrium.

This argument for a collective action agency is contested by the ideas of what Anderson (1992) calls the 'intransigent Right'. These ideas are closely associated with a quartet of 20th century thinkers, Strauss, Schmitt, Oakeshott and Hayek, and they plausibly now shape 'a large part of the mental world of end-of-the-century Western politics'. The lineage is, of course, much longer and, as Anderson suggests, Hayek (1962) himself traces the battlelines in the dispute back to the beginning of Enlightenment thinking:

> Hayek distinguished two intellectual lines of thought about freedom, of radically opposite upshot. The first was an empiricist, essentially British tradition descending from Hume, Smith and Ferguson, and seconded by Burke and Tucker, which understood political development as an involuntary process of gradual institutional improvement, comparable to the workings of a market economy or the evolution of common law. The second was a rationalist, typically French lineage descending from Descartes through Condorcet to Comte, with a horde of modern successors, which saw social institutions as fit for premeditated construction, in the spirit of polytechnic engineering. The former line led to real liberty; the latter inevitably destroyed it. (p. 9)

Some of the specific arguments of the 'intransigent Right' have turned on the difficulties associated with political decision making and State action. For instance, there are problems of inadequate knowledge which can mean that even the best intentioned and executed political decision generates unintended and undesirable consequences. Indeed this has always been an important theme in Austrian economics, featuring strongly in the 1920s debate over the possibility of socialist planning as well as contemporary doubts over the wisdom of more minor forms of State intervention.

Likewise, there are problems of 'political failure' that subvert the ideal of democratic decision making and which can match the market failures that the State is attempting to rectify. For example, Buchanan and Wagner (1977) and Tullock (1965) argue that special interests are bound to skew 'democratic decisions' towards excessively large bureaucracies and high government expenditures. Furthermore there are difficulties, especially after the Arrow impossibility theorem, with making sense of the very idea of something like the 'will of the people' in whose name the State might be acting (see Arrow, 1951, Riker, 1982, Hayek, 1962, and Buchanan, 1954).[1]

These, so to speak, are a shorthand list of the negative arguments coming from the political right against 'political rationalism' or 'social constructivism' – that is, the idea that you can turn social outcomes into matters of social choice through the intervention of a collective action agency like the State. The positive argument against 'political rationalism', as the quote above suggests, turns on the idea that these interventions are *not* even necessary. The failure to intervene does not spell chaos, chronic indecision, fluctuations and outcomes in which everyone is worse off than they could have been. Instead, a 'spontaneous order' will be thrown up as a result of evolutionary processes.

This is why evolutionary game theory assumes significance in the debate over an active State. It should help assess the claims of 'spontaneous order' made by those in the British corner and so advance one of the central debates in Enlightenment political thinking.

The next three sections set out the evolutionary approach using a repeated hawk–dove and pure coordination game. Section 7.3 draws some inferences from the evolutionary approach, focusing in particular on whether the conventions which emerge in evolutionary play can form the basis for a satisfactory account of equilibrium selection. Section 7.5 focuses on the evolutionary play of the prisoners' dilemma game. Section 7.6 connects some of the formal insights from the evolutionary approach to wider debates within the social sciences over power, morality and historical change. In particular, we suggest that the evolutionary approach can help elucidate the idea that power is mobilised through institutions and conventions. We conclude the chapter with a summing-up of where the issue of equilibrium selection and the debate over the State stands after the contribution of the evolutionary approach.

7.2 EVOLUTIONARY STABILITY

7.2.1 Symmetry in evolution

The equilibrium concept used most frequently in evolutionary game theory was developed by the biologist Maynard Smith (1982) (for a slight variation see Axelrod (1984)). His concern was with the evolution of phenotypes (that is, with the patterns of behaviour of a species) and not genotypes (the genetic basis of behaviour). In particular he was looking for phenotypes within a population which are evolutionary stable in the sense that they cannot be 'invaded' by some other phenotype. In these terms, an 'invasion' means that some other type of behaviour proves more successful and so agents adopt it. Since 'types of behaviour' translate in game theoretical terms as strategies, the search is for *evolutionary stable strategies* (ESSs) – the term used by Maynard Smith.

The basic idea behind this equilibrium concept is that an ESS is a strategy which when used among some population cannot be 'invaded' by another strategy because it cannot be bested. So when a population uses a strategy I, 'mutants' using any other strategy J cannot get a toehold and expand among that population. To be specific, let us define the expected utility for a player (in the biological literature the equivalent to 'utility' is, of course, reproductive fitness) from using strategy I when the other player uses strategy J as $E(I,J)$.

Definition: Strategy I is an **evolutionary stable strategy** when the following two conditions hold:

197

$$E(I, I) \geq E(J, I) \text{ for all strategies } J \quad\quad (7.1)$$
Either $E(I, I) > E(J, I)$ or $E(I, J) > E(J, J)$
for all strategies J (7.2)

These conditions follow naturally from the basic idea sketched above. The first condition must hold if I is to be an equilibrium strategy: it must be at least as good a reply to itself as any other strategy, otherwise people will drift away from its use. The second condition must hold if the strategy is not to be prone to invasion by another strategy. To see why, observe that when (7.1) holds as an equality, a population playing I might be invaded by an individual playing J in the sense that a J-player would fare no worse than the I-players in these circumstances. To preclude a successful invasion of J-players, then either I must be strictly better than J when playing against I or, if this does not hold, I must be better when playing a J than J is when playing itself.

To illustrate how this idea might be applied in the social sciences consider a variant of the 'chicken' or 'hawk–dove' game (see Schotter (1981) and Sugden (1986) for more detailed applications). Let us suppose that two people interact over a disputed piece of property which is worth 2 utils to both players. Each player has the same set of options: they can either act aggressively, like a 'hawk', or they can acquiesce like a 'dove'. When both act as 'doves', they share the disputed resource. When one is 'hawkish' and the other is 'dove'-like, the 'hawk' gets the resource, while if both are 'hawks' they just fight. The pay-offs from such an interaction are given in Figure 7.1.

		Player C	
		Hawk	Dove
Player R	Hawk	−2, −2	2, 0
	Dove	0, 2	1, 1

Figure 7.1

Mainstream game theory would distinguish three Nash equilibria here: (Hawk, Dove), (Dove, Hawk) and a mixed strategy Nash equilibrium where each player plays hawk with probability of $\frac{1}{3}$. To develop the evolutionary treatment of this game, we suppose that people from some population randomly interact with each other in this manner. This is, if you like, a version of Hobbes's nightmare where there are no property rights and everyone you come across will potentially claim your goods. We also assume that individuals do not know what is the best strategy to pursue (which is highly probable since there are three Nash equilibria and even mainstream game theory offers no clear guidance on which to select). Instead people here just start employing *some* strategy, or a probabilistic mix of strategies, and they adjust their strategies using a learning process of trial and error.

To be specific, there are two ways to introduce learning. Either we can imagine that there is some proportion p $(0 < p < 1)$ of the population using the hawk strategy and some proportion playing dove $(1 - p)$, and assume that people switch between the use of the two strategies depending on how well they fare using one rather than the other. Or we can suppose that each person uses a mixed strategy and adjusts the probability mix based on his or her experience using each pure strategy (i.e. increasing p when the use of the hawk strategy is actually yielding better returns than the dove strategy and vice versa). Whichever story is told, the analysis is fundamentally the same. People are rational because they learn in the rough and ready sense that they adjust their strategies in the light of experience so as to move towards the strategy which shows the greatest pay-off in the repeated play of this game. Of course, such rationality need not reflect conscious learning: in the biological case it is ordinarily thought to arise because those who are fittest reproduce faster. The parallel here is that those who receive lower pay-offs in the long run tend to emulate those who receive high pay-offs.

To see how the use of the strategies will evolve under this learning process, consider the expected returns from each strategy when the probability of meeting a hawk is p (either because this is the proportion of the population currently opting for this strategy or because this is the average probability mix of strategies employed by people in the population):

$$E(H) = p(-2) + (1 - p)2 = 2 - 4p$$
$$E(D) = p(0) + (1 - p)1 = 1 - p$$

(Recall from Chapter 2 that the Nash equilibrium in mixed strategies NEMS requires that $E(H) = E(D)$ which, of course, leads to $p = \frac{1}{3}$.) Thus the expected return from being a hawk exceeds that of a dove when $p < \frac{1}{3}$ and so will encourage people to change to more hawk-like behaviour (that is, p will rise). Conversely when $p > \frac{1}{3}$, the expected return from being a dove is greater than that of a hawk and p will fall. Hence the conclusion that evolution will lead to a situation where one-third of the population are likely to use the hawk strategy, since any smaller likelihood and p rises (and any greater likelihood and p falls).

In fact, $p = \frac{1}{3}$ is an ESS (and this is implicit in what has already been said). To appreciate the point formally, suppose I is the strategy $p = \frac{1}{3}$ and J is any other strategy under which a player chooses H with probability p' $(p' \neq \frac{1}{3})$. $E(I, I) = E(J, I)$ in these circumstances, since with $p = \frac{1}{3}$ the expected return from H is the same as D and so *any* probability combination of them will yield the same expected return. From (7.2) we know that $p = \frac{1}{3}$ is an ESS only if $E(I, J) > E(J, J)$. But,

$$E(I, J) = p[-2p' - 2(1 - p')] + (1 - p)(1 - p') = \frac{4}{3} - 2p'$$
$$E(J, J) = p'[-2p' + 2(1 - p')] + (1 - p')^2 = 1 - 3p'^2$$

Through inspection, $E(I, J)$ always exceeds $E(J, J)$ and, therefore, condition (7.2) holds: *mixed strategy $p = \frac{1}{3}$ is an ESS.* In passing, it is worth recalling that the Nash equilibrium mixed strategy of this game is also given by $p = \frac{1}{3}$. So, perhaps somewhat surprisingly, the evolutionary play of this symmetric game provides support for the Nash equilibrium mixed strategy (NEMS) concept – see Chapter 2.

7.2.2 Asymmetrical evolution: role-specific behaviour

Biologists are also interested in the evolution of new phenotypes, and so they have studied the evolution of these games when new strategies (new phenotypes) for playing a game emerge. One way in which a new strategy arises without altering the structure of the game is by conditioning the play of an existing strategy on an extraneous feature of the interaction (that is, extraneous to the game theoretical representation). For instance, the extraneous feature of the interaction might be the respective girth, height, age, etc., of the players and it could be used to divide the players into either role R (because they are fat, tall, old, etc., depending on what extraneous feature is mobilised) or role C (when they are respectively thin, short, young, etc.). The new behavioural rule would then take the form of 'if you are assigned R then play strategy x ; and if you are C play strategy y'. Such a game is now said to be played *asymmetrically* in recognition of the fact that the players have learned to differentiate themselves and assign each person to a different role. Once this happens learning also becomes more nuanced as it is role specific. Nevertheless the evolution of this asymmetrically repeated game under the influence of such learning can be studied easily.

We suppose that p is now the probability that role R players will play 'hawk' (H), while q is the probability that role C players will play 'hawk'. Letting $E(X|K)$ mean the 'expected returns of a player who has characteristic K from choosing strategy X', the expected returns to role R and role C players from playing each strategy are now given by

$$E(H|R) = q(-2) + (1 - q)2 = 2 - 4q$$
$$E(D|R) = q(0) + (1 - q)1 = 1 - q$$
$$E(H|C) = p(-2) + (1 - p)2 = 2 - 4p$$
$$E(D|C) = p(0) + (1 - p)1 = 1 - p$$

With the same learning rule as before, we can infer that p will be adjusted upwards by role R players when $q < \frac{1}{3}$ and vice versa; and q will be adjusted upwards by role C players when $p < \frac{1}{3}$ and vice versa. Figure 7.2 plots these dynamics.

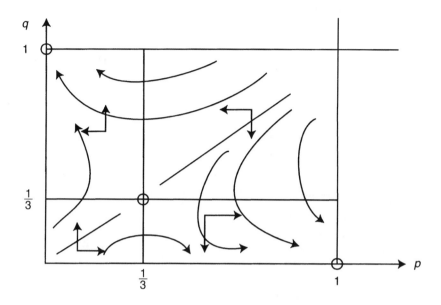

Figure 7.2

Inspection of this phase diagram reveals one unstable Nash equilibrium for the (p, q) pair at $(\frac{1}{3}, \frac{1}{3})$ and two Nash stable equilibria at $(1, 0)$ and $(0, 1)$ (the former is unstable because all trajectories (bar one) lead away from it[2]). So, discounting the unstable Nash equilibrium, the asymmetric version of the game evolves to a situation where either role R will always play hawk and C play dove, or vice versa. This is an interesting result. Before·we discuss it, the formal analysis needs to be completed by demonstrating that the two stable equilibria are ESSs.

As before, conditions (7.1) and (7.2) must be satisfied, only in these circumstances a strategy must be interpreted as a (p, q) pair and not just a singular probability p, as was the case under the symmetric version of the game. Strategies $(1, 0)$ and $(0, 1)$ clearly qualify under these conditions because the best response when your opponent is playing hawk with certainty is to play dove and vice versa. Now consider $I = (\frac{1}{3}, \frac{1}{3})$ (which is the NEMS from Chapter 2) and $J = (p', q')$, where $J \neq I$. Is I an ESS? Since $E(I, I) = E(J, I)$ here, the crucial condition that must be satisfied for stability is the second part of (7.2), that is

$$E(I, J) - E(J, J) = 3(p' - \tfrac{1}{3})(q' - \tfrac{1}{3}) > 0$$

However, this condition will only be satisfied if both p' and q' exceed $\frac{1}{3}$ or if both are less than $\frac{1}{3}$. For any other combinations of (p', q'), strategy $I = (\frac{1}{3},$

$\frac{1}{3}$) can be invaded. Thus it is not an ESS, a conclusion which adds to our suspicion in Chapter 2 that the Nash equilibrium in mixed strategies (NEMS), despite its theoretical interest, would not eventuate in reality.

7.3 SOME INFERENCES FROM THE EVOLUTIONARY PLAY OF THE HAWK–DOVE GAME

7.3.1 Four comments

This is enough of the technicalities, let us turn to some general inferences which can be drawn from the playing of games in an evolutionary setting.

Evolutionary stability and the Nash equilibrium

Firstly, to return to the discussion of the Nash equilibrium concept (see Chapter 2), all ESSs are Nash equilibria but not all Nash equilibria are ESSs. Hence, evolutionary game theory provides *some* justification for the Nash equilibrium concept (see also section 7.7). Paradoxically, though, the Nash equilibrium concept begins to look more plausible on this account once an imperfect form of rationality is posited. In other words, it is *not* being deduced as an implication of the common knowledge of rationality assumption which has been the traditional approach of mainstream game theory.

The lure of asymmetry

Secondly, and more specifically, there is the result that although the symmetrical play of this game yields a unique equilibrium, it becomes unstable the moment role playing begins and some players start to recognise asymmetry. Since creative agents seem likely to experiment with different ways of playing the game, it would be surprising if there was never some deviation based on an asymmetry. Indeed it would be more than surprising because there is much evidence to support the idea that people look for 'extraneous' reasons which might explain what are in fact purely random types of behaviour (see the adjacent box on winning streaks).

Formally, this leaves us with the old problem of how the solution to the game comes about. However, evolutionary game theory does at least point us in the direction of an answer. The phase diagram in Figure 7.2 reveals that the selection of an equilibrium depends critically on the initial set of beliefs (as summarised in an initial (p, q) pair). For some beliefs, namely those in the north-west and south-east quadrants, this is sufficient to determine which Nash equilibrium is selected. However, for other possible beliefs, namely those in the south-west and north-east quadrants, the selection of an equilibrium will also depend on the precise learning rule (that is, the precise way in which p and q are adjusted upwards/downwards) as this will determine whether beliefs evolve into the north-west or south-east quadrants. To put these observations rather less blandly, since rationality on this account is only responsible for the general impulse towards mimicking profitable behaviour, the history of the game depends in part on what are the idiosyncratic and unpredictable (non-rational, one might say, as opposed to irrational) features of individual beliefs and learning.

Box 7.1

WINNING AND LOSING STREAKS?

People often refer to winning or losing streaks to describe a process whereby one win (loss) leads to another because confidence grows (falls), making another win (loss) even more likely and so on. However, there are very few examples of so-called winning streaks which are not what would be expected statistically from a team which has a constant chance of winning each game (Joe DiMaggio's famous hitting run in baseball appears to be one such exception). The attribution of a causal process (the growth or decline of confidence which affects performance) to explain what is a purely random phenomena seems to be part of a general human cognitive tendency which imposes or seeks explanations for events which are in fact purely driven by chance (see Kahneman, Slovic and Tversky, 1982). If, as a species, we like to impose a deterministic order on events to render them intelligible, even when none exist (and the best description comes from the operation of chance), then it seems likely that the symmetrical version of these games (where we play and expect to encounter others playing strategies probabilistically) will yield to an asymmetrical deviation because this affords a deterministic 'explanation' of our behaviour.

Another example of this kind of attribution surfaces with moral luck. Driving at speed through a town is liable to produce accidents with some frequency for the simple reason that there are always people who inadvertently step onto the road. It is a matter of luck whether this happens to one speedster rather than another (because such inadvertent moves occur randomly) and yet we typically hold the person involved in an accident morally culpable in a way that a mere speedster is not. It is as if we believe that the person involved in the accident has done something more than speed to make the accident happen, but this is often not the case.

Conventions

Thirdly, it can be noted that the selection of one ESS rather than another embodies a *convention* in the sense of Lewis (1969). What sustains the practice of role R players, say, conceding while role C players take the lot (e.g. $p = 0$, $q = 1$), is simply the players' prediction that this is what will happen because, given these predictions, such behaviour maximises the pay-offs of each. The alternative prediction, that role R players get the lot while C players concede ($p = 1$, $q = 0$), could equally well be sustained provided this alternative set of predictions was held by the population. Thus the behaviour at one of these ESSs is *conventionally* determined and, to repeat the earlier point, we can plot the emergence of a particular convention with the use of this phase diagram. It will depend both on the presumption that agents learn from experience (the rational component of the explanation) and on the particular idiosyncratic (and non-rational) features of initial beliefs and precise learning rules.

Of course, this observation will only worry game theorists if these idiosyncrasies make some significant difference in the sense that they not only contribute to equilibrium selection but the characteristics of one equilibrium differ significantly from those of the others as well. This leads directly to the next observation.

Inequities

Fourthly, the selection of one equilibrium rather than another potentially matters rather deeply. In effect in the hawk–dove game over contested property, what happens in the course of moving to one of the ESSs is the establishment of a form of property rights. Either those playing role R get the property and role C players concede this right, or those playing role C get the property and role R players concede this right. This is interesting not only because it contains the kernel of a possible explanation of property rights (on which we shall say more later) but also because the probability of playing role R or role C is unlikely to be distributed uniformly over the population. Indeed, this distribution will depend on whatever is the source of the distinction used to assign people to roles. Thus, for instance, the distribution of property is likely to be very different in a society where the assignment to roles depends on sex and age as compared with, say, height. In the one either the tall or the short people will be respectively advantaged and disadvantaged. Whereas in the other, it could be old females who are marginalised while the young males rule the roost; or some other hierarchical combination of these age and sex differences.

7.3.2 The origin of conventions and the challenge to methodological individualism

The question, then, of how a source of differentiation gets established becomes rather important. Some evolutionary game theorists have tried to explain the selection of some extraneous feature by appealing to the idea of

---

Box 7.2

PROMINENCE AND FOCAL POINTS IN SOCIAL LIFE

Thomas Schelling conducted a series of experiments on his students which reveal a surprising capacity for people to coordinate their decisions. As far as formal game theory is concerned the experiments pose in sharp relief the problem of equilibrium selection which we have been discussing, yet it seems people are able, in practice, to solve the problem by finding some aspect of the situation prominent in a way that formal game theory overlooks. Here is a flavour of those early experiments (see Schelling, 1963).

(1) Name 'heads' or 'tails'. If you and your partner name the same, you both win a prize.
    36 people chose heads and only 6 chose tails.

(2) You are to meet somebody in New York City. You have not been instructed where to meet; you have no prior understanding with the person on where to meet; and you cannot communicate with each other. You just have to guess where to go.
    The majority selected Grand Central Station.

(3) You were told the date but not the hour of the meeting in (2). At what time will you appear?
    Virtually everyone selected 12.00 noon.

(4) You are to divide $100 into two piles, labelled A and B. Your partner is to divide another $100 into two piles labelled A and B. If you allot the same amounts to A and B respectively as your partner, each of you gets $100. Otherwise both of you get nothing.
    36 out of 41 divided the sum into two piles of $50 each.

As Schelling suggests:

> These problems are artificial, but they illustrate the point. People can often concert their intentions or expectations with others if each knows that the other is trying to do the same. Most situations . . . provide some clue for coordinating behaviour, some focal point for each person's expectation of what the other expects him to expect to be expected to do. Finding the key . . . may depend on imagination more than on logic; it may depend on analogy, precedent, accidental arrangement, symmetry, aesthetic or geometric configuration.

(p. 57)

---

prominence or salience (see Schelling, 1963). Some aspects of the social situation just seem to stand out and these become the 'focal points' around which individuals coordinate their decisions (see Box 7.2 for some evidence of our surprising capacity to coordinate around focal points). So, for example, Sugden (1986, 1989) argues that conventions spread from one realm to another by analogy. 'Possession' for instance is prominent or salient in property games like hawk–dove with the result that it seems 'natural' to play hawk in some disputed property game now when you seem to 'possess' the property while non-possession naturally leads to the play of dove. In fact evolutionary biologists lend some support to this particular idea because they find that a prior relationship (rather than size or strength) seems to count in disputes between males over females in the animal world (see Maynard Smith, 1982, and Wilson, 1975). But, they also draw attention to the apparent 'salience' of sex in the natural world as a source of differentiation; so it seems unlikely that a single characteristic can, on its own, explain the emergence of these crucial conventions.

There is a further and deeper problem with the concept of salience based on analogy because the attribution of terms like 'possession' plainly begs the question by presupposing the existence of some sort of property rights in the past. In other words, people already share a convention in the past and this is being used to explain a closely related convention in the present. Thus we have not got to the bottom of the question concerning how people come to hold conventions in the first place.[3] Indeed, the implicit assumption of prior sharing extends also to shared ways of projecting the past into the present. In this particular instance, the appeal to prior 'possession' relies on what is a probably innocuous sharing of the principle of induction. But, in general, the shared rules of projection are likely to be more complicated because the present situation rarely duplicates the past and so the sharing must involve rules of imaginative projection.

There are two ways of taking this observation. The first is to acknowledge that in any social interaction that we might be interested in people actually do come to it with a background variety of shared conventions (witness Box 7.2). So, of course, we cannot hope to explain how they actually achieve a new coordination without appealing to those background conventions. In this sense, it would be foolish for social scientists (and game theorists, in particular) to ignore the social context in which individuals play new games.

This, so to speak, is the weak form of acknowledging that individuals are socially located and if we leave it at that then it will sit only moderately uneasily with the ambitions of game theory, in the sense that game theory must draw on these unexplained features of social context in its own explanations. However, it could also be a source of more fundamental questioning. After all, perhaps the presence of these conventions can only be accounted for by a move towards a Wittgensteinian ontology, in which case mainstream game theory's foundations look decidedly wobbly. To prevent this drift a more robust response is required.

The alternative response is to deny that the appeal to shared prominence or salience involves either an infinite regress or an acknowledgement that individuals are necessarily ontologically social (i.e. to concede the practical

206

Box 7.3

EATING DINNER

Take candlesticks, the place settings and all the other frippery out of eating dinner in company and ask: what is left? It is not implausible to imagine that what is left is something like a hawk–dove game. Humans apparently are quite unique as a species in sharing their dinners. By contrast, most species eat 'on the hoof', so to speak, with food only ever taken to another place for consumption when there are immobile young which have to be fed. The point about such dinners is that, once the food is on the table, it becomes a potentially contested resource in exactly the manner captured by the hawk–dove game. Yet rarely do we observe 'fighting' breaking out. In practice, as we all know, property rights over the food are established by conventions: what we call 'manners' or more generally the rituals of eating. Or as Visser (1992) so nicely puts it: 'behind every ritual with respect to eating lies a simple concern of each person to be a diner and not a dish'.

The emergence of 'manners' here is not unsurprising from an evolutionary perspective. It is the ESS which our analysis leads us to expect. However, we have no way of predicting how the convention with respect to manners will operate. Salience might be invoked in a non-question-begging way, if it was biologically based. But in this case we should expect similar conventions to arise around the activity of dining between peoples who have very similar perceptual apparatus. Yet, as Visser (1992) marvellously demonstrates, this is not what we observe. The rituals of eating are richly varied across time and space: from the vestiges of sacrifice, the formalism of the Oxbridge 'high table', to the Malawian perception that westerners value peanuts most highly because they are one of the few foods they hold in both hands.

point that we all come with a history, but deny that this means methodological individualism is compromised). Along these lines there are at least two ways in which, as an ideal type exercise, one might explain a shared salience in one of two other ways without conceding any ground on methodological individualism. Firstly, salience could be biologically based (and therefore shared) in a certain bias in our perceptual apparatus. This, of course, is always a possibility. However, we doubt that biology can be the whole story because it would not account for the variety of human practices in such games (see Box 7.3).

Secondly a source of prominence could be explained if it emerges from an evolutionary competition between two or more candidate sources of distinction. This seems a natural route to take (and it is the one taken by Lewis (1969)). It is also of more general interest because there will be many actual settings where an appeal to a shared social context will not unambiguously point to one source of prominence. However, it also seems likely to reproduce an earlier problem/conclusion in a different form. Namely, that the initial distribution of beliefs (now regarding salience) will be crucial in determining which source of salience eventually acquires the allegiance of the population as a whole. We shall see!

7.3.3 The conflict of conventions

To see why this is likely, consider a situation where there are two competing sources of differentiation which generate two types of conventions. Let us say one distinguishes players according to age and instructs the young to concede to the old, while the other convention distinguishes according to height and instructs the short to concede to the tall. The basic intuition is easy to grasp. One convention will emerge as the dominant one and its selection depends critically on the initial number of people who subscribe to each convention. The reason is simple. We are dealing with conventions which, by their very nature, work and become stronger the larger the number of adherents. Thus once the balance tips in the direction of one convention, it quickly develops into a bandwagon. But the rub is: what does the tipping?

To make this clear, consider how the pay-off to the use of a particular convention will depend on the numbers adhering to it. The convention will tell you what is actually the best action to take provided you come across someone who also adheres to your convention (for instance, if you are old and you come across a young person who subscribes to the age convention, the best action is to play hawk). The convention, however, will lead you to take an inferior action when you come across someone who subscribes to a different convention and that convention indicates a different course of action. Of course, another convention will not always do this. For instance, in our example some young people are also taller than some old people and so the two conventions will sometimes point to the same pattern of concession for your opposing player. Nevertheless for any given overlap between conventions of this sort, the probability of coming across someone who is going to play the game in a contrary manner (that is, play hawk to your hawk), and who thus turns your action into an inferior one, will depend on the number of people who subscribe to the contrary convention. In other words, as the numbers using your convention rise so it becomes increasingly likely that it will guide you to the best action. If people switch between conventions based on expected returns, then eventually one convention will emerge as the dominant one.

This conclusion reinforces the earlier result that the course of history depends in part on what seem from the instrumental account of rational behaviour to be non-rational (and perhaps idiosyncratic) and therefore features of human beliefs and action which are difficult to predict mechanically. One can interpret this in the spirit of methodological individualism at the expense of conceding that individuals are, in this regard, importantly unpredictable. On the one hand, this does not look good for the explanatory claims of the theory. On the other hand, to render the individuals predictable, it seems that they must be given a shared history and this will only raise the methodological concern again of whether we can account for this sharing satisfactorily without a changed ontology. In summary, if individuals are afforded a shared history, then social context is 'behind' no one and 'in' everyone and then the question is whether it is a good idea to analyse behaviour by assuming (as methodological individualists do) the separability of context and action.[4]

There is a further wrinkle to this analysis which is worth mentioning precisely because the issue of competition between conventions is interesting for actual social settings as well as ideal-type reconstructions in our models. The return from the use of a convention for a particular individual will depend not only on the proportions of the population subscribing to it, but also on the frequency with which it is assigned the dominant role. Thus the general population movement towards the emerging convention is liable to be taking place against a backdrop of cross movements which take, to use the earlier example, the old to the age convention and the short to the height convention. In fact, these cross movements could be very influential in establishing which convention becomes more popular.

To see the point a little more sharply, suppose the two conventions have an equal number of adherents. The expected return from the use of each convention is the same when every person has a 50% chance of being dominant under each convention. Now suppose one convention actually allocates the advantage of being dominant more unequally than the other. This will encourage some from the equal convention to the unequal one (namely, those who think they will benefit under the unequal convention more than 50% of the time). At the same time, those who lose out under the unequal convention will be attracted to the equal one. The relative movement of population will be determined initially by the movements which are sparked by the differing characters of each convention with respect to the distribution of the advantage of dominance.

Expressions (7.3) and (7.4) illustrate this point. We assume that in the context of the hawk–dove game in Figure 7.1 there are two conventions (π and ϕ). We define the following probabilities:

p – the probability of a π-person interacting with a fellow π-person = proportion of π-persons.
q – the probability of a ϕ-person interacting with a fellow ϕ-person = proportion of ϕ-persons.
k – the proportion of all interconvention interactions in which the

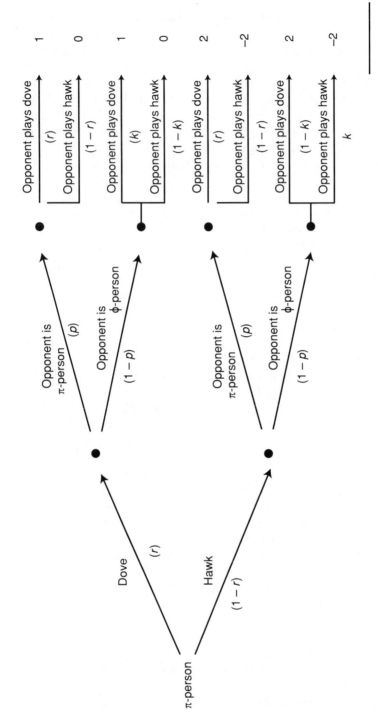

Probabilities in brackets under arrows

Figure 7.3

players are instructed by their (different) conventions to play in the same way.

r – the probability that a π-person will be instructed by π to play 'dove'.

s – the probability that a ϕ-person will be instructed by ϕ to play 'dove'.

In Figure 7.3 we have the tree diagram which enumerates all possibilities for a π-person who meets in a hawk–dove game a stranger who must subscribe to one of the two conventions π or ϕ.

The following expression for our π-player's expected returns follows from the above tree diagram:

$$\begin{aligned}
E^{\pi} &= r.p.r.1 + r.p.(1 - r).0 + r.(1 - p).k.1 + r.(1 - p).(1 - k).0 \\
&\quad + (1 - r).p.r.2 + (1 - r).p.(1 - r).(-2) + (1 - r).(1 - p).k.(-2) \\
&\quad + (1 - r).(1 - p).(1 - k).2 \\
&= r[pr + (1 - p)k] + 2(1 - r)[pr + (1 - p)(1 - k)] - \\
&\quad 2(1 - r)[p(1 - r) + (1 - p)k]
\end{aligned} \tag{7.3}$$

An analogous calculation leads to

$$\begin{aligned}
E^{\phi} &= s[qs + (1 - q)k] + 2(1 - s)[qs + (1 - q)(1 - k)] - \\
&\quad 2(1 - s)[q(1 - s) + (1 - q)k]
\end{aligned} \tag{7.4}$$

Close inspection of these expressions reveals that there is a wide range of k, r and s values for which E^{π} and E^{ϕ} are both increasing functions of p and q respectively. This confirms the earlier observation that population movements may create a bandwagon effect in favour of one convention once it emerges as the one offering the superior expected returns. Why? The reason is that, under random pairings of players, and provided E^{π} increases when p increases, the higher the value of p (i.e. the proportion of π-persons) the greater the expected returns for π-persons. And the higher the expected returns, the more people will have an incentive to adopt convention π. Hence the bandwagon effect. For this to happen, however (that is, for E^{π} to be an increasing function of p), it can be shown that the following condition must hold:[5]

$$k > [(3r^2 - 8r + 4)/(4 - 5r)] \tag{7.5}$$

Of course a similar condition applies for convention ϕ, namely that for E^{ϕ} to be increasing with q,

$$k > [(3s^2 - 8s + 4)/(4 - 5s)] \tag{7.6}$$

Inequalities (7.5) and (7.6) tell an interesting story. Consider for instance what happens when $r = \frac{2}{3}$, or $s = \frac{2}{3}$; that is, when the conventions recommend that a player plays 'dove' with the same probability that symmetrical evolution would recommend (see section 7.2.1). Then the right hand side of the inequalities is zero, and the expected returns from each convention will be increasing functions of the number of people following it, provided of course $k > 0$; that is, provided that there is at least a tiny possibility that an opponent following a different convention to yours will play the same strategy as you when the two of you meet.

So, we see that, beginning with only one convention for everyone, the original symmetrical convention may divide in two (π and ϕ). In other words, a second discriminating characteristic may come into play and, as it gathers more adherents, those who already adhere to it will benefit (provided $k > 0$). Which convention will do better for its adherents? We cannot tell in the abstract. What we can tell is that the adherents of one convention will do better while those of the other will do worse. The reason is that when there are only two conventions, $p = 1 - q$ (that is, when a person switches towards one convention he or she automatically abandons the other convention), and thus when some people start switching to π (for example) those who follow π will do better while ϕ-followers will suffer. An interesting corollary of this is that a convention which can skew its followers' interactions towards fellow users of the convention will be better able to survive than one that does not.

To demonstrate another point simply, let us assume that pairings are random: so p is the proportion of the population following π, and it equals $1 - q$. Furthermore, let p equal 0.5. The expected returns for an individual with a $1 - r = 1 - s$ chance of the dominant role under each convention are now identical, placing the group of people as a whole on a knife-edge ready for the bandwagon to roll towards one or another convention. Now imagine how the knife-edge is disturbed when one convention does not give every individual following it the same chance of being assigned the dominant role (that is, when r and s are not the same for all π-persons and ϕ-persons respectively).

Of course, for the population as a whole there will always be a $1 - r = 1 - s$ chance of being given the dominant role under each convention at any one time, as the per capita expected return to the followers of each convention is still identical. Nonetheless the distribution of that return can vary across the followers in repeated play because particular individuals may be assigned to the dominant role more or less often than the group-wide $1 - r = 1 - s$ figure. For instance, under the putative height convention, the shortest person among the population is always assigned to the dominant role while the tallest person is always given the subordinate role. This is captured above through the possibility that an individual's r or s probabilities (see equations (7.3) and (7.4)) need not be the same as the average group figure. Thus even though the per capita expected returns have been assumed equal, individuals will be encouraged to switch to the convention offering them personally the higher expected probability of playing the dominant role (for example, the tallest person may adopt the age-based convention). Since the subjective calculation of one's personal r and s values is made difficult by the fact that it depends on who else switches with you, it would be pure serendipity if these rough and ready estimates yielded flows which balanced exactly. The population sits so precariously on the knife-edge that the bandwagon is bound to roll.

7.3.4 Conventions, inequality and revolt

One final comment is worth making on the theme of distribution. By its very nature, we have seen that abiding by a convention makes sense to each individual when others also subscribe to that convention. However, this does not mean that it is in the interest of each person, or indeed to a majority of persons, to move from a situation where there are no conventions (that is, the symmetric ESS) to one where there is a convention (that is, one of the asymmetric ESSs). Under the symmetrical ESS in the original hawk–dove game, the expected return of each individual in our example is $\frac{2}{3}$. (If each plays hawk with probability $\frac{1}{3}$ and dove with probability $\frac{2}{3}$, then the expected returns for each player equal $(\frac{1}{3})[-2(\frac{1}{3}) + 2(\frac{2}{3})] + (\frac{2}{3})[0.(\frac{1}{3}) + 1(\frac{2}{3})] = \frac{2}{3}$.) Under the asymmetrical convention, you will get 2, which is the hawk's payment, when in the dominant role (which on average is half of the time) and 0, the dove's payment, when in the subordinate role. On average, the payment will equal 1. In general, when your particular chance of being given the dovish role is r, your expected return from that convention is $(1 - r)2$.

Thus the introduction of a convention will benefit the average person, but if you happen to be so placed with respect to the convention that you only play the dominant role with a probability of less than $\frac{1}{3}$, then you would be better off without the convention. This result may seem puzzling at first: why do the people who play a dominant role less than $\frac{1}{3}$ of the time not revert to the symmetric play of the game and so undermine the convention? The answer is that even though the individual would be better off if everyone quit the convention, it does not make sense to do so individually. After all, a convention will tell your opponent to play either H or D, and then instruct you to play D or H respectively; and you can do no better than follow this convention since the best reply to H remains D and likewise the best reply to D is H. It is just tough luck if you happen to get the D instruction all the time!

We take the force of this individual calculation to be a powerful contributor to the status quo and it might seem to reveal that evolutionary processes yield to stasis. The underlying point here is that discrimination may be evolutionary stable if the dominated cannot find ways of challenging the social convention that supports their subjugation. This conclusion is not necessarily right because there are other potential sources of change. The insight that we prefer to draw is that *individual* attempts to buck an established convention are unlikely to succeed, whereas the same is not true when individuals take collective action. Indeed when a large number of individuals take common action in pursuit of a new convention then this can tip the individual calculation of what to do for the best in favour of change.

A potential weakness of evolutionary game theory has just become apparent. Once the bandwagon has come to a standstill, and one convention has been selected, the theory cannot account for a potential subversion of the established convention. Such an account would require, as we argued in the previous paragraph, an understanding of political (that is, collective) action based on a more active form of human agency than the one provided by instrumental rationality. Can evolutionary game theory go as far? We will return to this question in section 7.6.

To summarise, we should expect a convention to emerge even though it may not suit everyone, or indeed even if it short-changes the majority. It may be discriminatory, inequitable, non-rational, indeed thoroughly disagreeable, yet some such convention is likely to arise whenever a social interaction like hawk–dove is repeated. Which convention emerges will depend on the shared salience of extraneous features of the interaction, initial beliefs and the way that people learn. In more complicated cases where there is competition between conventions, a convention's chances of success will also depend on its initial number of adherents, on how it distributes the benefits of coordination across its followers and on its ability to skew interactions towards fellow users. In particular, one would not expect a convention which generated relative losers and which confined them to the interactive margins (that is, placed them in a position where they were less likely to interact with their fellow adherents) to last long. Or to put the last point even more simply, where conventions create clear winners and losers, two conventions are more likely to co-exist when communication between followers of different conventions is confined to the winners of both. Finally, to undermine discriminatory conventions, individuals' action stands no chance of success, unless it is part of collective action.

7.4 COORDINATION GAMES

In his *Discourse on the Origin and Foundations of Inequality among Men*, Rousseau famously sketched the parable of the stag hunt. The tale has been variously interpreted, but it is common to see it as a coordination game (see, for instance, Lewis, 1969). On this reading each person faces a choice between hunting a stag (which will only be successful when the whole group joins the hunt) and trapping a hare (which can be successfully undertaken individually). A share in the stag is regarded as better than a hare and so the situation where all hunt the stag is superior for all (economists would say 'Pareto dominates') to the situation where each traps hare. The situation is reminiscent of Cephu in section 5.4, although it is quite different because

214

Cephu preferred to act individualistically when others joined the common hunt thus creating a free rider problem (and indeed some have interpreted Rousseau in this way, see Waltz (1965)).

Under the coordination game interpretation, a two-person stag hunt might be captured by the pay-offs in Figure 7.4.

		Player C	
		Stag	Hare
Player R	Stag	3, 3	0, 2
	Hare	2, 0	2, 2

Figure 7.4

The evolutionary analysis of this repeated game can be conducted in the same way as hawk–dove. Suppose your hunting partner is drawn randomly from the group that you belong to, and assume that initially there is a probability p that he or she will play 'stag'. The probability p can, as before, be given two interpretations: either everyone is playing mixed strategies or this is the proportion of the population who have opted for this strategy. It is easy to calculate that when $p > \frac{2}{3}$, the expected return from playing 'stag' exceeds that of 'hare'; and so with our evolutionary learning scheme people will switch to 'stag'. Thus p rises to 1. Alternatively when $p < \frac{2}{3}$, 'hare' looks better and p falls to 0. In short, either the group will end up coordinating on stag hunting or on hare trapping.

It is tempting to think that the stag hunt is the more likely of the two outcomes because it is an outcome which makes everyone better off compared with hare trapping (notice how in the Stag–Stag equilibrium both are better off than in the Hare–Hare equilibrium). There are at least two arguments along these lines and both need careful handling. One appeals to the idea of salience and suggests in effect that 'pay-off'-dominant solutions are salient in such settings. Some salience of pay-off dominance is difficult to dispute, but should we assume it is more than other sources of salience, for instance like risk dominance? In this example risk dominance points to hare trapping for the following reason. There are two Nash equilibria in pure strategies and since each will commend itself as strongly as the other when others choose it, you have no way of deciding whether to expect that people will play stag or hare. In these circumstances of uncertainty over what to expect (and hence the name risk dominance), you should assign a 50–50 chance to the play of both strategies. In which case the expected return from 'hare' exceeds that of 'stag'. Thus 'hare' might appear salient; and once again we get into the question of competing

Box 7.4

COORDINATION AMONG MBA STUDENTS

We asked a class of 95 MBA students to choose an integer between (and including) 1 and 10 on the basis that their choice would determine their final grade. The formula translating their choice of integer into a grade was: $11 \times$ (MIN) $-$ OWN, where MIN is the lowest integer chosen by anyone in the class and OWN one's own choice. It follows that if each chose 10, then they would all get 100%. Notice that this is a pure coordination problem: if you expect all others to choose λ (where λ is any integer in the [1, 10] interval) your best strategy is to choose λ yourself (check that if we substituted MIN with AVER, where AVER is the average of all the integers chosen in the class, then the game is of a prisoners' dilemma/free rider nature). Hence, *any* integer between 1 and 10 is, potentially, a Nash equilibrium strategy. Moreover, $\lambda = 10$ is the Nash equilibrium that dominates all others (in the sense that everyone is better off if it is selected).

In our little experiment only two chose 10 while 78 chose 1. The dismal result was that no one received more than 10% when everyone could have managed 100%. Why did they eschew the higher, pay-off-dominant choice? The answer might lie with what we referred to earlier as risk dominance. Put simply, if you fear that *one* member of your group will defect (choose integer 1, or hunt a hare in Rousseau's story) then you will also defect. It turns out that coordination games may be free of the inherent antagonism of prisoners' dilemmas but, nevertheless, agents need to be reassured that cooperation will be forthcoming before it becomes possible. This is why Amartya Sen refers to these interactions as *common assurance* games. A similar idea is central to Keynes' scepticism about the capacity of economic agents to coordinate prices of commodities and labour (i.e. wages) in a way that everyone is better off (and unemployment is eliminated). This scepticism leads to his advocacy of an interventionist government economic policy (see Box 7.5 for more).

saliences (for some evidence on how people respond to coordination games, see box 7.4). This leads into the second line of argument.

Suppose initial beliefs or the initial choice of strategies is random in all social groups facing such problems. Statistically this will produce $p > \frac{2}{3}$ for some social groups. So it seems highly likely that some groups will initially hunt stag even if others are hare trapping. But surely the groups stuck in the hare trapping equilibrium will 'learn' from the more successful groups and so switch to stag hunting. There are two ways in which the 'learning' might take place. One is through demonstration effects and the other is through the effects of 'competition'. Demonstration effects are not as obvious or as powerful as they might seem at first. Even when you notice that other groups do better, it will not make sense for you individually to switch to stag hunting. It only makes sense when more than two-thirds of your group also make the switch. In other words, there is still the same coordination problem for members of the group.

Turning to competition, in so far as people can move between groups, it may do the trick because then people will be drawn to the stag hunting groups at the expense of the hare hunting ones. However, there are often barriers to movement between social groups and the competition is confined to contacts between members of groups which subscribe to different conventions. In these cases, the 'competition' might persuade you to switch convention. The condition for this, though, is again rather demanding: two-thirds of your interactions must take place with people who subscribe to the stag convention. Interestingly, this suggests a rather similar conclusion to the hawk–dove game. The influence of contacts with other conventions will be maximised when those contacts are concentrated on a small subgroup because this will increase the subgroup's proportion of contacts with another convention.

There are also clear examples where groups have got stuck in what seems to be the lesser equilibrium of a coordination game. So these theoretical doubts about the likelihood of pay-off-dominant solutions have their practical counterparts (see Box 7.5 on the QWERTY keyboard and other coordination failures).

Box 7.5

QWERTY AND OTHER COORDINATION FAILURES

Have you ever wondered how the QWERTY arrangement of keys emerged as the standard for keyboards (and typewriters)? (It is called QWERTY because these are the first six letters on the top row.) One might think that it represents some optimal arrangement for typing fast and efficiently, otherwise it would not have stood the test of time. However, the QWERTY system is regularly outperformed in speed and time trials by another arrangement, the Dvorak and Dealey keyboard.

In some sense, it is hardly surprising that the QWERTY arrangement is not very efficient because, while the basic four row configuration was designed to overcome some early technical problems, the location of the letters across these rows was devised in part as a sales gimmick to promote the sales of a Remington machine called a Type Writer (the top row of letters allowed the sales representatives to type out, apparently effortlessly, the brand's name). What is surprising is that people continue to use it today, despite its failings, to operate state of the art computers. So why do people stick with it? Well, plausibly because it remains the best course of action so long as everyone is still producing and buying

QWERTY machines and acquiring the skills to use those machines. After all, it pays employers to buy these machines when everyone else uses them because the employer thereby gains access to a large pool of workers with the skills to use these machines; and likewise it pays workers to acquire the skills to operate these machines because this secures access to most job opportunities when employers have bought these machines. Thus, the selection of a key configuration has all the hallmarks of a coordination problem because it pays to do what others do; and in this instance, it seems that we have failed to coordinate on the best solution.

The occurrence of Keynesian unemployment is also often interpreted as a coordination failure (see also Box 7.4, Cooper and Johns, 1988, and Hargreaves Heap, 1992). It arises when nominal prices (and wages) fail to adjust immediately to nominal demand shocks (that is, shocks, like changes in the money supply, which, in principle, require changes in all nominal prices to preserve the original equilibrium position). It can be regarded as a coordination failure because the selection of a price is like playing a coordination game. Under certain circumstances, no change is the best response when all other prices remain constant, while a change is the best response when all other prices are changed. Thus there are (at least) two Nash equilibria and one is better than the other. The 'all change' outcome dominates 'no change' when there is a deflationary nominal demand shock as the latter generates an increase in unemployment, yet it seems that economic agents often fail to select them.

Another illustration of how recessions and booms in production can be interpreted as different Nash equilibria in a coordination context comes from Diamond's (1982) trading game. In a simple version, people produce either a high or a low amount of the commodity in which they specialise and they take it to a market to exchange with goods produced by other people. The choice between high and low production depends on the individual's expectations regarding the opportunities for trade in the market. If the opportunities are restricted because everyone else has chosen low production levels, then trading opportunities are poor (making low production the best option). Conversely, if others choose high production levels the trading opportunities are good (making high production the best strategy). Thus each will want to choose high when everyone else is expected to choose high, and each individual will want to choose low when everyone else is expected to choose low. In other words, we have two Nash equilibria, one associated with a boom and the other with a recession.

7.5 THE EVOLUTION OF COOPERATION IN THE PRISONERS' DILEMMA

Does evolutionary game theory encourage optimism with respect to the prospects of cooperation in the repeated prisoners' dilemma? The first part of an answer comes from section 6.3. To recap on the setting, imagine players are randomly drawn in pairs from a population to play an indefinitely repeated prisoners' dilemma game. In section 6.3 we showed that any strategy which cooperated with a tit-for-tat (τ) would be superior to any of the other two broad types of strategy in these indefinitely repeated games provided the probability of the game being repeated was sufficiently high. Strategy τ offers one example of a strategy which specifies cooperation with someone else playing τ but it is not the only one. Always cooperate (C) is another and it would fare just as well as τ. Thus a C-player could do as well as a τ-player in a group of τ-players (in other words the first part of condition 7.2 is not satisfied). For τ to be an ESS in these circumstances τ would have to do better against a group of C-players than C (the second part of condition 7.2). But, of course, it does not: it does as well as C but no better. Thus τ can be invaded by a C, and even though there is no incentive for Cs to grow since they fare no better, this means τ is not an ESS.

This looks a rather worrying result for those who argue in the tradition of spontaneous order that cooperation can emerge without some form of supra-individual intervention since a group of Cs is easily invaded by defectors (D). Hence, those who overcame the dilemma by becoming followers of strategy τ could drift to a state of playing C unconditionally and thus soon yield to a situation where cooperation can be destroyed even by a minuscule group of defectors. Nevertheless τ can be turned into an ESS through a simple and perhaps realistic change to the analysis (see Sugden, 1986).

Recall the idea of a trembling hand in section 2.7.1 and suppose that players make mistakes sometimes. In particular, when they intend to cooperate they occasionally execute the decision wrongly and they defect. In these circumstances, playing τ punishes you for the mistake endlessly because it means that your opponent defects next round in response to your mistaken defection. If in the next period you cooperate, you are bound to get zapped. If you follow your τ–strategy next time, then you will be defecting while your opponent will be cooperating and a frustrating sequence of alternating defections and cooperations will ensue. One way out of this bind is to amend τ to τ' whereby, if you defect by mistake, then you cooperate twice afterwards: the first time as a gesture of acknowledging your mistake and the second in order to coordinate your cooperative behaviour with that of your opponent. In other words, the amended tit-for-tat instructs you to cooperate in response to a defection which has been provoked by an earlier mistaken defection on your part.

Strategy τ' is now a unique best reply to τ' and so is an ESS provided mistakes are sufficiently rare. To see why suppose a panic attack, or a plain mistake, makes you defect just once and that it is as likely to affect you as your opponent. If this happens, you are clearly better off through τ' rather than τ because you avoid the alternation of defection and cooperation. Even though strategy C would do equally well as a reply to τ', if your opponent made the mistake (last period) then you know that your opponent will cooperate in the next two rounds no matter what you do this period. Thus your best response *in this round* is to defect (and not cooperate as a C would). That is, you follow what your opponent did last period. In short, your best reply to τ' is to play τ'.

Thus τ' is an ESS, albeit not the only one. For example D (i.e. 'always defect') is also an ESS here since it is also the best reply to itself in these circumstances. Thus although we might explain the emergence of cooperation spontaneously, we are back in the situation where there are several ESSs and not all generate cooperation. So we would like to know what determines the chances of one rather than another being selected. For instance, in a competition between τ and D, which is more likely to result? Formally, the problem is akin to the selection of a Nash equilibrium in a pure coordination game. To appreciate this, suppose partners are randomly selected from a population which has people who subscribe to both convention τ' and D. Let the probability that the game will be repeated between the players be p. If two players playing according to strategy τ' are selected (and to keep the calculation simple assume that they do not make any mistakes) then, from equation (6.1), we know they expect returns $3/(1 - p)$. When two Ds are selected each will expect a return of $2/(1 - p)$; and so on. Thus the pay-off matrix in Figure 7.5 represents the possibilities for a row player (the column player's pay-offs are analogous).

		Player C	
		τ'	D
Player R	τ'	$3/(1 - p)$	$1 + 2p/(1 - p)$
	D	$4 + 2p/(1 - p)$	$2/(1 - p)$

Figure 7.5

Assuming that $p > \frac{1}{2}$, there are two Nash equilibria strategies (we ignore mixed strategies): (τ', τ') and (D, D). Notice that the former corresponds to a higher pay-off for both. Thus we formally have a coordination game like the one discussed in section 7.4. The conclusions drawn there carry over intact: there will be some critical probability of encountering a τ' player (q) which, if exceeded, will favour the (τ', τ') equilibrium; any lower probability will encourage people to switch to the (D, D) convention. The critical q can be calculated in the usual way by comparing the expected returns to be had from following each convention:

$$E(\tau') = q[3/(1 - p)] + (1 - q)[1 + 2p(1 - p)];$$
$$E(D) = q[4 + 2p/(1 - p)] + (1 - q)[2/(1 - p)]$$

As before it will be tempting to think that the superior cooperative convention will be more likely to emerge but, as before, there are good reasons for believing that its emergence is not guaranteed.

7.6 POWER, MORALITY AND HISTORY: HUME AND MARX ON SOCIAL EVOLUTION

7.6.1 Conventions as covert social power

In 1795 Condorcet wrote:

> force cannot, like opinion, endure for long unless the tyrant extends his empire far enough afield to hide from the people, whom he divides and rules, the secret that real power lies not with the oppressors but with the oppressed.
>
> (1979, p.30)

Runciman (1989) is a recent work in social theory which places evolutionary processes at the heart of social analysis. In this section, we aim to give some indication of how the evolutionary analysis of games might make a similar contribution. We do so by focusing more narrowly and briefly on the relation, which our analysis in this chapter elucidates, between evolutionary processes and the debates in social science regarding power, history and functional explanations. We begin with the concept of power: that is, the ability to secure outcomes which favour one's interests when they conflict in some situation with the interests of another.

It is common in discussions of power to distinguish between the overt and the covert exercise of power. Thus, for instance, Lukes (1974) distinguishes three dimensions of power. There is the power that is exercised in the political or the economic arena where individuals, or firms, institutions, etc., are able to secure decisions which favour their interests over others quite overtly. This is the overt exercise of power along the first dimension. In addition, there is the more covert power that comes from keeping certain items off the political agenda. Some things simply do not get discussed in the political arena and in this way the status quo persists. Yet the status quo advantages some rather than others and so this privileging of the status quo by keeping certain issues off the political agenda is the second dimension of power. Finally, there is the even more covert power that comes from being able to mould the preferences and the beliefs of others so that a conflict of interest is not even latently present.

The first dimension of power is quite uncontentious and we see it in operation, in fact, whenever the State intervenes. In these cases, there will be political haggling between groups and issues will get settled in favour of some groups rather than others. Power is palpable and demonstrable in a way that it is not when exercised covertly. Not unsurprisingly, the idea of the covert exercise of power is more controversial. It is interesting, however, that the analysis of 'spontaneous order' developed in this chapter suggests how the more covert form of power might be grounded. Indeed, and perhaps somewhat ironically, it is precisely because we can see that active State intervention and 'spontaneous orders' are in some respects alternative ways of generating social outcomes that we can also see that both must involve the settling of (potential) conflicts of interest. In short, just as we have seen that the State does not have to intervene to create an order because order can arise 'spontaneously', so we can see that power relations do not have to be exercised overtly because they too can arise 'spontaneously'.

To see this point in more detail, return to the hawk–dove property game. There is a variety of conventions which might emerge in the course of the evolutionary play of the game. Each of them will create an order and, as we have seen, it is quite likely that each convention will distribute the benefits which arise from clear property rights differently across the population. In this sense, there is a conflict of interest between different groups of the population which surfaces over the selection of the convention. Of course, if the State were consciously to select a convention in these circumstances then we might observe the kind of political haggling associated with the overt exercise of power. Naturally when a convention emerges spontaneously, we do not observe this because there is no arena for the haggling to occur, yet the emergence of a convention is no less decisive than a conscious political resolution in resolving the conflict of interest.[6]

Evolutionary game theory also helps reveal the part played by beliefs, especially the beliefs of the subordinate group, in securing the power of the dominant group (a point, for example, which is central to Gramsci's notion of hegemony and Hart's contention that the power of the law requires voluntary cooperation). In evolutionary games, it is the collectivity of beliefs, as encoded in a convention, which is crucial in sustaining the convention and with it the associated distribution of power. Nevertheless, we can see how it is that under the convention 'the advantaged will not concede', the beliefs of the 'disadvantaged' make it instrumentally rational for the 'disadvantaged' to concede their claims. The figure of Spartacus captured imaginations over the ages, not so much because of his military antics, but because he personified the possibility of liberating the slaves from the beliefs which sustained their subjugation. This is especially interesting because it connects with this analysis and offers a different metaphor for power. This is scarcely power in the sense of the power of waves, wind, hammers and the like to cause physical changes. Rather, this is the power which works through the mind and which depends for its influence on the involvement or agreement of large numbers of the population (again connecting with the earlier observation about the force of collective action).

In conclusion, beliefs (in the form of expectations about what others will do) are an essential part of a particular convention in the analysis of 'spontaneous order' and they will mobilise power along Lukes's second dimension. The role of beliefs in this regard is not the same as Lukes's third dimension. In comparison, Lukes's third dimension of power operates with respect to the substantive character of the beliefs: that is, what people hold to be substantively in their interest (in our context this means the game's pay-offs) or what they regard as their legitimate claims and so on. At first glance the evolutionary analysis of repeated games will not seem to have much relevance for this aspect of power since the pay-offs are taken as given; but there is one which we develop next.

7.6.2 The evolution of predictions into moral beliefs: Hume on morality

Aristotle wrote in *Nicomachean Ethics* that

> moral virtue comes about as a result of habit . . . . From this fact it is plain that none of the moral virtues arises in us by nature; for nothing that exists by nature can form a habit contrary to its nature. The stone, for instance, which by nature gravitates downwards, cannot be induced through custom to move upwards, not even when we try to train it. . . . Neither by nature, then, nor contrary to nature do the virtues arise in us; rather we are furnished by nature with a capacity for receiving them, and are perfected in them through custom.

Sugden (1986, 1989) argues in a similar fashion that playing these evolutionary games gives rise to our moral beliefs. Sugden's argument actually looks back to Hume by offering an account of his contention that justice is an artificial rather than a natural virtue. On Hume's account mere conventions of the sort we have been discussing annex virtue to themselves and so become norms of justice. In contrast to Kant who thinks that 'the majesty of duty has nothing to do with the enjoyment of life' (*Critique of Practical Reason*), Hume sees morality as the reification of conventions whose *raison d'être* is to satisfy desires. We not only feel that we should follow them because it is in our interest to, which is the character of any convention, but we also feel that others *ought* to be obliged to follow them as well. Furthermore, we begin to feel that we, ourselves, *ought* to follow them. This extension to others (and then back to ourselves), making the following of a convention a (quasi-)moral obligation, is what turns a convention into a norm of justice. We have already noted that norms often do seem to have this quasi-moral character (with the result that they do more than merely coordinate, see section 5.4) and Hume offers an explanation of how this happens. He argues that we are interested in the use of the norm by others, even when it does not affect us, because we have a natural sympathy for others and this produces a concern that people should follow

223

conventions that work for the benefit of human society. However, there is a second, implicit, reason: conventions which have the capacity to turn themselves into moral norms enjoy greater evolutionary stability than others.[7] (Of course this is only a good thing if the conventions in question are ones which we want preserved.) In short, the injustice of breaches in a convention offend us because they are 'prejudicial to human society'. (See Chapter 8 for a discussion of some experimental evidence which does find that selection of an equilibrium in games of conflict is often associated with shared moral beliefs. Of course, this evidence leaves open the question of whether the beliefs are prior to the game or are generated within the game, as Hume suggests.)

Hence Hume's argument presupposes that conventions operate in the interest of human society. This is worrying for Sugden because it makes moral principles depend on an appeal to social welfare. Firstly, he doubts along with Hayek and Nozick that there is such a thing as 'society' which has 'interests' by which we can judge any convention – the 'myth of social justice', in the lingua of the 'intransigent right'. There are only individuals pursuing their own diverse goals, doubtless informed by a variety of views of the good. Secondly, it is clear that some conventions do not operate in the interest of all. As we have seen in the repeated hawk–dove game, a convention can be established which is not better for all even though it means people are better off on average (or most people are better off). As a result, Sugden argues differently that the moral sense of 'ought' which we attach to the use of a convention comes partially from sympathy that we directly feel for those who suffer when a convention is not followed and partially because we fear that the person who breaches the convention with others may also breach it with us when we may have direct dealings at some later date. This, Sugden believes, is sufficient to explain why individuals have an interest in the observance of a convention in dealings which do not directly affect them.

There is another line of argument which is open to his position. The annexing of virtue can happen as a result of well-recognised patterns of cognition. Recall the box on winning streaks earlier in this chapter: people, it seems, are very unhappy with events which have no obvious explanation or validation, with the result that they seek out reasons even when there are none. The prevailing pattern of property rights may be exactly a case in point. There is no obvious reason that explains why they are the way they are and since they distribute benefits in very particular ways, it would be natural to adjust moral beliefs in such a way that they can be used to 'explain' the occurrence of those property rights. Of course, like all theories of cognitive dissonance removal, this story begs the question of whether the adjustment of beliefs can do the trick once one knows that the beliefs have been adjusted for the purpose. Nevertheless, there seem to be plenty of examples of dissonance removal in this fashion, which suggest this problem is frequently overcome. Thus, whichever argument is preferred, moral beliefs become endogenous and we have an account of power in the playing of evolutionary games which encompasses Lukes's third dimension.

7.6.3 Gender, class and functionalism

Our final illustration of how evolutionary game theory might help sharpen our understanding of debates around power in the social sciences relates to the question of how gender and race power distributions are constituted and persist. The persistence of these power imbalances is a puzzle to some. Becker (1976), for instance, argues that gender and racial discrimination are unlikely to persist because it is not in the interest of profit maximising employers to undervalue the talents of women or black workers. Those who correctly appreciate the talents of these workers, so the argument goes, will profit and so drive out of business the discriminating employers. On first reading the point may seem convincing. However, the persistence of gender and race inequalities tells a different story and evolutionary game theory may provide an explanation of what is wrong with Becker's argument.

For example, suppose sex or race are used as a coordinating device to select an equilibrium in some game resembling hawk–dove. Groups which achieve coordination will be favoured as compared with those that do not and yet, as we have seen, once a sexist or racist convention is established, it will *not* be profitable for an individual employer to overlook the signals of sex and race in such games. Contrary to Becker's suggestion, it would actually be the non-racist and non-sexist employers who suffer in such games because they do not achieve coordination.

Of course, one might wonder whether sex or race seem to be plausible sources of differentiation for the conventions which emerge in the actual playing of such games. But it is not difficult to find support for the suggestion. Firstly, there are examples which seem to fit exactly this model of convention embodying power (see the adjacent box). Secondly, the biological evidence is instructive and it does suggest that sex is a frequent source of differentiation in the biological world. The point is that, since an initial differentiation has a capacity to reproduce itself over time through our shared commitment to induction, it would not be surprising to find that an early source of differentiation like sex has evolved into the gender conventions of the present. Thirdly, there is some support from the fact that gender and race inequalities also seem to have associated with them the sorts of beliefs which might be expected of them if they are conventions on Sugden/Hume's account. For example, it is not difficult to find beliefs associated with these inequalities which find 'justice' in the arrangement, usually through appeal to 'natural' differences; and in this way what starts as

Box 7.6

WHO GETS THE BEST JOBS IN WEST VIRGINIA?

Faludi (1992) recounts the case of the American Cyanamid Willow Island plant. This is located in West Virginia where there has traditionally been extreme competition for jobs because the area has one of the highest unemployment rates. Until the 1970s its workforce was predominantly male. Indeed the relatively high paid production lines had apparently never hired a woman until 1973 when the Federal government 'put American Cyanamid on notice to open its factory doors to women or face legal action'.

Men at the plant were most resistant to the idea, claiming that it was 'hard work' and 'no place for a woman'; and the personnel officers warned against having to 'work midnights with a bunch of horny men'. Nevertheless women were hired on to the production line under Federal pressure and the men complained: for instance, 'Women shouldn't be in here working, taking jobs away from men.' One woman worker was told: 'if you were my wife, you'd be home darning my socks and making my dinner'. The foreman complained that 'women were a safety risk because they could get [a] teat caught in the centre feed'. And so on.

Faludi continues with the story:

As the women's numbers mounted, so did the reprisals. One day the women arrived at work to find this greeting stencilled into a beam over the production floor: SHOOT A WOMAN, SAVE A JOB. Another day, the women found signs tacked to their lockers, calling them whores . . . in two separate incidents, women fended off sexual assaults.

(p. 480)

In 1976 the plant abruptly stopped hiring women. That same year back at headquarters, company executives decided to develop a foetal protection policy. American Cyanamid had never demonstrated a strong desire to protect factory workers in the past . . . . Suddenly though management was worried about the reproductive hazards in the factory. . . . Dr Robert Clyne quickly drafted a policy statement that would prohibit all women of child bearing age from working in production jobs that exposed them to any of twenty nine chemicals. . . . Clyne did not consider reproductive hazards for men.

(p. 482)

Two women stayed in the production department by complying with the regulations through sterilisation operations. When they returned to work they were branded: 'men in the department jeered that the women had been spayed . . . . The management's attitude was little better: its own literature referred to the women as neutered' (p.486). Eventually they were laid-off in the early 1980s.

a difference related to sex or race is spun into the whole baggage of gender or racial differentiation.

Finally, in so far as this analysis of gender and racial stratification does hold some water, then it would make sense of the exercises in consciousness raising which have been associated with the Women's movement and various Black movements. On this account of power through the working of convention, the ideological battle aimed at persuading people not to think of themselves as subordinate is half the battle because these beliefs are part of the way that power is mobilised. In other words, let us assume that consciousness raising political activity is a reasonable response to gender/race inequality. What account of power would make such action intelligible? The account which has power working through the operation of convention is one such account and we take this as further support for the hypothesis.

The relation between class and gender/racial stratification is another issue which concerns social theorists (particularly Marxists and Feminists) and again an evolutionary analysis of this chapter offers a novel angle on the debate. Return to the hawk–dove game, and recover the interpretation of the game as a dispute over property rights. Once a convention is established in this game, a set of property relations are also established. Hence the convention could encode a set of class relations for this game because it will, in effect, indicate who owns what and some may end up owning rather a lot when others own scarcely anything. However, as we have seen a convention of this sort will only emerge once the game is played asymmetrically and this requires an appeal to some piece of extraneous information like sex or age or race, etc. In short, the creation of private property relations from the repeated play of these games depends on the use of some other asymmetry and so it is actually impossible to imagine a situation of pure class relations, as they could never emerge from an evolutionary historical process. Or to put this slightly differently: asymmetries always go in twos!

This understanding of the relation has further interesting implications. For instance, an attack on gender stratification is in part an attack on class stratification and vice versa. Likewise, however, it would be wrong to imagine that the attack on either if successful would spell the end of the other. For example, the attack on gender stratification may leave class stratification bereft of its complement, but so long as there are other asymmetries which can attach to capital then the class stratification will be capable of surviving.

Of course, these suggestions are no more than indicators of how the analysis of evolutionary games might sharpen some debates in social theory. We end with one further illustration (again in outline) of this potential contribution. It comes from the connection between this evolutionary analysis and so-called functional explanations (see Box 3.3).

In effect, the explanation of gender and racial inequalities using this evolutionary model is an example of functional argument. The difference between men and women or between whites and blacks has no merit in the sense that it does not explain why the differentiation persists. The differentiation has the unintended consequence of helping the population to coordinate its decision making in settings where there are benefits from coordination. It is this function of helping the population to select an equilibrium in a situation which would otherwise suffer from the confusion of multiple equilibria which explains the persistence of the differentiation.

Noticing this connection is helpful because functional explanations have been strongly criticised by Elster (1982, 1986b). In particular, he has argued that most functionalist arguments in social science (and particularly those in the Marxist tradition) fail to convince because they do not fill in how the unintended consequences of the action help promote the activity which is responsible for this set of unintended consequences. There has to be a feedback mechanism: that is, something akin to the principle of natural selection in biology which is capable of explaining behaviours by their 'success' and not by their 'intentions'. The feedback mechanism, however, is present in this analysis and it arises because there is 'learning'. It is the assumption that people shift towards practices which secure better outcomes (without knowing quite why the practice works for the best) which is the feedback mechanism responsible for selecting the practices. Thus in the debate over functional explanation, the analysis of evolutionary games lends support to van Parijs's (1982) argument that 'learning' might supply the general feedback mechanism for the social sciences which will license functional explanations in exactly the same way as natural selection does in the biological sciences.

7.6.4 The evolution of predictions into ideology: Marx against morality

On Marx's graveside, Friedrich Engels compared Marx's achievement in social theory with Darwin's contribution to biology. Marx, one presumes, would have been gratified by the analogy. So how would he rate evolutionary game theory (which is rather Darwinian in content)? And what would his reaction be to the idea that morals are merely reified conventions?

Before offering our answers, let us first comment on the similarities and differences between the two approaches: on the one hand we have the blend of Hume with evolutionary game theory (which we will label H&EVGT) (see again Sugden (1986, 1989) for this position) while, on the other, there is Marx. Beginning with the similarities, both canvass a materialist theory of norms and morals. Such materialist theories can be juxtaposed to idealist explanations of morals (as in, for example, Plato or Kant) in that they trace morals in material conditions, rather than looking for them in some realm of ideas independent of material conditions. We already saw in sections 7.3.4, 7.6.1 and 7.6.2 how, according to H&EVGT, conventions evolve in order to fill the gap left open by the indeterminacy of the hawk–dove game, a process of evolution which, later, bestowed virtue on these conventions thus creating moral beliefs. Therefore moral beliefs are shaped in response (and in accordance) to the problem of distributing pay-offs in hawk–dove-like situations. Moreover, different distribution conventions lead to different conceptions of what is 'proper' behaviour. People may *think* that their beliefs on such matters go beyond material values (i.e. self-interest, which in our context means pay-offs); that they respond to certain universal ideals about what is 'good' and 'right', when all along their moral beliefs are a direct (even if unpredictable) repercussion of material conditions and interests. H&EVGT and Marx agree on this and both are deeply suspicious of moral judgements which are presented as objective (i.e. as moral facts). Indeed most of the ideas developed on the basis of H&EVGT in the preceding pages would find Marx in agreement. After all, we have suggested that evolutionary game theory reveals several insights with respect to social life which sound quite like observations that Marxists might make: the importance of taking collective action if one wants to change a convention; how power can be covertly exercised; how beliefs (particularly moral beliefs) may become endogenous to the conventions we follow; how property relations might develop functionally; and so on.

So the major similarity is that both see morals as illusory beliefs which are successful only as long as they remain illusory. From that moment onwards, the two traditions diverge. On the side of H&EVGT, Hume thinks that such illusions play a positive role (in providing the 'cement' which keeps society together) in relation to the common good. So do neo-Humeans (like Sugden) who are, of course, less confident that invocation of the 'common good' is a good idea (as we mentioned in section 7.6.2) but who are still happy to see conventions (because of the order they bring) become entrenched in social life even if this is achieved with the help of a few moral 'illusions'. On the other side, however, Marx insists that moral illusions are never a good idea (indeed he dislikes all illusions). Especially since, as he sees it, their social function is to help some dreadful conventions survive (recall how in section 7.3.4 we showed that disagreeable conventions may become stable even if they are detrimental to the majority). Marx believed that we can (and should) be liberated from illusory moral beliefs, from what he called 'false consciousness'.

So far, however, the difference between the two camps (H&EVGT and Marx) is purely based on value judgements: one argues that illusory morals are good for all, the other that they are not. In this sense, both can profitably make use of the analysis in evolutionary game theory. Indeed, as we have already implied in section 7.3.4, a radical political project grounded in collective action is as compatible with evolutionary game theory as is the neo-Humeanism of Sugden (1986, 1989). But is there something more in Marx than a left wing interpretation of evolutionary game theory? We think there is.

To see what this 'something more' is, we must first look at what type of interests are served by conventions and morals. In the case of Hume and evolutionary game theory (what we labelled H&EVGT) we saw that the relevant interests were those of the individual. H&EVGT starts with a study of individual action (as for instance in the analysis of the hawk–dove game) based on self-interest (i.e. the pay-offs of the game). Then, once conventions come into being (following the inability of self-interest and instrumental rationality alone to guide the individual) they start evolving. Indeed a process of natural selection gets to work: individuals selecting conventions which increase their pay-offs (on average) and conventions fading or dominating depending on how many individuals (guided by self-interest) switch to them. Finally, the established (stable) conventions acquire moral weight and even lead people to believe in something called the common good – which is most likely another illusion brought about by the observation that individuals who consistently follow the convention *all* do better.[8] In summary, H&EVGT begins with a behavioural theory based on the *individual interest* and eventually lands on its agreeable by-product: the *species interest*. There is nothing in between the two types of interest. By contrast, Marx posits another type of interest in between: class interest.

Marx's argument is that humans are very different from other species because we produce commodities in an organised way before distributing them. Whereas other species share the fruits of nature (hawk–dove games are therefore 'naturally' pertinent in their state of nature), humans have developed complex social mechanisms for *producing* goods. Naturally, the norms of distribution come to depend on the structure of these productive mechanisms. They involve a division of labour and lead to social divisions (classes). Which class a person belongs to depends on his or her location (relative to others) within the process of production. The moment collective production (as in the case of Cephu and his tribe in Chapter 5) gave its place to a separation between those who owned the tools of production and those who worked those tools, then groups with significantly different (and often contradictory) interests developed.

An analysis of hawk–dove games, along the lines of H&EVGT, helps explain the evolution of property rights in primitive societies. Once these rights are in place and social production is under way, each group in society (e.g. the owners of productive means, or those who do not own tools, land, machines, etc.) develops its own interest. And since (as H&EVGT concurs) conventions evolve in response to such interests, it is not surprising that different conventions are generated within different social groups in response to the different interests. The result is conflicting sets of conventions which lead to conflicting morals. Each set of morals becomes an ideology.[9] Which set of morals (or ideology) prevails at any given time? Marx thinks that, inevitably, the social class which is dominant in the sphere of production and distribution will also be the one whose set of conventions and morals (i.e. whose ideology) will come to dominate over society as a whole.

To sum up Marx's argument so far, prevailing moral beliefs are illusory products of a social selection process where the driving force is not some subjective individual interest but objective class interest rooted in the technology and relations of production. Although there are many conflicting norms and morals, at any particular time the morality of the ruling class is uniquely evolutionary stable. The *mélange* of legislation, moral codes, norms, etc., reflects this dominant ideology.

But is there a fundamental difference between the method of H&EVGT and Marx? Or is it just a matter of introducing classes in the analysis without changing the method? This is a controversial question. On the one hand we have those who think that, in terms of method, there is no difference.[10] They would, for example, argue that classes are essentially a by-product of individual interactions (just as the consequences for the species in H&EVGT are a by-product of individual interactions). On the other hand, there are others who argue (with Marx) that social relations are *primarily* (though not deterministically) constitutive of the individual.[11] In the latter case, Marx's introduction of classes in the theory of society is of major ontological significance and distinguishes his method to that of H&EVGT.

So, how would Marx respond to evolutionary game theory if he were around today? He would, we think, be very interested in some of the radical conclusions in this chapter. However, he would also speak derisively of the materialism of H&EVGT. Marx habitually poured scorn on those (e.g. Spinoza and Feuerbach) who transplanted models from the natural sciences to the social sciences with little or no modification to allow for the fact that human beings are very different to atoms, planets and molecules.[12] We mention this because at the heart of H&EVGT lies a simple Darwinian mechanism (witness that there is no analytical difference between the models in the biology of John Maynard Smith and the models in this chapter). Marx would probably claim that the theory is not sufficiently evolutionary because (a) its mechanism comes to a standstill once a stable convention has evolved, and (b) of its reliance on instrumental rationality which reduces human actions to passive reflex responses to some (meta-physical) self-interest. He would ask:

> How is it that you can explain moral beliefs in materialist terms, but you avoid a materialist explanation of beliefs about what people consider to be their own interest? If they are capable of having illusions about the

former (as you admit), surely they can have some about the latter! If morals are socially manufactured, then so is self-interest.

Of course there is always the answer that self-interest feeds into moral beliefs and then moral beliefs feed back into self-interest and alter people's desires. And so on. But that would be too circular for Marx. It would not explain where the process started and where it is going. By contrast, his version of materialism (which he labelled historical materialism) starts from the technology of production and the corresponding social organisation. The latter entails social classes which in turn imbue people with interests; people act on those interests and, mostly without knowing it, they shape the conventions of social life which then give rise to morals. The process, however, is grounded on the technology of production at the beginning of the chain. And as this changes (through technological innovations) it provides the impetus for the destabilisation of the (temporarily) evolutionary stable conventions at the other end of the chain.

Two questions remain: how useful is Marx's contribution to the debate on evolutionary theory and, further, how relevant is the latter to those who are engaged in debates around Marxism? Our answer to the first question is that Marx seems aware of the ontological problem to which we keep returning from Chapter 2 onwards: the need for a model of human agency richer than the one offered by instrumental rationality.[13] Especially in his philosophical (as opposed to economic) works, Marx argued strongly for an evolutionary (or more precisely historical) theory of society with a model of human agency which retains human activity as a positive (creative) force at its core. In addition, Marx often spoke out against mechanism; against models borrowed directly from the natural sciences (astronomy and biology are two examples that he warned against). It is helpful to preserve such an aversion since humans are ontologically different to atoms and genes. Of course Marx himself has been accused of mechanism and, indeed, in the modern (primarily Anglo-Saxon) social theory literature he is taken to be an exemplar of 19th century mechanism. Nevertheless he would deny this, pointing to the dialectical method he borrowed from Hegel and which (he would claim) allowed him to have a scientific, yet non-mechanistic, outlook. Do we believe him? As authors we disagree here. SHH does not, while YV does.

The answer to the second question in the opening sentence of the previous paragraph is trickier. As authors we think we disagree (again), but we are not sure on what! SHH is quite enthusiastic about evolutionary game theory (on the basis of the impressive results of previous sections), even though he concedes that without a new ontology (a better model of human agency) we cannot take the theory much further. YV, on the other hand, also enjoys evolutionary game theory but is pessimistic about the prospects of transforming a mechanical materialism (i.e. a theory based on instrumental rationality plus biology) into something more wholesome. Our discomfort with each other is made worse by the possibility that we may not really disagree. Perhaps our disagreement needs to be understood in terms of the lack of a shared history in relation to these debates – one of us embarking from an Anglo-Saxon, the other from a (south) European, tradition. It was, after all, one of our important points in earlier chapters that game theorists should not expect a convergence of beliefs unless agents have a shared history!

7.7 CONCLUSION

We began this chapter with three concerns about mainstream game theory. Two were theoretical in origin: one related to the model of rational agency employed and the other was the problem of pointing to solutions in the absence of a clear-cut equilibrium. The third arose because game theory has some controversial insights to offer the debate on the role and function of collective agencies (such as the State). Evolutionary game theory has thrown light on all three issues and it is time now to draw up a balance sheet.

On the first two issues, we have found that evolutionary game theory helps explain how a solution comes about in the absence of an apparent unique equilibrium. However, to do so it has to allow for a more complex notion of individual agency. This is not obvious at first. Evolutionary game theory does away with the more demanding (and complex) assumption of common knowledge of what it is rational to do and, instead, assumes that agents blunder around on a trial and error basis. This learning model, directed as it is instrumentally by pay-offs, may be more realistic but it is not enough to explain equilibrium selection. Instead, if we are to explain actual outcomes, individuals must be socially and historically located in a way that they are not in the instrumental model. 'Social' means quite simply that *individuals have to be studied within the context of the social relations within which they live and which generate specific norms.* When this is not enough to explain their current beliefs and expectations then, of course, we have to look to the individual idiosyncrasies and eccentricities (in belief and action) if we are to explain their behaviour.

Thus evolutionary game theory, like mainstream game theory, needs a changed ontology (which will embrace some alternative or expanded model of human agency) if it is to yield explanations and predictions in many of the games which comprise the social world. We have left open the question of what changes are required. Nevertheless, it is entirely possible that the change may make a nonsense of the very way that game theory models social life. For example, suppose the shared sources of extraneous belief which need to be added to either mainstream or evolutionary game theory in one form or another come from the Wittgensteinian move, sketched in section 1.2.3. Or, imagine a model in which preferences and beliefs (moral and otherwise) are simultaneous by-products of some social process rooted in the development of organised production – as in Marx's model in section 7.6.4. These theoretical moves will threaten to dissolve the distinction between action and structure which lies at the heart of the game theoretical depiction of social life because it will mean that the structure begins to supply reasons for action and not just constraints upon action. On the optimistic side, this might be seen as just another example of how discussions around game theory help to dissolve some of the binary oppositions which have plagued some debates in social science – just as it helped dissolve the opposition between gender and class earlier in this chapter. However, our concern here is not to point to required changes in ontology of a particular sort. The point is that some change is necessary, and that it is likely to threaten the basic approach of game theory to social life.

Turning to another dispute, that between *social constructivism* and *spontaneous order* within liberal political theory, two clarifications have occurred. The first is that there can be no presumption that a spontaneous order will deliver outcomes which make everyone better off, or even outcomes which favour most of the population. This would seem to provide ammunition for the social constructivists, but of course it depends on them believing that collective action agencies like the State will have sufficient information to distinguish the superior outcomes. Perhaps all that can be said on this matter is that, if you really believe that evolutionary forces will do the best that is possible, then it is beyond dispute that these forces have thrown up people who are predisposed to take collective action. Thus it might be argued that our evolutionary superiority as a species derives in part precisely from the fact that we are pro-active through collective action agencies rather than reactive as we would be under a simple evolutionary scheme.

Secondly, on the difficult cases where equilibrium selection involves choices over whose interests are to be favoured (i.e. it is not a matter of selecting the equilibrium which is better for everyone), then it is *not* obvious that a collective action agency like the State is any better placed to make this decision than a process of spontaneous order. This may come as a surprise, since we have spent most of our time here focusing on the indeterminacy of evolutionary games when agents are only weakly instrumentally rational. But the point here is that the indeterminacy of equilibria when agents are instrumentally rational arises as much as a problem for collective action (see Chapter 4) as it does for the repeated play of evolutionary games. To see this, one need only model the political process as a game between different agents. Some aspects of this process are bound to resemble a bargaining game, since there are 'spoils'/gains of collective action to be distributed, in which case the potential problem of indeterminacy resurfaces (see Chapter 4).

In other words the very debate within liberal political theory over social constructivism versus spontaneous order is itself unable to come to a resolution precisely because its shared ontological foundations are inadequate for the task of social explanation. In short, we conclude that not only will game theory have to embrace some expanded form of individual agency, if it is to be capable of explaining many social interactions, but also that this is necessary if it is to be useful to the liberal debate over the scope of the State.

8

WATCHING PEOPLE PLAY GAMES
Some experimental evidence

8.1 INTRODUCTION

So far in this book we have been subjecting almost every theoretical proposition of game theory to scrutiny. The result has been a sequence of challenges and defences of the theory's predictions about how rational people would play the games under study. What would be more natural then than to ask real people to play these games under controlled (laboratory) conditions so that we can observe their actual behaviour? Would this not cut through the maze of arguments surrounding the appropriateness of the various assumptions, such as CKR (Common Knowledge of instrumental Rationality), CAB (Common Alignment of Beliefs) and the resultant Nash equilibrium, the marriage of backward induction and CKR, as well as the initial assumption that players are exclusively instrumentally rational? Indeed our reflections on the assumptions of game theory are based on mental experiments of the sort: 'How would I behave in this situation? What would I expect my opponent to do?' Such introspection is a type of proto-experiment. Well-organised experiments involving many people is the next step.

In fact several central propositions in game theory have been systematically tested through laboratory experiments. In this chapter we report on some of the results. Most experiments are typically organised around one particular type of game and then the observed behaviour of individuals and groups is used to test a number of hypotheses. Faithful to this format, we begin the discussion in section 8.2 with evidence on backward induction (see Chapter 3). Does the marriage of CAB (the assumption that beliefs will always remain consistently aligned) with backward induction (see sections 3.2 and 3.3) predict how well people play these games? Or will they deviate from the theory's predictions, as we described in section 3.4? In section 8.3 we turn to the prisoners' dilemma (see Chapters 5 and 6), in particular the finitely repeated version. How relevant are the stories about the possibility of cooperation in section 6.5? In section 8.4 we investigate games of coordination (which feature more than one Nash equilibrium) and report on some experimental results which raise eyebrows amongst those who expect the 'best outcome' (that is, the Nash equilibrium which is best for all players) to materialise simply because no one has an incentive to sabotage it (for the relevant theoretical discussion see section 7.4). Then in section 8.5 we look at some of the bargaining games discussed earlier in Chapter 4. How well does the Nash bargaining solution and Nash backward induction explain actual offers and demands between bargainers? Finally section 8.6 discusses games in the genre of the hawk–dove contests which featured in Chapter 7 (but also in Chapter 4). Our own experimental data reveals evolutionary patterns which go beyond the predictions of evolutionary game theory. Section 8.7 concludes.

Before we proceed with the experimental findings, a word of caution is in order. The idea of conducting tests in laboratories is liable to conjure up thoughts of authoritative science. It might seem that, at last, we shall *know* whether people behave in the way that game theory predicts. Unfortunately

---

Box 8.1

WHO DO YOU TRUST?

Different people may play games differently. So, who do you trust? Whose behaviour should you use as the benchmark by which you will judge a theory? Do you choose at random? And what if the randomly chosen group of experimental subjects behave contrary to the theory which you favour? You may be tempted to conclude that yours is not a 'good' sample. But what is a 'good' sample? Should you go about looking for one in the way that opinion pollsters do (seeking a representative cross section of the population), or should you screen people so that the more 'rational' are admitted in the laboratory? Indeed experimental physicists go to great lengths to remove all 'impurities' from the laboratory prior to their experiments. Why not do the same here and disqualify less than instrumentally rational people since game theory does not claim to predict their behaviour? This is fine, provided you realise that you have ended up judging people according to the theory, rather than vice versa. Moreover, unlike physics, the criteria for the 'quality' of the subjects, or of the environment in the laboratory, cannot be objective (e.g. less dust, no gravity, etc.). By having subjectively to decide what they are, you cannot avoid instilling your prejudices (as the experimenter) in the data. Thus the subjective choice of criteria determining who qualifies as a good subject is very likely to affect how well the theory will fare. And since as an honest experimenter you do not want to have this type of influence over the 'data', you cannot even trust yourself!

---

matters are not quite that simple. There are major philosophical problems associated with interpreting empirical evidence, particularly in the social sciences, and game theory experiments are no exception (see Hargreaves Heap and Varoufakis (1994) as well as Box 8.1). This does not mean that we should turn our back on empirical evidence. What it does mean is that our interpretation of results must be cautious and that, ultimately, laboratory experiments may only be telling us how people behave in laboratories.

8.2 BACKWARD INDUCTION

Recall the centipede game in Figure 3.6. The unique subgame perfect Nash equilibrium (SPNE), which was arrived at through Nash backward induction, instructed either player to end the game at the first opportunity. Would people act this way? Or would they play across in a bid to reach the higher pay-offs on the right hand side of the centipede?

Aumann (1988) suggested a simple experiment. Place two piles of money on a table. One pile is much larger than the other. Then ask one of two players, say R, either to take one of the two piles or to pass. If she 'takes', the game ends with R collecting the money in that pile and C getting nothing. If she 'passes', the amount in each pile is multiplied by 10 and then C chooses to 'take' or to 'pass'. If he passes, the piles are multiplied by 10 again. Imagine there are six rounds and the piles initially contain $10 and 50c. In the second round they would be worth $100 and $5 respectively. By the sixth round, player C will have a choice between $1 million and $50,000. In all probability, R can expect $50,000 if they reach round 6. Yet Nash backward induction (and the SPNE concept) suggests that R will take the $10 at the beginning (see sections 3.3 and 3.4).

McKelvey and Palfrey (1992) conducted a very similar experiment (with, understandably, lower potential pay-offs). In seven sessions each involving between 18 and 20 subjects, they found that only in 37 out of 662 such games did the SPNE prediction (i.e. that the first player would 'take' the largest pile thus ending the game) come true. In all other cases the game entered the latter stages and both players ended up with more money than predicted. Could this be because the game was repeated and players established some way of communicating to each other a readiness not to abscond? The experimental design does not leave room for such an explanation. Players were told that they will only be matched with the same person once. Indeed it was common knowledge that no subject i was ever matched with any other subject who had previously played someone who had played someone who had played i. This should, in principle, have eliminated cooperative behaviour (of the tit-for-tat variety).

Of course game theory's SPNE prediction rests on two assumptions: players are instrumentally rational and they are subject to CKR (i.e. common knowledge of their instrumental rationality). Thus the experiment, at best, tests the joint hypothesis formed by these assumptions and does not clarify which particular assumption has been invalidated by the results. Of course, the game theorist can then explain the predictive failure by arguing that CKR was not in place! If there is a positive probability that your opponent is the type of person who eschews subgame perfection calculations (i.e. an altruist who despises penny-pinching) and who is inclined to 'pass' so that both can move to the more lucrative part of the game, then a logic similar to that in section 6.5 could explain why it is that people do not 'take' immediately. Recall that this explanation is known as a *sequential equilibrium* (see sections 3.4 and 6.5.3) and goes like this: in the presence of a possibility that your opponent expects you to be an altruist, it may be an equilibrium strategy to behave like an altruist, even if you are not. As the game moves on, both you and your opponent will be increasingly tempted to reveal your true colours by 'taking' the largest pile and ending the game. Thus, as the game progresses beyond a certain stage, only genuine altruists continue to pass.

McKelvey and Palfrey (1992) observed that 9 out of 138 subjects passed at every opportunity (genuine altruists?). By contrast only one subject always took the largest pile. This seems to support the sequential equilibrium view which suggests that, in the presence of altruists and therefore of uncertainty about who is an altruist, people will mix their strategies, at least in the earlier stages of the game (see Box 6.3 for a related example). Also the fact that games tended to end earlier the more games the players had played before, suggests a type of learning which leads closer to the SPNE prediction.

However, when the data is examined more closely, the theory looks decidedly shaky. Firstly, there was a significant proportion (between 15% and 25%) who chose the obviously dominated strategy of passing in the penultimate and in the last rounds. Moreover, there was no evidence that the mixed strategies involved were compatible with the sequential equilibrium explanation (which is of course the only explanation game theory can offer of why people passed). For example, some subjects 'took' the lesser pile at the last node and then 'took' the largest pile on the first occasion in the next game. Much of the observed behaviour is impossible to rationalise even by resorting to the possibility of altruistic individuals or Bayesian updating across games. To quote the authors:

> Rational play cannot account for some sequences of plays we observe in the data, even with a model that admits the possibility of altruistic players.

(McKelvey and Palfrey, 1992)

Similar results are reported by Camerer and Weigelt (1988) in another experimental study which targeted the sequential equilibrium explicitly (as opposed to the SPNE). In their experiments they tested the equilibrium theory of reputation building in section 6.5 (and Box 6.3). They found that *some* of the intuitively appealing aspects of the sequential equilibrium story are confirmed by actual behaviour. However, this is not the same as saying that support was given to the more specific predictions about the exact rules by which people select their mixed strategies as the end of the horizon (i.e. the last repetition of the game) approaches. Their own interpretation of the fact that behavioural data is all over the place (compared with the neat predictions of the theory) is that people come into the laboratory with heterogeneous 'homemade priors'; that is, with all sorts of private beliefs about the probability that an altruist will pass; or a strong defender will fight; or an opponent is altruistic, strong, etc.

8.3 REPEATED PRISONERS' DILEMMAS

The earliest recorded attempt to test game theory happened in 1950 when two Rand Corporation researchers, Flood and Dresher, asked two friends (Almen Alchian, an economist at UCLA, and John Williams, a colleague at Rand) to play the prisoners' dilemma game exactly 100 times. Recall from section 6.2 that, in such a finitely repeated version of the prisoners' dilemma, the unique subgame perfect Nash equilibrium SPNE predicts defection throughout in exactly the same way that in the game discussed by Aumann (1988) (and tested by McKelvey and Palfrey) in the previous section the SPNE recommended 'taking' at the first opportunity. The results were rather spectacularly different from what John Nash (also a colleague at Rand) expected, but very similar to those McKelvey and Palfrey (1992) found 34 years later: mutual defection occurred in only 14 plays and mutual cooperation occurred in 60 plays.

Was it that Alchian and Williams were not instrumentally rational, or was it that they had no CKR? Or was it simply that they thought their partner thought there was some probability that they are the type of person who makes a habit of playing tit-for-tat regardless of the game theoretical calculus – in which case they would profit from playing along with that expectation? (The latter is of course the same sequential equilibrium logic discussed in the previous section and in section 6.5.)

However the result is interpreted, it was not an auspicious beginning for experimental game theory because both assumptions (of instrumental rationality and CKR) are central to mainstream game theory. Things have not improved since that time, at least as far as empirical support for CKR is concerned. There is a large experimental literature which has replicated this basic result (see for instance Rapoport and Chammah, 1965, and Selten and Stoecker, 1986) and this has set an agenda for exploring the source of this 'surprisingly' cooperative behaviour. The basic explanation canvassed is the sequential equilibrium story. Since we have rehearsed it in the previous section, we will only mention three papers which give it some credence:

Selten and Stoecker (1986), Kahn and Murnighan (1993) and Andreoni and Miller (1993).

In summary, cooperation prevails in the finitely repeated prisoners' dilemma against the force of Nash backward induction. So, CKR seems absent even when experimenters do their best to create enough common knowledge of pay-offs and rules to give CKR its best shot (see Box 8.3 for an example of how degrees of common knowledge could be induced in the laboratory). Instead we observe that players insist on entertaining doubts about the motives and character of each other. Indeed, the evidence from these experiments suggests not only that players do entertain doubts about motives, but that they have good reason to entertain such doubts for two reasons. Firstly because there are some players who are unconditionally cooperative or 'altruistic' in the way that they play this game and, secondly, because whether someone is cooperative or not seems to be determined by one's background, rather than by how clever (or rational) he or she is (see adjacent box on the curse of economics). In this sense, the evidence seems to point to a falsification of the assumption of instrumentally rational action based on the pay-offs (and with it common knowledge of this rationality) rather than an inability to use the principle of backward induction.

Box 8.2

THE CURSE OF ECONOMICS

Frank, Gilovich and Regan (1993) found that students who have been majoring in economics are less likely to cooperate in the prisoners' dilemma than other students. Also, they were much more prone to abscond on undertakings to cooperate and they were the most pessimistic about the prospect that others would cooperate. As a result, the group of economists secured a significantly lower level of pay-offs than the rest. Frank also showed that this is not the result of self-selection (i.e. the less cooperative by nature choosing economics subjects) but of the experience of studying economics. Should we be pleased, as economists, that our students seem to gravitate towards the logic of dominance reasoning or should we despair that the spread of economics thus makes cooperation in society more difficult to achieve because it encourages people to think that rational action amounts to a simple form of instrumental calculation?

In short, the experiment is a testament to the potential power of any theory to shape the world that we live in by influencing the way that people think of themselves; and it serves to remind us that we can quite legitimately be concerned not only with whether game theory predicts actual behaviour well, but also with whether its model of individuals and their social interactions is actually desirable.

8.4 COORDINATION GAMES

Consider the following situation (as described in Halpern (1986)). Two divisions of an army are stationed on two hill-tops overlooking a valley in which an enemy division can be clearly seen. It is known that if both divisions attack simultaneously they will capture the enemy with none, or very little, loss of life. However, there were no prior plans to launch such an attack, as it was not anticipated that the enemy would be spotted in that location. How will the two divisions coordinate their attack (we assume that they must maintain visual and radio silence)? Neither commanding officer will launch an attack unless he is sure that the other will attack at the same time. Thus a classic coordination problem emerges.

Imagine now that a messenger can be sent but that it will take him about an hour to convey the message. However, it is also possible that he will be caught by the enemy in the meantime. If everything goes smoothly and the messenger gets safely from one hill-top to another, is this enough for a coordinated attack to be launched? Suppose the message sent by the first commanding officer to the second read: 'Let's attack at dawn!' Will the second officer attack at dawn? No, unless he is confident that the first commanding officer (who sent the message) knows that the message has been received. So, the second commanding officer sends the messenger back to the first with the message: 'Message received. Dawn it is!' Will the second officer attack now? Not until he knows that the messenger has delivered his message. Paradoxically, no amount of messages will do the trick since confirmation of receipt of the last message will be necessary regardless of how many messages have been already received.

We see that in a coordination game like the above, even a very high degree of common knowledge of the plan to attack at dawn is not enough to guarantee coordination (see Box 8.3 for an example of how different degrees of common knowledge can be engendered in the laboratory). What is needed (at least in theory) is a consistent alignment of beliefs (CAB) about the plan.[1] And yet this does not exclude the possibility that the two commanding officers will both attack at dawn with very high probability. How successfully they coordinate will, however, depend on more than a high degree of common knowledge. Indeed the latter may even be unnecessary provided the time of the attack is carefully chosen. The classic early experiments by Thomas Schelling on behaviour in coordination games have confirmed this – see Box 7.2.

Schelling's experiments draw the conclusion that players have a surprising capacity to coordinate their behaviour by drawing on shared senses of prominence, or salience, to select a particular equilibrium once the game has been embedded in some shared social context. Just like people seem to converge on 12.00 noon as the time to meet others when no prior arrangement has been made, our commanding officers would (in all probability) find it easier to communicate a willingness to launch an attack at dawn rather than at any other time – even if the messenger got lost or was captured. In other words, even mild doses of common knowledge will do the trick provided the plan is salient in some other way.

Experiments with coordination games have been very useful in this sense. They illustrate the importance of extraneous information (e.g. the non-rational salience of 'dawn' or 'heads' or of number 7, etc.) since it is

---

Box 8.3

DEGREES OF COMMON KNOWLEDGE IN THE LABORATORY

Two players are located at different computer terminals. Before asked to choose their strategies (for example, in a coordination game like the one in Figure 8.1) one of them, say R, is given an opportunity to send the following message to player C: 'I will choose R2. Please choose C2 so that we can get the high pay-off!' Let us assume that she is not allowed to send any other message. If the electronic network is set up in a way that a confirmation is sent automatically upon receipt of *any* message (including a confirmation), then almost immediately after R has sent her message, an infinity of confirmations will be exchanged between the two terminals. If there is a number at the top of each screen relating the number of messages received, then (provided the message is sent) that number will be increasing *ad infinitum*. Here the laboratory version of common knowledge that R plans to play R2. It follows that if a message is not received by C, then R obviously does not intend to play R2 and this is why she did not send any message (recall that she is not allowed to send the message: 'I will play R1. Please choose C1.').

Less than infinite common knowledge can be easily introduced. Imagine that every time a computer sends a message (or a confirmation) there is a positive, yet small, probability ε that the message will be lost in the system. If a message does not arrive then the communication is severed. Thus non-receipt of the above message may mean two things: (a) that R intends to play R2 but her message was lost; (b) that R does not intend to play R2 and for this reason never sent the message. Even when ε is very small and most messages get through, there is still some residual uncertainty. Then the number on the players' screen is significant. If, for example, it reads 25 on C's screen, this means that 25 messages have been received by C (25th-order common knowledge). Nevertheless, player R still faces *some* uncertainty: given that she sent 25 messages, and there are only 24 received messages on her screen, she does not know whether C did not get message 25 or whether C got that message but his confirmation has been lost. The only way of eliminating uncertainty resulting from less than infinite-order common knowledge is when $\varepsilon = 0$. (See Rubinstein (1989) for a perfect equilibrium solution which cuts through this uncertainty.)

---

easy to show that the degree of coordination depends on how strategies (which are identical in every other sense) are presented to subjects. For example, if in a 2 × 2 coordination game as the one below the two strategies are 'Attack at dawn' and 'Attack at 3.45 am' the former always wins hands down. But even when there is no such 'framing', subjects still manage to discover some salience.

	C1	C2
R1	1, 1	0, 0
R2	0, 0	1, 1

Recall Schelling's finding that when he asked people to choose between 'Heads' and 'Tails' most chose 'Heads' for no apparent reason (as this was not a game and there were no pay-offs). In the above coordination game, people whose first language is (say) English may find that (R1, C1) has greater salience than (R2, C2) for the simple reason that their eye has been trained to read rows first and from left to right. Similarly for people of a Chinese or a Korean background (R2, C2) may offer a great attraction. Indeed this is what we found to be the case in similar experiments reported in greater detail in section 8.6. Whereas the bulk of subjects were attracted by strategies R1 and C1, a subset of subjects who had Chinese, Japanese and Korean as their first language tended towards R2 and C2.

Behaviour in coordination games has recently been studied by Cooper *et al.* (1990) in a way which directly addresses the use of extraneous information as well as some of our earlier concerns. In particular they devised a series of games to test the following three hypotheses:

(a) The outcome will be a Nash equilibrium.
(b) The Pareto-dominant Nash equilibrium will be selected.[2]
(c) Dominated strategies are irrelevant to equilibrium selection.

To illustrate their technique consider one of their games in Figure 8.1.
This is basically a coordination game with two Nash equilibria ((R1, C1) and (R2, C2)), one of which – i.e. (R2, C2) – is better than the other in the

	C1	C2	C3
R1	+350, 350−	350, 250	700, 0
R2	250, 350	+550, 550−	+1000, 0
R3	0, 700	0, 1000−	600, 600

Figure 8.1

244

	C1	C2	C3
R1	$^+1, 0^-$	−1, −1	−1, −1
R2	0, 0	$^+0, 1^-$	$^+601, 0$
R3	−1, −1	$−1, 601^-$	600, 600

Figure 8.2

Pareto sense (see note 2 for a definition of Pareto improvement). However, the game also includes a third strategy choice (R3, C3) which is strategically dominated for both players – i.e. neither R3 nor C3 is a best response to any of the strategies of C and R respectively. Yet the strategically dominated strategy pair (R3, C3) yields an outcome which is more lucrative for both players, when compared with the two Nash equilibria.

The authors experiment with games like the one in Figure 8.1 in order to test their three hypotheses. Their results show that:

Firstly, in games with this strategic structure agents *do* select Nash strategies, even though there is a third non-Nash strategy available which is better for both. (Notice that the third strategy imparts some of the character of a prisoners' dilemma to the game.)

Indeed they found that only about 1% of their subjects chose their third strategies. Is this result sufficiently general? We suspect that it is not. If for instance the matrix was changed to that in Figure 8.2 we suspect that, even though the strategic structure of the game would remain intact (notice that the location of the ($^+$) and ($^-$) signs labelling the players' best replies has not changed), there would be a greater tendency for players to play the non-Nash strategies R3 and C3. Indeed our own experiments confirm this (see section 8.6).

Secondly, players may or may not select the Pareto-superior Nash equilibrium.

Indeed in the game of Figure 8.1 they did – that is, they played their second strategy yielding (550, 550) more often. But it seems that this was so not because of the superiority of (R2, C2) over (R1, C1) but because of the fact that, if you play your second strategy when your opponent has played his or her third, then you stand to gain a much higher pay-off: 1000. However, once more this result seems hardly generalisable. When the authors changed the matrix in Figure 8.1 so that the 1000 pay-off was substituted with a 0, the 'worse' Nash equilibrium (R1, C1) – i.e. the Pareto-dominated one – was played 83% of the time while (R2, C2) was only played 26% of the time. We suspect that the same would have happened if the strategic

	C1	C2	C3
R1	+360, 360−	340, 250	700, 0
R2	250, 340	+350, 350−	+1000, 0
R3	0, 700	0, 1000−	600, 600

Figure 8.3

structure of Figure 8.1 was maintained but the pay-offs changed to those in Figure 8.3.

Thus in experiments, Pareto superiority does not seem to be a general criterion which players use to select between Nash equilibria (see also Chapter 7). In conclusion, so far it seems that the way people actually play these games is neither directly controlled by the strategic aspects of the game (i.e. the location of the best response marks (+)and (−) in the matrix) nor by the size of the return from coordinating on non-Nash outcomes such as (R3, C3): it is a so-far-unexplained mixture of the two factors that decides.

> **Thirdly**, although mainstream game theory treats dominated strategies as irrelevant under CKR, it seems that players do use them as a cue for conditioning their behaviour.

In the game of Figure 8.3, it is the fact that the second strategy does so much better against the third strategy than does the first (1000 as compared with 700) which may explain why the players opt for the Nash equilibrium (R2, C2) rather than for (R1, C1). In other words, from a mainstream game theoretical point of view the information contained in the third row and column is, strictly speaking, 'extraneous' to the interaction, yet players share this extraneous information and are able to use it in a way which enables them to coordinate their choice of one particular Nash equilibrium. (For an example of how game theory can explain this, see section 2.7.1.)

In conclusion, experiments with coordination games show that people sometimes coordinate more often than the theory can explain (recall Schelling's results as well as the coordinated attack example) whereas at other times (and depending on framing and social context, as well as on the exact pay-offs) they fail to coordinate at all on what the theory considers to be a natural equilibrium.

8.5 BARGAINING GAMES

Experiments with bargaining games have been used to test both the Nash bargaining solution and the solution by Rubinstein (1982) – see Chapter 4. We begin with a discussion of one test of these solutions.

One of the difficulties with testing the Nash solution to the bargaining problem is that it requires knowledge of the players' utility functions and these are not readily observable. Roth and Malouf (1979) devised an ingenious way of overcoming this problem, which we shall briefly describe as it has been used in a number of later experiments testing behaviour in a variety of games. They asked players in pairs to bargain over the distribution of 100 lottery tickets. In the experiment the distribution of these lottery tickets determines the probability of each player receiving a 'high' and 'low' prize. Thus when R gets 60 tickets and C 40 that means R 'wins' a 60% chance of her 'high' prize and a 40% chance of her 'low' prize; whereas C gets a 40% chance of his 'high' prize and a 60% chance of his 'low' prize. The high and low prizes need not be the same for both players (for instance, R's possible prizes might be $100 and $10; and C's possible prizes might be $200 and $10). Finally if the players fail to agree on a distribution of the lottery tickets, then each will receive their 'low' prize with certainty. Thus the players are bargaining with each other in order to increase their respective *chances* of getting their 'high' prizes.

Why all this? Because in this way, if we ask people to bargain over these 100 lottery tickets, we know what the theory predicts they will do *even if we have no idea of their utility functions* (e.g. we do not know how risk averse they are, how keen they are to get their hands on $1, etc.). The reason is this: we know that a cardinal utility function is arbitrary,[3] and so we can set the utility of each player's 'high' prize equal to, say, 1 and the utility of the low prize equal to, say, 0. But because they are not bargaining over utilities, but over probabilities of receiving certain utilities (i.e. lottery tickets), we do not need to know how much that fictitious 1 is valued by different players. Hence they are not bargaining over 1 unit of utility but over chances of getting whatever it is that they prefer. Formally, their agreement entails a distribution of lottery tickets which will divide the expected gain of 1 util between the two. What that 1 means to each one of them is neither here nor there. All that matters is that each values one extra lottery ticket exactly the same as the other because it gives him or her an extra 1% chance of getting what they want. Figure 8.4 illustrates the various possible combinations of expected utility which are available if they agree. The Nash solution selects the outcome which maximises the product of the expected utility gains and the geometry (or the mathematics) in this instance is clear: they should agree on an equal division of the lottery tickets.

In the case where R's high pay-off is $100 and her low is $10, with C's pay-offs $200 and $10 respectively, Roth and Malouf (1979) found that solutions clustered around two distributions when the players knew the value of each other's prizes: the Nash solution giving the same number of lottery tickets to each (thus a 50–50 chance to each) and the distribution which produced an equal expected gain (in our example that would give 66.6% to R and 33.3% to C as C's high prize is double R's). The latter solution is perhaps to be explained by the players' concern for equity. Thus there is partial support for the Nash solution, but it is not overwhelming. (Similarly dichotomous results are easy to replicate.) Nash seems to be one 'attractor', but only one among several distributions which players will agree to. Likewise, there seems to be some, though not overwhelming, support for the prediction that more risk averse players will concede more readily than risk neutral players (see Roth, 1988).

These days the non-cooperative approach to modelling the bargaining problem is becoming more popular (recall section 4.1) and tests of the Rubinstein (1982) solution (and therefore of the SPNE approach to bargaining) proliferate. Most popular are the truncated versions of Rubinstein's sequential non-cooperative model, i.e. ones with a deadline so that if no agreement in reached by round k neither gets anything. In the special case when $k = 1$, the game becomes an ultimatum game in which unless an offer is accepted immediately both lose. Guth, Schmittberger and Schwarz (1982) ran such an experiment. Although the SPNE solution is for the offering player to offer no more than a smidgen to the other player, the average offer was about 30% – a rather generous offer! The authors concluded that there is something wrong with the SPNE stories on how people bargain.

Binmore, Shaked and Sutton (1985) denied that much should be read in these results. For

> the one stage ultimatum game is a rather special case, from which it is dangerous to draw general conclusions. In the ultimatum game, the first player might be dissuaded from making an opening demand at, or close to, the optimal level, because his opponent would then incur a negligible cost in making an 'irrational' rejection. In the two-stage game, these considerations are postponed to the second stage, and so their impact is attenuated.

This criticism led to a fresh study in Guth and Tietz (1987).

In their new experiment, Guth and Tietz gave the game a second round. Again the bargainers' objective was to divide between them a certain sum. R would make a claim for $x, C could then can accept this or make a counter-claim. The catch, however, was that the sum to be divided shrunk if the bargaining reached the second round (that is, if C rejected R's offer). If C's offer was rejected by R in round 2, both players left the laboratory empty handed. Two versions of the experiment were run: one where the overall sum shrinks by 90% after C's rejection and one where it shrinks by only 10%. The SPNE prediction is that in the first version R offers a little bit more than 10%, while in the second she offers a bit more than 90%. In both cases C should accept these offers immediately so that the game does not enter the second round. Each player played the game twice: once as the R player and once as the C player. In the first version R players first offered

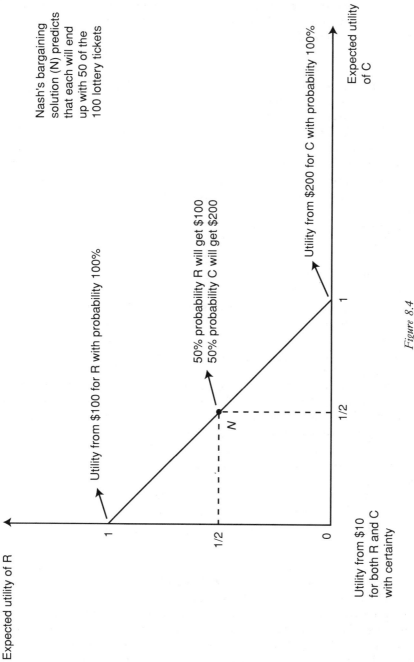

Expected utility of R

Nash's bargaining solution (N) predicts that each will end up with 50 of the 100 lottery tickets

Utility from $100 for R with probability 100%

50% probability R will get $100
50% probability C will get $200

Utility from $200 for C with probability 100%

Expected utility of C

Utility from $10 for both R and C with certainty

Figure 8.4

30% on average and then in the second play they offered 41%. In the second version R players first demanded 76% on average and then in the second play they demanded 67%. Here the conclusion that SPNE bargaining strategies are ignored even when there is more than one round.

Another response to Binmore, Shaked and Sutton (1985) is the experimental paper of Neelin, Sonnenschein and Spiegel (1988). Two experiments were reported: in the first, 80 subjects played two-period, three-period and five-period sequential, alternating offer, bargaining games, in that order, against different opponents. In the second, 30 subjects played three five-period games. The pie shrunk from $5 to different (lower values) in each of the three games. The authors summarise their findings as follows: 'Neither the Stahl[4]/Rubinstein nor the equal-split models predict the bargaining behaviour observed in our six games. A convenient summary of what we observed is that in each game the sellers offered the buyers the value of the second-round pie.' Thus we have the interesting (and unexpected) result that players played all these games as if they consisted of only two rounds (even when this was not so).

In a more recent study Ochs and Roth (1989) attempt to bring together the experiments mentioned above in a bid to examine the various claims under one roof. Their conclusions make for interesting reading: Firstly, the SPNE predictions 'that come from assuming that players' monetary payoffs are a good proxy for their utility payoffs are not at all descriptive of the results we observed. This is true . . . also of the qualitative predictions.' Secondly, there is a high frequency of disadvantageous counterproposals and moves (of the type we discussed earlier in sections 3.4.3 and 4.4.2). Thirdly, the observed behaviour, even though it does not fit the pattern predicted by the SPNE concept, displays a great deal of regularity. Fourthly, individuals' ideas about fairness seem to be both clear and 'highly sensitive to which the issue arises. . . . If ideas about fairness play a significant role in players' utility functions, their clarity would help account for the regular behaviour often observed within each of the previous experiments discussed here as well as in our own.'

The final conclusion fits nicely within the theme of our Chapter 4: 'Bargaining is a complex social phenomenon which gives bargainers systematic motivations distinct from simple income maximisation.'

Summary

In conclusion, we see that the SPNE predictions scarcely receive much encouragement from these results and again this raises a tricky issue of interpretation. These experiments, as well as those in section 8.2, involve a joint hypothesis test (that agents are instrumentally motivated by the pay-offs and that they apply the reasoning of Nash backward induction) and in principle the failure of either might account for the absence of clear support for the subgame perfect Nash concept. The tendency in the literature has again been to see these results as telling against the assumption of instrumental motivation. In particular, it is often argued that players have some notion of a just outcome which influences their behaviour in both the ultimatum game and the earlier tests on the Nash solution (and which is not captured in the description of the game). This seems plausible and might also help explain why in both types of experiments there is a surprising number of occasions when the players fail to agree on a distribution and so receive nothing; and of why the frequency of disagreement falls in face-to-face negotiations. The point is that when players do not share a sense of justice they are less likely to agree and it becomes less likely that a pair will come to share such a sense when bargaining does not involve face-to-face negotiation.

To phrase this conclusion slightly differently, but in a way which connects with the results in the next section, bargaining is a 'complex social phenomenon' where people take cues from aspects of their social life which game theory typically overlooks. Thus players seem to base their behaviour on aspects of the social interaction which game theory typically treats as extraneous; and when players share these extraneous reference points such behaviour becomes concerted. There are agreements, in other words, but they are typically not those which mainstream game theory expects because they are cued by these shared extraneous reference points. Not unsurprisingly, the chances of agreement on this view are bound to fall when players fail to share the social context which is provided by a face-to-face negotiation.

8.6 HAWK–DOVE GAMES AND THE EVOLUTION OF SOCIAL ROLES

In this section we report on our own experiments based on the five games in Figure 8.5. Games 1 and 4 are similar to the hawk–dove games in Chapter 7 in that, if any of the two players is to win something, only one will win while the other will collect a zero pay-off. Still, players have an incentive to 'concede' because this is better than a situation when both are going for the maximum pay-off (which is 5 in both games 1 and 4) and end up with −1. Games 2 and 3 are identical to game 1, while game 5 is identical to 4, provided we disregard the third strategies in these 3 × 3 games. Indeed, with CKR this is exactly what instrumentally rational players will do: they will ignore the third strategies of each player (R3 and C3) since they are not rationalisable: R3 is always a dominated strategy, while C3 is dominated in game 2 and, while it is not dominated in games 3 and 5, it drops out of these games by first-order CKR (that is, once C recognises that R will not play her dominated R3 strategy, C will never play C3). In this sense, the third strategies play a role similar to the third strategies in the game of Cooper et al. (1990) – see Figure 8.1.

The equilibrium analysis of these games can be found in sections 2.7.1 and 2.7.2. Briefly, game theory makes the following basic predictions:

(1) Game 1 is symmetrical and therefore, on average, R1 and C2 (R2 and C1) ought to be played with the same frequency. The NEMS scenario, in particular, has each player reaching for pay-off 5 with probability $\frac{6}{7}$.

(2) In game 2 strategies R3 and C3 will only be selected by mistake and strategies R1 and C1 will be played more often in game 2 than in game 1 (recall the perturbed game model in section 2.7.1). If the third strategies are played it will be by mistake, and thus the frequency with which R3 and C3 will be chosen should be the same across games 2 and 3 – i.e. the frequency of (random) errors.

(3) Moving to games 4 and 5, R1 will be played with probability $\frac{6}{7}$ and C1 with probability $\frac{2}{3}$ while in game 5, strategies R3 and C3 will be played with the same frequency as in games 2 and 3.

We tried the above games on a set of 138 volunteers (75 men and 63 women) each one of whom played every game four times. In total, each game was played 276 times. Our sample was divided into 13 groups each with size ranging from 8 to 14 participants (most groups comprised 10 to 12 players). Most of them, although not all, were university students (mainly undergraduates) from different faculties of Australian, Austrian, Greek and Hong Kong universities. None had taken courses in game theory. A small proportion of the participants were professional people, mostly with university degrees. As you can imagine, the ethnic mix of our sample is diverse as is their class, ideology and general outlook. The only thing we made sure they had in common was lack of exposure to game theory (see Boxes 8.1 and 8.2).

The details of the experimental procedure can be found in Varoufakis and Hargreaves Heap (1993). For now it suffices to say that, at the end of the session, the pay-offs of each player from each round and game were summed up and paid in Australian dollars (note: they were guaranteed a minimum of A$10 even though only one player earned less than $10 from the pay-offs; the average payment was $47 and the maximum A$98). Also, subjects played the games without knowing who they were playing against. They knew that they were playing against *someone* in their group but could not pinpoint that person. Moreover, in each round they played against someone else (so that the games were not of the repeated nature discussed in Chapter 6) and they occupied role R and C an equal number of times. Although each game (of the five we described above) was repeated four times, the fact that (a) they did not know their opponent and (b) they knew that in the next round their opponent would change, ensured that no player-specific reputation or signalling was possible. One can, however, argue that because the games were played by members of a group over and over again, social conventions may have emerged specific to that group.

	C1	C2
R1	+5, 0⁻	−1, −1
R2	−1, −1	+0, 5⁻

Game 1

	C1	C2	C3
R1	+5, 0	−1, −1	+10, −1
R2	−1, −1	+0, 5⁻	−1, −2
R3	−1, 10⁻	−2, −1	6, 6

Game 2

	C1	C2	C3
R1	+5, 0⁻	−1, −1	+10, −1
R2	−1, −1	+0, 5⁻	−1, −2
R3	−1, 1	−2, −1	6, 6⁻

Game 3

	C1	C2
R1	+5, 0⁻	−5, −1
R2	−5, −1	+0, 5⁻

Game 4

	C1	C2	C3
R1	+5, 0⁻	−5, −1	+10, −1
R2	−5, −1	+0. 5⁻	−1, −2
R3	−1, −1	−2, −1	6, 6⁻

Game 5

Figure 8.5

253

If this is so, then important evolutionary phenomena such as those discussed in the previous chapter would come into play. We think they did. Figure 8.6 summarises the aggregate results.

	Outcome (R1, C1)	Outcome (R2, C2)	Outcome (R3, C3)
Game 1	50 (34)	38 (34)	N/A
Game 2	77 (34)	0 (34)	67 (0)
Game 3	51 (34)	0 (34)	69 (0)
Game 4	39 (78)	98 (39)	N/A
Game 5	58 (78)	0 (39)	54 (0)

A summary of the incidents of Nash equilibria (R1, C1) and of (dominated) third ('cooperative') strategies (R3, C3). Each row of the table is the sum of the observations from the four rounds of each game. The numbers in brackets are the predictions based on the NEMS scenario (see section 2.7.2). In games 2, 3 and 5, these predictions are still valid if we assume common knowledge rationality (CKR).

Figure 8.6

We see immediately that the prediction that the third strategies will not be played in games 2, 3 and 5 (other than due to a random error) fails rather spectacularly. Despite being dominated, strategies R3 and C3 are not only played but players also manage to coordinate on them 67, 69 and 54 times respectively. Either most of our subjects were instrumentally irrational in concert, or they were motivated 'differently'. As far as prediction (1) is concerned, we found that in game 1 one of the two Nash equilibria (R1, C1) was prioritised by the players while the NEMS-predicted frequencies did not even come close. Turning to prediction (2) – the prediction (based on the perturbed version of game 2, see section 2.7.1) that (R1, C1) will be more prevalent because of the presence of the third strategies – the data offers the theory considerable support; notice how (R1, C1) becomes increasingly dominant in games 2 and 3. However, it appears that this support may be due to the 'wrong' reasons (as far as game theory is concerned) since the third strategies are clearly not chosen as a result of some random mistakes (or 'trembles'). The fact that the frequencies of cooperative moves in games 2 and 3 are not too dissimilar, is hardly supportive of the game theoretical view of those strategies. Instead, it is indicative that subjects refuse to abandon them even when it is evident that they are dominated. Finally, the data refutes the expectation that (R1, C1) would become more frequent in game 4 (compared with game 1).[5]

In the remainder of this section, we will focus on what we consider to be the two main conclusions. Firstly, in game 1 even though the matrix is symmetrical, the game is not played symmetrically. Indeed (R1, C1) seems to be more salient. Why? Recall the discussion in section 8.4 on salience in coordination games. There we suggested that for those who are used to reading from left to right, the (R1, C1) Nash equilibrium is naturally salient because it is the one they see first. Similarly, for those who are used to reading from right to left (e.g. Chinese) the second Nash equilibrium (R2, C2) may be more 'obvious' – indeed it is no longer seen as the 'second Nash equilibrium'. The evidence supports this hypothesis. We observed a number of subjects (13) whose first language was Chinese or Korean and who are used to reading matrices columns first. Unlike the rest of the population, they were not attracted to (R1, C1) as often as the others. Overall, Rs went for the $5 203 times as opposed to the Cs who were similarly ambitious 187 times. Within our sample of 13 Chinese and Korean subjects, we observed 29 choices of C2 and only 23 of R1. Of course this is a very small sample. Nevertheless it does illustrate a point already made several times in this book: the degree of observed coordination cannot be explained well enough without a contextual analysis that mainstream game theory treats as irrelevant.

Our second conclusion concerns the evolution of social roles in games 2, 3 and 5. Let us label strategies R3 and C3 as 'cooperative' (for it is obvious that they lead to a Pareto-superior outcome over the Nash equilibria). How does the propensity to 'cooperate' evolve as players move from the first round of game 2 to the last round of game 5? Figure 8.7 sheds light on this. Figure 8.7(a) tells the story of how R-players altered their behaviour while Figure 8.7(b) is dedicated to C-players. The first column records the number of cooperative moves (R3s for the Rs and C3s for the Cs). The second column records the number of occurrences of what we call *reflective cooperation*; that is, the number of times a player anticipated a cooperative strategy by his or her opponent/partner **and** chose to cooperate in response. We label this P3P3. In the case of Figure 8.7(a) (8.7(b)) P3P3 records the number of times an R (C) player anticipated C3 (R3) and chose R3 (C3). (We know what players anticipated because, prior to making their strategic choice, we had asked them to predict their opponent's move.) Finally, the third column records the number of cheating moves. For example, if in game 2 R expected C to play C3, and chose R1 in response to this expectation, she was obviously intent on some form of cheating (that is, taking advantage of the cooperative behaviour she expected from C).[6]

Notice the extraordinarily different trends in the two figures. Looking at game 2, there is no huge difference between the propensity of Rs and Cs either 'reflectively' to cooperate (this is measured by P3P3) or simply to 'cooperate'. The main observed difference in behaviour is in the propensity to cheat. This could be due to some accident or to the salience of the R role

(a) Row players

Row players	Cooperated – i.e. played R3	P3P3 – i.e. predicted C3 and then played R3	Cheat – i.e. predicted C3 and then played R1
Game 2	122	80	89
Game 3	89	76	130
Game 5	72	60	148

(b) Column players

Column players	Cooperated – i.e. played C3	P3P3 – i.e. predicted R3 and then played C3	Cheat – i.e. predicted R3 and then played C1
Game 2	134	77	60
Game 3	194	107	Meaningless
Game 5	190	127	Meaningless

Total number of choices in games 2, 3 and 5 = $138 \times 4 \times 3 = 1656$; total number of P3P3 choices = 527; average of P3P3 incidence = 32%; average for Rs = 26%; average for Cs = 38%.

Figure 8.7

for reasons already canvassed. However, as we move to game 3 the number of reflectively cooperative moves rise substantially for the Cs (from 77 to 107) while they drop by four for the Rs. By the time players move to game 5, Rs reflectively cooperate only 60 times in direct contrast to the Cs massive 127. The cheating data (third column in Figure 8.7) *partly* reveals what is happening: as Rs realise that the Cs are just as cooperative as before (if not more cooperative than before), and given the asymmetries in games 3 and 5 which favour the Rs, they cheat a lot more. This is unsurprising. But why do the Cs cooperate more in game 3 than they did in game 2? And why do they cooperate almost as often in game 5? Moreover, how can we explain that their tendency to cooperate reflectively (P3P3) rises all along?

It would be tempting to hypothesise that the Cs must be made of different 'stuff' than the Rs; that they have a different disposition to that of the meaner Rs. However, this explanatory avenue is not open to us. For the *Rs and the Cs are exactly the same persons!* If you recall the experimental design, each person was an R in one round and a C the next. So, we have

Box 8.4

ATHENS AND THE MELIANS

The 5th century BC historian Thucydides reports that in the course of its geopolitical struggle against Sparta, Athens dispatched a fleet with the specific order that the independently minded island-state of Melos be subdued or razed to the ground. In the dialogue entered into by representatives of the two sides following the arrival of the Athenian troops, the interplay between moral principles and strategic concerns underscored the rhetoric.

In an opening speech anticipating Aristotle's infamous pronouncement that 'The weaker are always anxious for justice and equality. The strong pay heed to neither' (*Politics*, s1318),[7] the Athenians demanded Melos' surrender. After all, they decried,

> on the one hand the principles of justice, encompassed in human reason, hinge on the equal capacity to compel, yet on the other hand, the strong actually do what is possible and the weak suffer what they must.
>
> (Thucydides, *The History of the Peloponnesian War*, Book 5, s89)

The Melians played their only card. They demanded that they be allowed to remain neutral and free for Athens' *own* sake:

> Then in our view (since you force us to base our arguments on self-interest, rather than on what is proper) it is useful that you should not destroy a principle that is to the general good – namely that those who find themselves in the clutches of misfortune should be justly and properly treated, and should be allowed to thrive beyond the limits set by the accurate calculation of their power. And this is a principle which does not affect you less, since your own fall would be visited by the most terrible vengeance, watched by the whole world.
>
> (Thucydides, *The History of the Peloponnesian War*, Book 5, s90)

Necessity invented a splendid, and highly prophetic, argument: when in the dominant position do to others what you would like to be done to you when weak. If you do not, you will live to regret it. Years later, these words may have resonated in Athenian ears as the Spartans were scaling the walls of Piraeus intent on destruction. The connection between this dialogue and the experimental results reported in this section is suggestive. Both the Melians and the C-players in our laboratory developed strategies with a moral content embarking from a position of strategic weakness. However, the experimental data comes with a splendid twist: the *same* players seem to have heeded the Melians' argument when in the weak role and adopted something like the Athenians' logic when in the dominant position (see section 7.6 for the relevant discussion on the evolution of morality.)

the following phenomenon: the same person who, on average, had the propensity to 'cheat' on a cooperative C in one round became that cooperative C in the next round – with increasing commitment! And even though he or she knew first hand how aggressive and unreliable (as a cooperator) the R role renders one!

Tantalisingly, no instrumental explanation of this phenomenon appears possible. Moreover, the evolutionary game theory of the previous chapter cannot help either. In our conclusion to Chapter 7 we emphasised that, even though evolutionary game theory makes a decisive step in the right direction in dropping the axiom of CKR (and CAB), this is not enough: a radical break with the exclusive reliance of instrumental rationality is also necessary. The data in Figure 8.7 reinforces that point. What we have here is an evolution of social roles. Players with the R label develop a different attitude towards reflective cooperation to those players with the C role *in spite of the fact that the Rs and the Cs are the same people.* In other words, the signal which causes the observed pattern of cooperation seems to be emitted by the label R or C. This reminds us of the discussion in Chapter 7 about the capacity of sex, race and other extraneous features to pin down a convention on which the structure of discrimination is grounded. Only in this case the experimental design, and in particular the fact that the roles are alternating continually, allows us to put the same thought more strongly: the observed differences in the behaviour of R- and C-players have *nothing* to do with personal characteristics (since the Rs and Cs are the same persons). So, unlike feminists who have had to argue that women's lesser social status is not due to an inherent physical or intellectual inferiority (but due to social formations), such debate is irrelevant in the case of R- and C-players: the differences in their behaviour and expectations are social constructions (see Box 8.4 for an ancient explanation of these differences).

8.7 CONCLUSION

Experimentation with game theory is good, clean fun. Can it be more than that? Can it offer a way out of the obtuse debates on CKR, CAB, NEMS, Nash backward induction, out-of-equilibrium behaviour, etc.? The answer depends on how we interpret the results. And as interpretation leaves plenty of room for controversy, we should not expect the data from the laboratory unequivocally to settle any disputes. Our suspicion is that experiments are to game theory what the latter is to liberal individualism: a brilliant means of codifying its problems and of creating a taxonomy of time-honoured debates.

There are, however, important benefits from experimenting. Watching people play games reminds us of their inherent unpredictability, their sense of fairness, their complex motivation – of all those things that we tend to forget when we model humans as bundles of preferences moving around some pay-off matrix. Moreover, we find that the social context (or structures) is terribly difficult to efface even when we sit people in front of computers and force them to exchange clinical messages in total isolation from each other. Indeed in some cases, after we have taken out as much of the social context as possible (through the design of the experiment), our subjects manage to create one afresh (e.g. the creation of social roles in the last section). Even if the only benefit from experiments is to keep theorists in touch with what real humans are like, they are worth the trouble.

POSTSCRIPT

The ambitious claim that game theory will provide a unified foundation for all social science seems misplaced to us. There is a variety of problems with such a claim which we have discussed in this book. Some are associated with the assumptions of the theory (for instance, that agents are instrumentally motivated and that they have common knowledge of rationality), some come from the inferences which are often drawn from these assumptions (as when it is assumed that common knowledge delivers consistently aligned beliefs) and yet others come from the failure (even once the controversial assumptions and the inferences are in place) to generate determinate predictions of what 'rational' agents would, or should, do in important social interactions.

At root we suspect that the major problem is the one that the experiments in the last chapter isolate: namely, that people appear to be more complexly motivated than game theory's instrumental model allows and that a part of that greater complexity comes from their social location.

We do not regard this as a negative conclusion. Quite the contrary, it stands as a challenge to the type of methodological individualism which has had a free rein in the development of game theory. Either this greater complexity and its social dimension must be coherently incorporated in an individualistic framework, or the methodological foundations will have to shift away from individualism.

Along the way to this conclusion, we hope also that you have had fun. Prisoners' dilemmas and centipedes are great party tricks. They are easy to demonstrate and they are amenable to solutions which are paradoxical enough to stimulate controversy and, with one leap of the liberal imagination, the audience can be astounded by the thought that the fabric of society (even the existence of the State) reduces to these seemingly trivial games – *Fun and Games*, as the title of Binmore's (1992) text on game theory neatly puts it. But there is a serious side to all this. Game theory is, indeed, well placed to examine the arguments in liberal political theory over the origin and the scope of agencies for social choice like the State. In this context, the problems which we have identified with game theory resurface as timely warnings of the difficulties any society is liable to face if it thinks of itself only in terms of liberal individualism.

NOTES

1 AN OVERVIEW

1 An ontological question addresses the essence of *what is* (its etymology comes from the Greek *onta* which is plural for *being*).
2 An epistemological question (*episteme* meaning the knowledge acquired through engagement) asks about *what is known* or about *what can be known*.
3 In fact, some economists prefer to talk solely about 'consistent' choice rather than acting to satisfy best one's preferences. The difficulty with such an approach is to know what sense of rational motivation, if it is not instrumental, leads agents to behave in this 'consistent' manner. In other words, the obvious motivating reason for acting consistently is that one has objectives/preferences which one would like to see realised/satisfied. In which case, the gloss of 'consistent' choice still rests on an instrumentally rational motivated psychology.
4 You will notice how the Rousseau version not only blurs the contribution of the individual by making the process of institution building transformative, it also breaches the strict separation between action and structure. In fact this difference also lies at the heart of one of the great cleavages in Enlightenment thinking regarding liberty (see Berlin, 1958). The stict separation of action and structure sits comfortably with the negative sense of freedom (which focuses on the absence of restraint in pursuit of individual objectives) while the fusion is the natural companion for the positive sense of freedom (which is concerned with the ability of individuals to choose their objectives autonomously).

2 THE ELEMENTS OF GAME THEORY

1 Pure strategies are contrasted with mixed strategies. Driving and walking to work in the previous chapter are examples of pure strategies. A mixed strategy involves a probabilistic mix of pure strategies. Thus driving to work with probability 0.5 and walking with probability 0.5 is an example of a mixed strategy. We shall always use the term Nash equilibrium to refer to an equilibrium in pure strategies; when the same solution concept involves mixed strategies we shall refer explicitly to it as a Nash equilibrium in mixed strategies (NEMS) - see section 2.7.2.
2 That R has a dominant strategy can be seen from the fact that both ($^+$) signs correspond to R1 (thus meaning that R1 is the best response to both C1 and

C2). That C does not have a dominant strategy is reflected by location of the ($^-$) signs on different columns.

3 To see why ε must exceed $\frac{7}{161}$, substitute $q = \frac{1}{14}$ into (2.5) and solve for ε.

4 Recall, however, that a Kantian defence would go much further than game theorists would tolerate: it will spill over into an argument in favour of action that is judged from a perspective external to that of the individual agent, recommending action on the basis of whether it is in the common good rather than on the basis of individual instrumental rationality. See Hollis (1987), especially the chapter on 'External and Internal Reasons'.

3 DYNAMIC GAMES

1 Of course, the whole game can also be thought of as a subgame in the same way a set can be thought of as a subset of itself.

2 For example, in section 2.3 we mentioned that Kant's reason also invites us to act on reasons external to our desires.

3 Our disagreement as authors returns in Chapter 7 when we discuss the potential usefulness of evolutionary game theory.

4 BARGAINING GAMES

1 What if an agent claims during pre-play negotiations that he or she will bid for the $1000? That would indeed be a significant signal. However, we are reminded that, in equilibrium, no one would have an incentive to make such a claim. It is not so clear that this is true. James Farrell has indicated that signalling one's intention to back down *can be credible* (see his 1987 paper). But for this to be so in equilibrium, a convevtion must be introduced; namely, that those who announce their intention to settle for the little money, do not change their minds later (and play R6 or C6).

2 Although David Gauthier invoked the Kalai and Smorodinsky bargaining solution in his 1986 book, he has retreated from the position expressed there. In a recent book (see Gauthier and Sugden, 1993) he seems convinced by game theorists' criticisms of his non-Nash bargaining theory: 'The argument in Chapter V of *Morals by Agreement* cannot stand in its present form' (p.178).

3 The Rubinstein demand coincides, of course, with the subgame perfect Nash equilibrium demand.

4 In this case, C values $100(1 - w)\%$ of the pie at $t = 2$ more than $100(1 - k)\%$ of the pie at $t = 1$. For this to hold, $\delta(1 - w) > (1 - k)$.

5 This is very similar to our critique of the Nash equilibrium in section 3.7.

6 Of course there is a great deal of opposition to this identification. For example, see Varoufakis (1991, pp. 266–8).

7 This is how Rawls derives his second principle of justice, the 'difference principle'. Rawls also argues that agents will agree to prioritise lexicographically his first principle of justice, which only allows arrangements to be considered if they respect each person's basic freedoms.

8 The only explanation for strikes would then be that at least one of the parties is irrational, or information is in short supply, or the institutional (legal) framework is not well suited to reaching agreement. In all three cases, industrial conflict is the result of some deficiency. But this only holds if the bargaining problem (at least in its pure, simple form) has a unique solution.

5 THE PRISONERS' DILEMMA

1 It is widely recognised that Wittgenstein's views in *Philosophical Investigations* are distinct from those he expressed earlier in his *Tractatus*. Thus this distinction.
2 The central difference to note here between Simon and Wittgenstein arises over the need or otherwise for these procedures or practices to be shared.

6 REPEATED GAMES AND REPUTATIONS

1 In so far as it is instrumentally rational, of course, to play Nash equilibrium strategies – see the discussion in sections 2.5 and 3.7.

7 EVOLUTIONARY GAMES

1 We focus on the neo-right (or 'intransigent right') critique of 'political rationalism' because (a) game theory brings such interventions in sharp focus and (b) they are prominent in many contemporary debates. This is not, however, to eschew the significant critique of the idea of a social contract (mediated by the State for the benefit of all) which comes from the Left. For instance, Marxists also reject the possibility of a national, or general, interest in the presence of class conflict. And feminists (see Pateman, 1988) demonstrate how the social contract can be seen as a social device for excluding half the population.
2 There will be one trajectory running from the south-west to the north-east where the pull of learning in both directions just pushes the group to $(\frac{1}{3}, \frac{1}{3})$.
3 In effect, this was precisely the point that Lewis (1969) was reacting against in the work of Quine. Quine was denying that language arises by convention because *conventions are agreements* and so language could not have originated by agreement because the notation of agreement between people presupposes a shared rudimentary language. Lewis's book is an attempt to show that convention does not presuppose agreement in this way.
4 Again there are many political angles here. For instance, Seyla Benhabib (1987) argues against the model of human agency found in methodological individualism by noticing that 'the conception of privacy is so enlarged that . . . relations of "kinship, friendship, love and sex" . . . come to be viewed as spheres of "personal decision making"', and so gender discrimination is hidden under a cloak of private preference satisfaction.
5 To see how the following inequality is arrived at, notice that the condition for E^{π} to be an increasing function of p is that the first-order derivative of E^{π} subject to p must be greater than zero. Differentiating E^{π} with respect to p and setting the derivative greater to zero yields inequality (7.5). Similarly for (7.6).
6 Against Lukes on this, it is sometimes argued that this is not so much evidence of the exercise of power covertly as an illustration of the structural influence on outcomes, see Giddens (1979). However, this is more of a semantic dispute than a substantive disagreement over the fact of influence.
7 Notice that this argument is of the functional variety – Box 3.3.
8 Perhaps the reason why they 'see' this common good is similar to the one which explains why some think they can discern winning streaks – see box 7.1
9 Marx defines ideology as 'a whole superstructure of different and characteristic feelings, illusions, ways of thinking and views of life' (*Collected Works II*).
10 This group includes Erik Olin Wright, Andrew Levine, Alan Carling, G.A.

Cohen, John Roemer. For an interesting recent exchange see the Spring 1994 issue of *Science and Society.*

11 Ellen Meiskin Wood (1989), W. Suchting (1993) and one of the authors of this book (!) seem to fit in this broad category.

12 Even though, it must be said, his collaborator Friedrich Engels was not so averse to such transplants.

13 That need manifests itself by the seemingly insoluble problem of selecting one out of multiple equilibria in most interesting games examined in this book.

8 WATCHING PEOPLE PLAY GAMES

1 Which is equivalent to infinite-order common knowledge of the plan.

2 A Nash equilibrium is Pareto dominant when it makes at least one player better off than any other Nash equilibrium without making anyone else worse off.

3 Up to any linear transformation.

4 They are referring to Stahl (1972) who offered an early version of a non-cooperative sequential bargaining model. In fact the only difference with Rubinstein (1982) is that Stahl postulated a fixed number of potential bargaining rounds.

5 A more disaggregated tabulation of our subjects' behaviour (see Varoufakis and Hargreaves Heap, 1993) reinforces the findings reported here.

6 Notice that the 'cheat' frequencies do not make much sense in the case of C players in games 3 and 5, since they have nothing to gain from not cooperating with a cooperative R.

7 All the translations from ancient Greek are the authors'.

BIBLIOGRAPHY

Admati, A. and M. Perry (1987) 'Strategic delay in bargaining'. *Review of Economic Studies*, LIV, 345–64.

Akerlof, G. (1980) 'A theory of social custom of which unemployment may be one consequence'. *Quarterly Journal of Economics*, XCIV, 749–75.

Akerlof, G. (1983) 'Loyalty filters'. *American Economic Review*, 73, 54–63.

Allais, M. (1953) 'Le comportement de l'homme rationnel devant le risque, critique des postulats et axiomes de l'ecole americaine'. *Econometrica*, 21, 503–46.

Anderson, P. (1992) 'The intransigent right at the end of the century'. *London Review of Books*, 24 September, 7–11.

Andreoni, J. and J. Miller (1993) 'Rational cooperation in the finitely repeated prisoner's dilemma: experimental evidence'. *Economic Journal*, 103, 570–85.

Aristotle (1987) *Nicomachean Ethics*, transl. J. Weldon. New York: Prometheus.

Aronson, E. (1988) *The Social Animal*. New York: W.H. Freeman.

Arrow, K. (1951) *Social Choice and Individual Values*. New Haven, CT: Yale University Press.

Ashworth, T. (1980) *Trench Warfare, 1914–18: the Live and Let Live System*. New York: Holmes and Meier.

Aumann, R. (1976) 'Agreeing to disagree'. *Annals of Statistics*, 4, 1236–9.

Aumann, R. (1987) 'Correlated equilibrium as an expression of Bayesian rationality'. *Econometrica*, 55, 1–18.

Aumann, R. (1988) 'Preliminary notes on integrating irrationality into game theory'. Mimeo, International Conference on Economic Theories of Politics, Haifa.

Aumann, R. and S. Hart (eds) (1992) *Handbook of Game Theory*. Amsterdam: North-Holland.

Axelrod, R. (1984) *The evolution of cooperation*. New York: Basic Books.

Bacharach, M. (1987) 'A theory of rational decision in games'. *Erkenntnis*, 27, 17–55.

Barry, B. (1976) *Power and political theory: some European perspectives*. London: Wiley.

Becker, G. (1971) *The Economics of Discrimination* Chicago: Chicago University Press.

Becker, G. (1976) *The Economic Approach to Human Behaviour*. Chicago: Chicago University Press.

Becker, G. (1986) 'The economic approach to human behaviour'. In J. Elster (ed.) *Rational Choice*. Cambridge: Cambridge University Press.

Benhabib, S. (1987) *Feminism as critique*. Minneapolis, MN: University of Minnesota Press.

Berlin, I. (1958) 'Two concepts of liberty', reprinted in *Four Essays on Liberty*. Oxford: Oxford University Press.

Bernheim, D. (1984) 'Rationalisable strategic behaviour'. *Econometrica*, 52, 1007–28.

Bernstein, J. (1984) 'From self-consciousness to community: act and recognition in the master–slave relationship'. In Z. Pelczynski (ed.).

Binmore, K. (1987) 'Nash bargaining theory I-III'. In K. Binmore and P. Dasgupta (eds) *The Economics of Bargaining.* Oxford: Blackwell.

Binmore, K. (1987/1988) 'Modeling rational players: parts I and II'. *Economics and Philosophy,* 3, 179–214 and 4, 9–55.

Binmore, K. (1989) 'Social contract I: Harsanyi and Rawls'. *Economic Journal* (Suppl.), 99, 84–103.

Binmore, K. (1990) *Essays on the Foundations of Game Theory.* Oxford: Basil Blackwell.

Binmore, K. (1992) *Fun and Games: A text on game theory.* Lexington, MA: D.C. Heath.

Binmore, K. and P. Dasgupta (eds) (1986) *Economic Organisations as Games.* Oxford: Blackwell.

Binmore, K. and P. Dasgupta (1987) *The Economics of Bargaining.* Oxford: Blackwell.

Binmore, K., A. Rubinstein and A. Wolinsky (1986) 'The Nash bargaining solution in economic modelling'. *Rand Journal of Economics,* 17, 176–88.

Binmore, K., A. Shaked and J. Sutton (1985) 'Testing non-cooperative bargaining theory'. *American Economic Review,* 78, 837–9.

Blau, P. (1964) *Exchange and Power in Social Life.* London: Wiley.

Brams, S. (1993) *A theory of moves.* Cambridge: Cambridge University Press.

Brennan, G. and J. Buchanan (1985) *The Reason of Rules: Constitutional Political Economy.* Cambridge: Cambridge University Press.

Brennan, G. and G. Tullock (1982) 'An economic theory of military tactics'. *Journal of Economic Behaviour and Organization,* 3, 225–42.

Buchanan, J. (1954) 'Individual choice in voting and the market'. *Journal of Political Economy,* 62, 334–43.

Buchanan, J. (1976) 'A Hobbesian re-interpretation of the Rawlsian difference principle'. *Kyklos,* 29, 5–25.

Buchanan, J. and R. Wagner (1977) *Democracy in Deficit: the Legacy of Lord Keynes.* London: Institute of Economic Affairs.

Camerer, C. and K. Weigelt (1988) 'Experimental tests of a sequential equilibrium reputational model'. *Econometrica,* 56, 1–36.

Carling, A. (1986) 'Rational choice Marxism'. *New Left Review,* 160, 24–62.

Carling, A. (1991) *Social Division.* London: Verso.

Casson, M. (1991) *The Economics of Business Culture.* Oxford: Clarendon Press.

Chislom, R. (1946) 'The contrary to fact conditional'. *Mind,* 55, 289–307.

Cho, I. (1987) 'A refinement of the sequential equilibrium concept'. *Econometrica,* 55, 1367–89,

Cho, I. and D. Kres (1987) 'Signalling games and stable equilibria'. *Quarterly Journal of Economics,* CII, 179–221.

Condorcet, J.A. (1979 [1795]) *Sketch for a History for the Progress of the Human Mind.* Connecticut: Hyperion Press

Cooper, R. and A. John (1988) 'Coordinating coordination failures in Keynesian models'. *Quarterly Journal of Economics,* 53, 441–63.

Cooper, R., D. DeJong, R. Forsythe and T. Ross (1990) 'Selection criteria in coordination games: some experimental results. *American Economic Review,* 80, 218–33.

Dawkins, R. (1976) *The Selfish Gene.* Oxford: Oxford University Press.

Derrida, J. (1978) *Writing and Difference* London: Routledge and Kegan Paul.

Diamond, P. (1982) 'Rational expectations business cycles in search equilibrium'. *Journal of Political Economy,* 97, 606–19.

Dixit, A. and Nalebuff, B. (1993) *Thinking Strategically.* New York: Norton.

Downs, A. (1957) *An Economic Theory of Democracy.* New York: Harper & Row.

Ellsberg, D. (1956) 'Theory of the reluctant duellist'. *American Economic Review,* 46, 909–23.

Ellsberg, D. (1961) 'Risk, ambiguity and the Savage axioms'. *The Economic Journal,* 64, 643–69.

Elster, J. (1982) 'Marxism, functionalism and game theory'. *Theory and Society,* 11, 453–82.

Elster, J. (1983) *Sour Grapes: Studies in the Subversion of Rationality.* Cambridge: Cambridge University Press.

Elster, J. (1984) *Ulysses and the Sirens.* Cambridge: Cambridge University Press.

Elster, J. (ed.) (1986a) *Rational Choice.* Cambridge: Cambridge University Press.

Elster, J. (1986b) *Making sense of Marx.* Cambridge: Cambridge University Press.

Elster, J. (ed.) (1986c) *The Multiple Self.* Cambridge: Cambridge University Press.

Elster, J. (1989) 'Social norms and economic theory'. *Journal of Economic Perspectives,* 3, 99–117.

Faludi, S. (1992) *Backlash.* London: Vontage.

Farrell, J. (1987) 'Cheap talk, coordination and entry'. *Rand Journal of Economics,* 18, 34–9.

Farrell, J. and R. Gibbons (1989) 'Cheap talk can matter in bargaining'. *Journal of Economic Theory,* 48, 221–37.

Festinger, L. (1957) *A Theory of Cognitive Dissonance.* Stanford, CA: Stanford University Press.

Flax, J. (1987) 'Postmodernism and gender relations in feminist theory'. *Signs,* 12, 621–43.

Foucault, M. (1967) *Madness and Civilisation.* London: Tavistock.

Frank, R., T. Gilovich and D. Regan (1993) 'Does studying economics inhibit cooperation?'. *Journal of Economic Perspectives,* Spring, 159–71.

Fudenberg, D. and E. Maskin (1986) 'The Folk theorem in repeated games with discounting or with incomplete information'. *Econometrica,* 54, 533–54.

Fudenberg, D. and J. Tirole (1989) 'Non-cooperative game theory for industrial organisation: an introduction and overview.' In R. Schmalensee and R. Willing (eds) *Handbook of Industrial Organization.* Amsterdam: North-Holland.

Fudenberg, D. and J. Tirole (1991) *Game Theory.* Cambridge, MA: Cambridge University Press.

Gauthier, D. (1986) *Morals by Agreement.* Oxford: Clarendon Press.

Gauthier, D. and R. Sugden (eds) (1993) *Rationality, Justice and the Social Contract.* Hemel Hempstead: Wheatsheaf.

Geanakoplos, J., D. Pearce and E. Stacchetti (1989) 'Psychological games and sequential rationality'. *Games and Economic Behaviour,* 1, 60–79.

Giddens, A. (1979) *Central Problems in Social Theory.* London: Macmillan.

Guth, W. and R. Tietz (1987) 'Ultimatum bargaining for a shrinking cake: an experimental analysis'. Mimeo.

Guth, W., R. Schmittberger and B. Schwarz (1982) 'An experimental analysis of ultimatum bargaining'. *Journal of Economic Behavior and Organization,* 3, 367–88.

Halpern, J. (1986) 'Reasoning about knowledge: an overview'. In J. Halpern (ed.) *Reasononing about knowledge.* Morgan Kaufman.

Hardin, R. (1982) *Collective Action.* Baltimore, MD: and Johns Hopkins University Press.

Hardin, R. (1988) *Morality within the Limits of Reason.* Chicago: Chicago University Press.

Hargreaves Heap, S. (1989) *Rationality in Economics.* Oxford: Blackwell.

Hargreaves Heap, S. (1991) 'Entrepreneurship, enterprise and information in economics'. In S. Hargreaves Heap and A. Ross (eds) *The Enterprise Culture*. Edinburgh: Edinburgh University Press.

Hargreaves Heap, S. (1992) *The New Keynesian Macroeconomics: Time, Belief and Social Interdependence*. Aldershot: Edward Elgar.

Hargreaves Heap, S. and Y. Varoufakis (1994) 'Experimenting with neoclassical economics'. In I. Rima (ed.) *Quantity and Measurement in Economics*. London: Routledge.

Harper, W. (1991) 'Ratifiability and refinement'. In M. Bacharach and S. Hurley (eds) *Foundations of Decision Theory*. Oxford: Basil Blackwell.

Harrison, G. and K. McCabe (1991) 'Testing noncooperative bargaining theory in experiments'. In R. Issac (ed.) *Research in Experimental Economics*. Greenwich: JAI Press.

Harsanyi, J. (1961) 'On the rationality postulates underlying the theory of cooperative games'. *Journal of Conflict Resolution*, 5, 179–96.

Harsanyi, J. (1966) 'A general theory of rational behaviour in game situations'. *Econometrica*, 34, 613–34.

Harsanyi, J. (1967/1968) 'Games with incomplete information played by Bayesian players'. *Management science*, 14, 159–82, 320–34 and 486–502.

Harsanyi, J. (1973) 'Games with randomly disturbed payoffs: a new rationale for mixed strategies'. *International Journal of Game Theory*, 2, 1–23.

Harsanyi, J. (1975a) 'The tracing procedure: A Bayesian approach to defining a solution for n-person non-cooperative games'. *International Journal of Game Theory*, 4, 61–94.

Harsanyi, J. (1975b) 'Can the maximin principle serve as a basis for mortality? A critique of John Rawls' theory'. *American Political Science Review*, 69, 594–606.

Harsanyi, J. (1977) *Rational Behaviour and Bargaining Equilibria in Games and Social Situations*. Cambridge: Cambridge University Press.

Harsanyi, J. (1982) 'Solutions of some bargaining games under the Harsanyi–Selton solution theory, Parts I–II. *Mathematical Social Sciences*, 3, 171–91, 259–79.

Harsanyi, J. (1986) 'Advances in understanding rational behaviour'. In J. Elster (ed.) *Rational Choice*. Cambridge: Cambridge University Press.

Harsanyi, J. and R. Selten (1972) 'A generalised Nash solution for two-person bargaining games with incomplete information'. *Management Science*, 18, 80–106.

Harsanyi, J. and R. Selten (1988) *A general theory of equilibrium selection in games*. Cambridge, MA: MIT Press.

Hayek von, F. (1937) 'Economics and knowledge'. *Economica*, 4, 33–54.

Hayek von, F. (1945) 'The use of knowledge in society'. *American Economic Review*, 35, 519–30.

Hayek von, F. (1960) *The Constitution of Liberty*. London: Routledge.

Hayek von, F. (1962) *The road to serfdom*. London: Routledge and Kegan Paul.

Hebdige, D. (1989) 'After the masses'. *Marxism Today*, January, 48–53.

Hegel, G.W.F. (1931) *The Phenomenology of Mind*, trans. J. Baillie. London.

Hegel, G.W.F. (1953) *Reason in History*, trans. R. Hartman. New York: The Library of Liberal Arts, Macmillan.

Hegel, G.W.F. (1965) *The Logic*, trans. W. Wallace, from *The Encyclopedia of the Philosophical Sciences*. London: Oxford University Press.

Hollis, M. (1987) *The Cunning of Reason*. Cambridge: Cambridge University Press.

Hollis, M. (1991) *Honour Among Thieves*. Proceedings of the British Academy.

Howard, M. (1971) *Paradoxes of rationality: theory of meta-games and political behaviour*. Cambridge, MA.: MIT Press.

Hume, D. (1888) *Treatise on Human Nature*, ed. L.A. Selby-Bigge. Oxford: Oxford University Press.

Kahn, L. and J.K. Murnighan (1993) 'Conjecture, uncertainty and cooperation in prisoner's dilemma games'. *Journal of Economic Behaviour and Organisation*, 22, 91–117.

Kahneman, D. and A. Tversky (1979) 'Prospect theory: an analysis of decision under risk'. *Econometrica*, 47, 263–91.

Kahneman, D., P. Slovic and A. Tversky (eds) (1982) *Judgment under uncertainty: heuristics and biases.* Cambridge, MA: Cambridge University Press.

Kalai, E. and M. Smorodinsky (1975) 'Other solutions to Nash's bargaining problem'. *Econometrica.* 43, 413–18.

Kant, I. (1788) *Critique of Practical Reason*, trans. and ed. L.W. Beck, *Critique of Practical Reason and Other Writings in Moral Philosophy*, Cambridge: Cambridge University Press, 1949.

Kant, I. (1855) *Critique of Pure Reason.* London: Bohn.

Keynes, J.M. (1936) *The General Theory of Employment, Interest and Money.* London: Macmillan.

Knight, F. (1971) *Risk, Uncertainty and Profit.* Chicago: Chicago University Press.

Kohlberg, E. and J.-F. Mertens (1986) 'On the strategic stability of equilibria'. *Econometrica*, 54, 1003–37.

Kreps, D. (1990) *Game Theory and economic modeling.* New York: Oxford University Press.

Kreps, D. and R. Wilson (1982a) 'Reputation and imperfect information'. *Journal of Economic Theory*, 27, 253–79.

Kreps, D. and R. Wilson (1982b) 'Sequential equilibria'. *Econometrica*, 50, 863–94.

Kreps, D., P. Milgrom, J. Roberts and R. Wilson (1982) 'Rational cooperation in the finitely repeated prisoner's dilemma'. *Journal of Economic Theory*, 27, 245–52.

Lewis, D. (1969) *Convention.* Cambridge, MA: Harvard University Press.

Luce, R. and H. Raiffa (1957) *Games and Decisions.* New York: Wiley.

Lukes, S. (1974) *Power: A radical view.* London: Macmillan.

Lukes, S. (ed.) (1986) *Power.* Oxford: Blackwell.

Lyotard, J.-F. (1984) *The Postmodern Condition: A Report on Knowledge.* Manchester: Manchester University Press.

MacKinnon, C. (1989) *Towards a Feminist Theory of the State.* Cambridge, MA: Harvard University Press.

Marx, K. (1972) *Capital: I–III.* London: Lawrence and Wishart.

Marx, K. (1979) 'The Eighteenth Brumaire of Louis Bonaparte'. In K. Marx and F. Engels *Collected Works.* London: Lawrence and Wishart.

Marx, K. and F. Engels (1979) *Collected Works.* London: Lawrence and Wishart

Maynard Smith, J. (1973) *On Evolution.* Edinburgh: Edinburgh University Press.

Maynard Smith, J. (1982) *Evolution and the Theory of Games.* Cambridge: Cambridge University Press.

Maynard Smith, J. and G. Price (1974) 'The theory of games and the evolution of animal conflict'. *Journal of Theoretical Biology*, 47, 209–21.

McKelvey, R. and T. Palfrey (1992) 'An experimental study of the centipede game' *Econometrica*, 60, 803–36.

McCloskey, D. (1983) 'Rhetoric of economics'. *Journal of Economic Literature*, 21, 481–517.

Milgrom, P. and J. Roberts (1982) 'Predation, reputation and entry deterrence'. *Journal of Economic Theory*, 27, 280–312.

Mirowski, P. (1986) 'Institutions as a solution concept in a game theory context'. In L. Samuleson (ed.), *Microeconomic Theory.* Boston: Kluwer.

Moulin, H. (1982) *Game Theory for the Social Sciences.* New York: New York University Press.

Myerson, R. (1978) 'Refinements of the Nash equilibrium concept'. *International Journal of Game Theory*, 7, 73–80.

Myerson, R. (1991) *Game theory: Analysis of conflict*. Cambridge, MA: Cambridge University Press.

Nash, J. (1950) 'The bargaining problem'. *Econometrica*, 18, 155–62.

Nash, J. (1951) 'Non-cooperative games'. *Annals of Mathematics*, 54, 286–95.

Nash, J. (1953) 'Two person cooperative games'. *Econometrica*, 21, 128–40.

Neelin, J., H. Sonnenschein and M. Spiegel (1988) 'A further test of non-cooperative game theory'. *American Economic Review*, 78, 824–36.

North, D. (1991) *Institutions, Institutional Change and Economic Performance*. Cambridge: Cambridge University Press.

Nozick, R. (1974) *Anarchy, State and Utopia*. New York: Basic Books.

Ochs, J. and A. Roth (1989) 'An experimental study of sequential bargaining'. *American Economic Review*, LXXIX, 355–84.

Olson, M. (1965) *The Logic of Collective Action*. Cambridge, MA: Harvard University Press.

Olson, M. (1982) *The Rise and Decline of Nations*. New Haven, CT: Yale University Press.

O'Neill, O. (1989) *Constructions of Reason*. Cambridge: Cambridge University Press.

Pateman, C. (1988) *The Sexual Contract*. Oxford: Polity Press.

Pearce, D. (1984) 'Rationalisable strategic behaviour and the problem of perfection'. *Econometrica*, 52, 1029–50.

Peters, T. and R. Waterman (1982) *In Search of Excellence*. London: Routledge.

Pettit, F. and R. Sugden (1989) 'The paradox of backward induction'. *Journal of Philosophy*, LXXXVI, 169–82.

Polanyi, K. (1945, 1957) *Primitive, archaic and modern economies*. London: Routledge and Kegan Paul.

Poundstone, W. (1993) *Prisoner's dilemma*. Oxford: Oxford University Press.

Prasnikar, V. and A. Roth (1992) 'Considerations of fairness and strategy: experimental data from sequential games'. *Quarterly Journal of Economics*, 865–88.

Quine, W. (1960) *Word and Object*. Cambridge, MA: MIT Press.

Rapoport, A. and A. Chammah (1965) *Prisoner's Dilemma*. Ann Arbor, MI. Michigan University Press.

Rasmussen, E. (1989) *Games and Information*. Oxford: Blackwell.

Rawls, J. (1971) *A Theory of Justice*. Cambridge, MA: Harvard University Press.

Reny, P. (1992) 'Backward induction, normal form perfection and explicable equilibria'. *Econometrica*, 60, 627–49.

Richardson, L. (1960) *Arms and Insecurity*. Chicago: Quadrangle.

Riker, W. (1982) *Liberalism against Populism*. New York: W.H. Freeman.

Roemer, J. (1980) *A General Theory of Exploitation and Class*. Cambridge, MA: Harvard University Press.

Roemer, J. (1988) 'Axiomatic bargaining theory on economic environments'. *Journal of Economic Theory*, 45, 1–31.

Roemer, J. (1989) 'Distributing health: the allocation of resources by an international agency'. WIDER Papers 71.

Roth, A. (1979) *Axiomatic Models of Bargaining*, Lecture Notes in Economics and Mathematical Systems No. 170. London: Springer-Verlag.

Roth, A. (1988) 'Laboratory experimentation in economics: a methodological overview'. *Economic Journal*, 98, 974–1031.

Roth, A. and M. Malouf (1979) 'Game theoretic models and the role of information in bargaining'. *Psychological Review*, 86, 574–94.

Roth, A., J. Murnighan, and F. Schoumaker (1988) 'The deadline effect in bargaining: some experimental evidence'. *American Economic Review,* 78, 806–23.

Rousseau, J-J. (1964) *The First and Second Discourses.* ed. R.D. Masters. New York: St Martin's Press.

Rubinstein, A. (1982) 'Perfect equilibrium in a bargaining model'. *Econometrica,* 50, 97–109.

Rubinstein, A. (1985) 'A bargaining model with incomplete information about preferences'. *Econometrica,* 53, 1151–72.

Rubinstein, A. (1986) 'A bargaining model with incomplete information'. In K. Binmore and P. Dasgupta (eds) *The Economics of Bargaining.* Oxford: Blackwell.

Rubinstein, A. (1989) 'The electronic mail game: strategic behaviour under "almost common knowledge"'. *American Economic Review,* 79, 385–91.

Runciman, W. (1989) *A Treatise on Social Theory, Volume 2: Substantive Social Theory.* Cambridge: Cambridge University Press.

Savage, L. (1954) *The Foundations of Statistics.* New York: Wiley.

Schelling, T. (1960, 1963) *Strategy of conflict.* Oxford: Oxford University Press.

Schotter, A. (1981) *Economic Theory of Social Institutions.* Cambridge: Cambridge University Press.

Selten, R. (1975) 'Re-examination of the perfectless concept for equilibrium in extensive games'. *International Journal of Game Theory,* 4, 22–5.

Selten, R. (1978) 'The chain store paradox'. *Theory and Decision,* 9, 127–59.

Selten, R. and R. Stoecker (1986) 'End behaviour in sequences of finite prisoner dilemma supergames'. *Journal of Economic Behaviour and Organization,* 7, 47–70.

Sen, A. (1967) 'Isolation, assurance and the social rate of discount'. *Quarterly Journal of Economics,* 80, 112–24.

Sen, A. (1970) 'The impossibility of a Paretian Liberal'. *Journal of Political Economy,* 78, 152–7.

Sen, A. (1977) 'Rational fools'. *Philosophy and Public Affairs,* 6, 317–44.

Sen, A. (1989) *Hunger and Public Action* (with J. Dreze). Oxford: Clarendon Press.

Shapley, L. (1953) 'A value for n-person games'. In H. Kuhn and A. Tucker (eds)

Shubik, M. (1984) *Game Theory in the Social Sciences.* Cambridge, MA: MIT Press.

Simon, H. (1982) *Models of bounded rationality.* Cambridge, MA: MIT Press.

Smith, A. (1976 [1795]) *The Theory of Moral Sentiments,* ed. D. Raphael and A. Macfie. Oxford: Oxford University Press.

Smith, H. (1994) 'Deciding how to decide: Is there a regress problem?'. In M. Bacharach and S. Hurley (eds) *Foundations of Decision Theory.* Oxford: Blackwell.

Sobel, J. (1985) 'A theory of credibility'. *Review of Economic Studies,* 52, 557–73.

Spence, M. (1974) *Market Signalling.* Cambridge, MA: Harvard University Press.

Spöhn, W. (1982) 'How to make use of game theory'. In W. Stegmuller *et al.* (eds) *Philosophy of Economics.* Berlin: Springer-Verlag.

Stahl, I. (1972) *Bargaining Theory.* Stockholm: Economic Research Institute

Stegmuller, W., W. Balzer and W. Spöhn (1982) (eds) *Philosophy of Economics.* Berlin: Springer-Verlag.

Stinchcombe, A. (1975) 'Natural selection'. In *The Idea of Social Structure: Papers in Honour of Robert K. Merton,* ed. L. Coser. Cambridge, MA and London: Harvard University Press.

Stinchcombe, A. (1978) *Theoretical Methods in Social History.* London: Academic Press.

Stinchcombe, A. (1980) 'Is the prisoner's dilemma all of sociology?'. *Inquiry,* 23, 187–92.

Suchting, W. (1993) 'Reconstructing Marxism'. *Science and Society,* 57, 133–59.

Sugden, R. (1986) *The Economics of Rights Cooperation and Welfare.* Oxford: Blackwell.

Sugden, R. (1989) 'Spontaneous order'. *Journal of Economic Perspectives*, 3, 85–97.

Sugden, R. (1991) 'Rational choice: a survey of contributions from economics and philosophy. *Economic Journal*, 101, 751–85.

Sugden, R. (1991a) 'Rational bargaining'. In M. Bacharach and S. Hurley (eds) *Foundations of Decision Theory*. Oxford: Blackwell.

Sutton, J., A. Shaked and K. Binmore (1986) 'An outside option experiment'. *American Economic Review*, 76, 57–63.

Taylor, M. (1976) *Anarchy and Cooperation*. Chichester: Wiley.

Thucydides (1955) *History of the Peloponnesian War*. Athens: Estia (in ancient Greek).

Titmuss, R. (1970) *The Gift Relationship*. London: Allen and Unwin.

Tullock, G. (1965) *The Politics of Bureaucracy*. Washington, DC: Public Affairs Press.

Tullock, G. (1992) 'Games and preference'. *Rationality and Society*, 4, 1, 24–32.

Turnbull, C. (1963) *The Forest People*. London: The Reprint Society.

Tversky, A. and D. Kahneman (1986) 'The framing of decisions and the psychology of choice'. In J. Elster (ed.) *Rational Choice*. Cambridge: Cambridge University Press.

van Huyck, R. Battalio and R. Beil (1990) 'Tacit coordination in games, strategic uncertainty and coordination failure'. *American Economic Review*, 80, 234–48.

van Parijs, P. (1982) 'Reply to Elster'. *Theory and Society*, 11, 496–501.

Varoufakis, Y. (1991) *Rational Conflict*. Oxford: Blackwell.

Varoufakis, Y. (1993) 'Modern and postmodern challenges to game theory'. *Erkenntnis*, 38, 371–404.

Varoufakis, Y. and S. Hargreaves Heap (1993) 'The simultaneous evolution of social roles and of cooperation: some experimental evidence'. Working Paper No. 184, Department of Economics, University of Sydney.

Visser, M. (1992) *The Rituals of Dinner*. London: Viking.

von Neumann, J. and O. Morgenstern (1944) *Theory of Games and Economic Behaviour*. Princeton, NJ: Princeton University Press.

Waltz, K. (1965) *Man, State and War*. New York: Columbia University Press.

Weber, M. (1922, 1947) *Economy and Society*, ed. G. Roth and C. Wittich. New York Bedminster Press (1968).

Wilson, E. (1975) *Sociobiology*. Cambridge: Cambridge University Press.

Wilson, R. (1985) 'Reputations in games and markets'. In A. Roth. (ed.) *Game Theoretic Models of Bargaining*. Cambridge: Cambridge University Press.

Wittgenstein, L. (1922) *Tractatus logico-philosophicus*. London: Routledge and Kegan Paul.

Wittgenstein, L. (1953) *Philosophical Investigations*. Oxford: Blackwell.

Wood, E.M. (1989) 'Rational choice Marxism: Is the game worth the candle?'. *New Left Review*, 177, 41–88.

Wright, E., A. Levine and E. Sober (1992) *Reconstructing Marxism*. London: Verso.

Yaari, M. (1981) 'Rawls, Edgeworth, Shapley, Nash: Theories of distributed justice reconsidered'. *Journal of Economic Theory*, 24, 1–39.

NAME INDEX

SUBJECT INDEX